MARY SI

Mary Sidney Herbert
Countess of Pembroke

an Elizabethan Writer

and her World

JULIA ALLEN

AND

CHRISTINE BENNETT

THE HOBNOB PRESS

First published in the United Kingdom

by The Hobnob Press,
8 Lock Warehouse, Severn Road, Gloucester GL1 2GA
www.hobnobpress.co.uk

British Library Cataloguing in Publication Data
A catalogue record for this book is available from the British Library

ISBN 978-1-914407-32-1

Typeset in Palatino Linotype 10/12 pt
Typesetting and origination by John Chandler

Biographical note

Julia Allen PhD is a historian and author with a particular interest in English literature and the development of ideas. She is an alumnus of the University of Manchester and has extensive experience of research, course consultancy and inter-disciplinary lecturing in the higher education sector.

Christine Bennett MA is a Literature specialist with a keen interest in all kinds of poetry. Since graduating from the University of Manchester she has had wide experience of teaching in both further and higher education. She has also been a Principal Examiner for English Language and Literature A-level, and is an author of several textbooks.

Contents

Preface

There is a wealth of information relating to the origin and spread of the Renaissance and Reformation which took place across the British Isles and Europe during the sixteenth century. Tudor England played a prominent role in this outburst of creativity which swept across many countries. It is rare for the spotlight to be on a woman making a contribution to that process but the story of Mary Sidney Herbert places the focus on an authoress and editor of significance in the Elizabethan era. During recent decades her work has been recognized as ground breaking. She wrote a dramatic version of the Antony and Cleopatra story which pre-dated Shakespeare, translated works of philosophy and it is widely agreed that her versification of the Psalms had an impact on the development of English poetry. Yet her publications have not been fully appreciated outside university departments of English and she has still has to make her way into works for a wider readership.

This book aims to present the narrative of Mary Sidney Herbert's life and achievements in an accessible form. A wide range of sources have been used to convey the context for her work. Material and evidence has been selected for inclusion to shine a light on her world and give an understanding of boundaries that had to be shifted and constraints overcome in order for her to carry out the task which she set herself. Initially, as a bereaved sister she aimed to edit the poetry and prose of her deceased brother, Sir Philip Sidney, in order to honour his name. Her achievements went further, but to understand how and why this happened, her writing must be considered against the background of the changing times brought about by the long reign of Elizabeth I. In presenting a developed picture of Mary's life and times the authors have included detailed literary analysis of her writing and also that of her brother Philip. As part of the purpose of unravelling the influence she had on the development of lyric poetry, her relative George Herbert is placed within the framework of this study.

Mary Sidney Herbert's story begins in the locality of Wilton, a small town in Wiltshire, where she started her adult life. It moves to a wider arena of national and international politics and religion. Her closest relatives worked in the service of the Tudor monarchs. At the same time, living on the fringes of court life, she was an outsider, an observer with an interest in the ethics of government. Her writing is extraordinary in the genres that she tackled. She was capable of writing sublime verse while her political translations give outstanding insight into how an Elizabeth woman understood her world.

List of illustrations

The authors have taken care to acknowledge the sources, attributions, copyrights and licenses for all the images included in the work. They wish to extend general thanks to all persons involved in creating the images and particular thanks to copyright holders who granted permissions when requested. All the public domain and unrestricted images were obtained via Wikimedia Commons unless otherwise stated.

p. 57   Stonehenge, ©Antoine Lamielle, CC BY-SA 4.0, https://creativecommons.org/licenses/by-sa/4.0

p. 65   Ramsbury Manor, reproduced with permission from *A History of the County of Wiltshire*, Volume 12, Victoria County History, London, 1983, ©University of London

p. 66   Navy engaging Armada, National Maritime Museum, Greenwich, London, CC-BY-NC-SA-3.0 http://creativecommons.org/licenses/by-nc-sa/3.0

p. 67   Robert Dudley, First Earl of Leicester, Steven van der Meulen, public domain, ©Yale centre for British art, released under Creative Commons license CC-BY-SA 2.0

p. 73   Ivy Church Priory ruins, Internet Archive Book Images, Allen County Public Library Genealogy Centre, no restrictions

p. 74   Frontispiece of *Silkwormes*, Early English Manuscripts, British Library, public domain

p. 92   Queen Elizabeth I, Marcus Gheeraerts the Elder, The Harley Foundation, Welbeck, Nottinghamshire, public domain

p. 107   Psalm 40, Philip Sidney, probably in his own hand, Philip and Mary Sidney, Trinity College Library, Cambridge, public domain

p. 123   George Herbert, Robert White, National Portrait Gallery, London, public domain

p. 124   George Herbert, Salisbury Cathedral, Richard Avery, public domain

p. 124   Herbert memorial window, Salisbury Cathedral, photograph by Christine Bennett, no permission required

p. 129   St Andrew's Church, Bemerton, ©Nick Macneill, license CC BY-SA 2.0

p. 139   The Old Rectory, Bemerton, ©Chris Talbot, license CC BY-SA 2.0

p. 142   Mary Sidney, engraving by B Reading after S van der Passe, The Wellcome Collection, London, https://wellcomecollection.org/works/fzck8xqc license CC-BY-SA 4.0

p. 145   Baynard's Castle in the 1600s, The British Library, London, no restrictions

p. 163   Houghton House, APB-CMX at English Wikipedia, public domain

p. 164   Salisbury Cathedral, ©Nick Macneill, license CC BY-SA 2.0

1
Origins

Beginning with a funeral

On a winter's day in February 1587 London witnessed the spectacle of one of the most lavish funerals ever to be observed in the city. On 16 February that year the Countess of Pembroke, Mary Sidney Herbert, was burying her beloved eldest brother Sir Philip Sidney. Seven hundred mourners were present that day. The entourage processed from Westminster to Sidney's final resting place in St Paul's churchyard. It is unlikely that Mary was present at the event in the capital as women were discouraged from attending funerals, so Philip's wife, Frances Walsingham, would not have been present either. The family were represented by Philip's father-in law, Sir Francis Walsingham, and Robert Sidney the younger brother of Philip and Mary. Extensive preparations had been made for the occasion including providing clothes for dozens of men from the Sidney retinue in matching uniforms made for the purpose using yards of cloth befitting the status of each mourner. Sixteen yards of the black cloth were allocated for a duke or earl, six for a baron, five for a knight and four for a yeoman or servant. Black cloth covered the hearse. The cost of the event, borne by Sir Francis Walsingham, is said to have led to Walsingham's financial ruin. Mary and Philip's uncle, Robert Dudley, Earl of Leicester, was buried the following year. His was a smaller affair but was known to have cost three thousand pounds. At a time when what was considered to be a respectable living for a labourer was just six to eight pence a day and for a craftsmen, eight to ten pence, such opulence is likely to have attracted attention. It was unusual for the funeral service of a commoner to take place at St Paul's Church and in terms of the participation of the public it has been said that the occasion was not rivalled until the state burial of Winston Churchill in the 20th century. St Paul's was a highly prestigious venue which was sadly destroyed in the Great Fire of London which occurred almost eighty years later.

Philip had died in October the previous year, 1586, aged just thirty-one. He had received a wound to the thigh inflicted in the battle of Zutphen in the Netherlands, sometimes referred to as being situated in the Low Countries (comprising of the Netherlands, Belgium and French Flanders); the country was locked in a war for independence against

Spain. English Protestant soldiers fought alongside their European allies in an attempt to expel the Catholics, whom they regarded as a mutual enemy. Robert Dudley, long-term favourite of the queen, had been commissioned by Elizabeth I to lead six thousand troops to support the Netherlands. For this particular battle Leicester had chosen his nephew Philip to fight at his side. Reinforcements from the Spanish side were travelling towards the English stronghold at Zutphen when Leicester decided to try to intercept them. This proved to be unsuccessful and many men were lost on the English side while Philip sustained his injury charging into a line of enemy soldiers. His distraught family must have felt their distress was amplified by the knowledge that had he worn his full armour on that day he might have left the field of battle unharmed. Instead he had rushed into the fray with his body exposed, and in particular his thighs without protection. Initially there were hopes of a recovery as the young soldier responded well to rest and the care he received away from the battlefield. However optimism was dashed when the injury became gangrenous and Philip's health went into a steep decline with family and friends standing by unable to effect a cure: he perished without returning to his home.

If Mary and the rest of the family had access to a document which is readily available today, *The Manner of Sir Philip Sidney's Death,* then their distress may have been increased. The authorship is anonymous although it is thought that the writer was a clergyman. He was present by Philip's bedside from the time when he received his injury until his death. The writer was in a position where he had responsibility for encouraging the patient to ensure that his soul was prepared for the life beyond death. The poignancy of the narrative emerges hundreds of years after the event. It is a demonstration of sixteenth century religious belief and a very touching account of a man facing his own demise. One section in particular, as Philip approached the end of his life, stands out as offering up a reflection on the character of the man:

> Perceiving that death did approach, he did with a few and short sentences (for it was grievous for him to speak much) exhort his two brothers in his affectionated manner, giving them instruction in some points, and namely to learn by him that all things here are vanity. His speech failing, he made signs with his hands to be still spoken unto, and could then less endure that I could make any intermission. Even as one that runs a race, when he comes near to the end, doth strain himself most vehemently, so he would have all the help that might be, to carry him forward now to the very end of this his race unto God.[1]

The anonymous narrator reports these words that Sidney wanted him to convey to his brothers as being his last speech. If he had a message relating to his wife and young child perhaps the nature of the sentiment was too personal to record. What is illustrated most clearly are the close bonds with his siblings and it is to them that Philip addresses his final judgement

---

[1] Anon in Duncan-Jones, 2008,

Thomas Lant engraving of the funeral procession of Sir Philip Sidney: the hearse.

on life. This intriguing warrior, poet, diplomat and philosopher might have disappeared into obscurity if his sister had not been determined that it should not happen. Exactly how much was known about his death outside his circle is not known. Back in England the war and its causes must have seemed very far from the realities of poor Londoners eking out a living. Life in Tudor times was notoriously harsh for those living from hand to mouth as hunger and disease were rife. It would be fascinating to know if onlookers at the funeral had any understanding of the war in which Philip had been engaged. There had been tragedy enough to concern them in England. A little more than twenty years before Philip's funeral with the extravagant display of grief more than twenty thousand citizens had died of a highly contagious plague that hit London and the surrounding area in 1563. The victims of that tragedy were buried in mass graves.

Funerals of the elite were not an uncommon sight in London. It was an established tradition to put on a good show and express the material wealth and prosperity of a family at the death of a loved-one; serving to reinforce the social standing of participants and sending a message regarding wealth and influence. Some effort was required to sustain powerful alliances. The College of Arms was in control of funeral pageantry and insisted upon a strict observance of the rules associated with hierarchy. Sidney was not a peer of the realm so the College were not concerned with the designation of titles in this instance. It was within the remit of this institution to ensure that the inheritance of titles followed a rigid precedent. The ceremony would also have involved charity for the poor. Ronald Strickland argues that by these means funerals were used to reinforce social norms with the contrast of the wealth of the nobility and the neediness of the poor emphasizing their reliance on the 'generosity' of their masters[1]. During later decades the ease with which elegies

1   Strickland, R, 1990.

could be written and printed for mourners was thought to be a reason for the reduction of the numbers enacting the procession. The increase in printing, therefore, allowed the printed word to produce a different way of representing the power and influence of an individual. Meanwhile the extent of the Sidney parade was staggering even by the standards of the day. As well as bearing the cost of the event Walsingham made the arrangement for the funeral for his son-in-law. Walsingham was, of course, one of the most powerful men in the land, in charge of Elizabeth's security and espionage. He shared the same religious outlook as the Sidney family and losing a close relative and a significant political ally was a disaster for him. For Mary the loss of her eldest brother was a cause for profound sorrow and much of the evidence emerging from her life story points towards his having been the person with whom she shared the most understanding and affection; the death proved to be something of a watershed for her.

Thomas Lant engraving of the funeral of Philip Sidney: mourners.

Philip Sidney had fought his last battle. He had embodied the ideal of a Protestant prince, highly educated and willing to take up the sword for the defence of the new religious ideas spreading across Europe. The funeral procession through England's most populous city reinforced the legendary status which Philip had already begun to acquire with his associates making every effort to show that Philip's death would not go unnoticed and that the conflict for which he had given up his life was a just and necessary war. There was widespread mourning at the court of Elizabeth and beyond. His very public commitment to Dutch independence had made him a popular figure in Holland and the European comrades wanted him to be buried on their soil but Queen Elizabeth insisted that his remains should be returned to the country of his birth. On the day of the funeral his Dutch supporters joined the party following the hearse through London; at the front of the procession walked Mary's husband, the Earl of Pembroke, and her uncles. Also present was a servant of the family, one Thomas Lant. Thanks to him Mary was able to see visual representations of her brother's funeral as Lant made a series of engravings depicting the event. Mary was grieving tucked away in the family home in the country, a condition which apparently lasted for nearly two years before, at some point, anguish transformed to energy and creativity and Mary Sidney formed her response to the death of Philip. What is so fascinating for the purposes of this story is how the tragedy of her brother's death, at such a young age, perhaps propelled her into becoming a significant woman in the world of English literature.

When the funeral took place Mary Sidney was just twenty-five years of age. In this book Mary Sidney Herbert will be referred to as Mary or Mary Sidney when her full name and title is not used, although she took her husband's family name – Herbert – after their marriage. This will distinguish her from other women also called Mary who form part of this story. Piecing together information from numerous written sources which emerged during her lifetime it is possible to gather the kind of thinking which motivated her in planning her emergence into public life. There is a wealth of material relating to the Sidney family and her uncle Robert Dudley alone, with the latter attracting a huge amount of attention from historians, in part because of his close relationship with Queen Elizabeth. Mary might have wished that Dudley had been more cautious with the safety of his nephew but the Earl of Leicester had been known to take risks in the past. As the favourite of the queen there had been speculation for years that they might marry or that they had an intimate relationship, although actual evidence to suggest the latter did not exist.

Robert Dudley had first met the future queen when he was eight and the Princess Elizabeth had been clear then and on subsequent occasions that she would never marry. Theirs was an unusual dependency which was once characterized as more like being brother and sister than queen and courtier. When Queen Mary approached the end of her reign and it became apparent that she would not survive, Robert Dudley made preparations to support Elizabeth in case there was a challenge to her succession. His reward was to become Master of the Horse: a prestigious position which placed him close to the daily activity of the queen. However, the lack of freedom to leave the side of the queen without special permission, which was hardly ever forthcoming, took its toll on Dudley and in later life he bitterly lamented not having autonomy or recognition as the consort of the queen. She released him for service overseas when, by the standards of the day, he was ageing and his inexperience on the field of battle limited his success. It is likely that Mary Sidney contemplated the impact of the odd circumstances upon Dudley as he became especially embroiled in difficulties to do with inheritance and succession. Did the queen's affection for him prevent her from marrying someone more suitable, thus inhibiting the birth of an heir? He married a noble woman Amy Robsart on 4 June 1550 but the pressure exerted on him by Elizabeth to remain by her side at court meant that he spent little time with his wife. When Robsart died of a broken neck ten years later there was speculation that she had either taken her own life or that she was murdered by her own husband. The coroner's verdict was death by misadventure but the belief in the possibility of his guilt stayed with Dudley for his life time. The complexities of his political and personal

Mary Sidney Herbert as a young woman.

behaviour as a member of the Privy Council and de facto semi partner to the queen only ended with his sudden death in 1588.

Having regarded difficulties faced by her close family in association with the monarch, it is highly unlikely that Sidney harboured any unrealistic notions of the legacy that would be attached to the name of her brother, without the intervention of someone who would keep him in the public eye for a period of time. The tributes to him poured in immediately after his death but his actions in the face of the enemy would be regarded as heroic for a fleeting moment. Mary was also aware that like his uncle, but for different reasons, there were ambiguities in the position that he found himself in before going to war. However, his great achievements that could not be disputed were literary and were in document form, in Mary's possession, and it was

Sir Philip Sidney.

to these that she turned in response to his untimely loss. Brother and sister had worked together on some of their writing projects but, in the main, at the time of his death it was Philip's work that formed a collection of material, not yet in the public domain, that was ready and waiting to enter the literary environment. There is no doubt that Mary was already engaged in literary ventures before the events of 1587. She was, for example, writing a translation of the psalms with her brother. After the funeral and a period of mourning, Mary Sidney decided that the Sidney voice would not be lost and that she would preserve the legacy of her brother through making public his writing. At the same time she sought ways of encouraging support for the cause for which he died through her own ability to write and express herself. Thus Mary Sidney became integrated into a literary network that was, at least in part, of her own making. She promoted his work and found ways of writing in her own name that could gain acceptance in the Elizabethan world, hence taking her place in the history of the development of English literature.

The 'back story': The Sidney family and their relationship with the English monarch: from Henry VIII to Elizabeth I.

The account of Mary Sidney Herbert, her network and the impact on the world of literature has to be told against the background of the English monarchy and the Reformation. It was an age when the religious beliefs of the monarch had an impact on the politics of the day. Religion was deeply entwined with the way that people thought about the world. Mary and Philip Sidney grew up in an environment where their security and livelihoods were dependent upon the favours and support of the monarch. Religion was also hugely important in the political thinking of the kings and queens and in the way in which they dealt with their subjects: the populace of the kingdom. For the purpose of shedding light on Mary Sidney's life the changes that began to unfold during the reign of Henry VIII (1509-1547) need to be understood as he was a key figure in the English Reformation. Within the context of British history the credit for starting the Reformation is generally given to Henry and the argument with the pope over the king's desire to set Catherine of Aragon aside as his queen, in favour of marriage to Anne Boleyn. The rift in the Christian church within England that followed Henry's rejection of the influence of the pope in this matter caused turmoil as, according to the king, the power of Rome had to be obliterated in England. Henry set about destroying the institutions, such as the abbeys and monasteries, capable of challenging his own authority and upholding allegiance to the vicar of Rome. This is the period which is frequently called the English Reformation: a time when the church was reformed in such a way that the king became head of the church in England rather than the pope from his base in Rome.

For many English people, eventually including Mary Sidney and her brother Philip though, this just covers a very limited aspect of the Reformation and is a small part of the story of religious change across Europe. Henry had entered a very personal conflict with the pope but across the seas in Europe there was a rejection of papal power on an entirely different basis. Across the English Channel change was taking place that was not just based on the whim of a king. In Europe prominent religious leaders challenged the laws of Roman Catholicism and called for a reformed church for reasons to do with the practice of religion rather than a desire for a divorce. The nature of the protests on the continent led to the movement being named as Protestantism. Protests against the old church were mainly to do with leadership and the way the Bible was used in preaching, teaching and worship. There was also a conviction that corruption had gained a foothold in the church with the selling of indulgences. Indulgences were sold by corrupt church officials and operated on the basis of an individual paying for a pardon or penance in order, it was believed, to shorten their time in hell or purgatory, a place of limbo after death. In the pre-Reformation world purgatory had become the terror associated with the anticipation of an after-life. There was a widespread belief that it was a place of torture: a 'chamber of horrors', where sins committed on earth caught up with the individual and called for a purging of the soul which would involve much discomfort and pain. A desire to avoid a lengthy period in such a dwelling was a strong motivating force which was readily taken advantage of by unscrupulous priests.

During his lifetime Henry largely held on to the main teachings and forms of worship of the old church whilst in Europe leaders such as Martin Luther and John Calvin emerged to shape and define the newly changing Protestant way of organising their churches. In England the groups of people who wanted this sort of change, such as the Sidney and Dudley families, began to be called Reformers or Protestants. Throughout the sixteenth century the Protestant movement in Europe gathered momentum leading to battles with the Roman Catholic Church; the conflict became known as the Protestant Wars. But the influence of men such as Luther and Calvin was not confined to mainland Europe. European Protestants brought their ideas to the British Isles and merchants, courtiers, soldiers and others from a variety of walks of life travelled to Europe and became sympathetic to the new church in Europe. They wanted the English church to transform along the lines of the European churches: it would involve a greater understanding of the theology, or the changes in the new way of thinking about God, and quite probably a lesser role for the monarch. This is where Mary Sidney and her family enter the story once more. Mary and her set had particular views on the Christian faith: as Reformers they were highly sympathetic to the views of the followers of the European religious leader, John Calvin. Those who adopted his reformist ideas came to be known as Calvinists. Some of the key differences between the beliefs of Calvinists were that the church can guide but is not essential for individual salvation; there is no need for priests to act on the behalf of individuals in communicating with God. In other words the lines of communication are open to all and rituals of the church are to be performed in vernacular languages. Everyone is equal in the sight of God so prayers of priests and noblemen do not hold more power and, according to God's plan, every person is predestined for salvation or damnation

Education designed for Prince Edward and its influence on Sidney family tradition

The ideas and beliefs imbibed by the Sidneys and the origin of the passions that were to have such an influence on Mary and her siblings, including Philip, possibly began with the education their parents Henry Sidney 1529-1586 and Mary Dudley 1530-1586, received. Henry VIII is well known for the atrocities he inflicted on his family, and the nation, but one very real and positive point about his legacy was the emphasis that he put on the education of his son and daughters. Henry Sidney was educated alongside Henry's only son Prince Edward, and Mary Dudley (Mary Sidney Herbert's mother) received a parallel education at court. Before Edward VI succeeded his father Henry to the throne, the king was so concerned about the health and safety of his precious heir he appointed special officers in the royal household to take responsibility for the welfare of the prince and to provide an environment

Princess Elizabeth

which it was believed would allow for the optimal development of the future king. Hence Sir William Sidney was made Chamberlain in 1539 and his son, Henry Sidney, was one of eight boys allowed to join Edward in his 'Royal' school. They became close friends. Robert Dudley also attended the highly select little school. When King Henry died in 1547 Edward was just nine years of age. His mother's brother the Duke of Somerset was appointed as his protector. A rival for the post was John Dudley who was, and remained, a close adviser of the young king. It was in 1551 that his daughter Mary Dudley married Henry Sidney. So Mary Sidney Herbert's parents had spent many of their formative years in the close company of Henry VIII's son Edward. The fact that both parents had this exceptional benefit seems to go a long way towards explaining the high value put on literacy and intellectual achievement in the Sidney household.

So the choice of tutors for the young prince Edward also had great significance for the Sidney children who were the progeny of this marriage. In the first instance Henry selected Sir Richard Cox, headmaster of Eton and canon of Westminster to teach at the little school in the palace. Later, during preparations to go to war with France in 1544, Henry Tudor made his current and last wife Katherine Parr regent general to lead in his absence. At this stage Katherine took the princess Elizabeth under her wing and brought her under the same roof as her half-brother Edward. The evidence depicts the queen taking an intimate interest in the education of her charges and these two motherless youngsters developed affection for their step-mother. Prince Edward is said to have written loving letters to Katherine and referred to her as 'my dearest mother'. Princess Mary Tudor was also at court as were the daughters of Dudley (including Mary Dudley later to become mother to our Mary Sidney); Elizabeth's tutors Roger Ascham and Anthony Cooke also joined the team at the palace responsible for the shaping of beliefs in young minds. All of the men thus employed shared a common interest with Queen Katherine: their aim was the conversion of England into a Protestant nation and their intention was to take their cause further than the idiosyncratic break with Rome achieved by King Henry VIII.

Popular histories of the period typically see Henry's wives in terms of whether or not their marriages ended in their being set aside or beheaded. Interest in Katherine Parr is sometimes seen just in terms of the fact that she outlived her husband. Her influence on the trajectory of the Reformation has frequently been ignored altogether which has led to an incomplete understanding of the dynamics of religious change in which she was heavily involved. What is particularly intriguing about this episode though is that this highly educated woman with a penchant for the Reformed faith was able to choose a new tutor for Edward to work alongside Cox. He was Sir John Cheke, Regius Professor of Greek at Cambridge and one of the most eminent humanist scholars of his day. The appointment of this man had consequences for the elite pupils in the school at Hampton Court. The prince and his companions received a rigorous humanist education under the auspices of Cheke. He taught his pupils to analyse the Bible as if they were interrogating classical

Hampton Court Palace

texts. They learnt Greek and Latin and French was taught by Cheke's nephew, a Calvinist scholar. It was a training designed for the ideal Protestant prince planned by Cheke, as he himself was devoted to the cause. By the time of their marriage Henry Sidney and Mary Dudley had absorbed the humanist teaching of the Reformation which was heavily influenced by European Protestantism. A small but touching detail which gives some insight into the priorities of the Sidney household that came about in response to their privileged education is that Henry, Mary's father, had kept a 'chronicle' of his learning which he later shared with his family. On one page, side by side, verses written in Latin by Henry can be seen next to English verses written by Mary Dudley. This provides a revealing insight into the Sidney love of the arts and learning[1] which they passed on to their own children.

The transition from Edward VI to Mary Tudor

When Edward became king after the death of his father in 1547, it marked the beginning of a short reign as he died at the age of sixteen in 1553. Today historians have collected ample evidence to show that the importance of Edward's short reign might have been understated with his being dismissed as a boy king. Edward had to mature quickly and it is argued that he had developed his own stance on certain issues by the time of his illness and death. It is argued in particular that his views on religion were well formed and he had begun to take England down the route of a Protestantism that was closer to that practised amongst Protestants in Europe before he was stopped in his tracks. It is safe to say that this would have been the preferred choice for Edward's school friend Henry Sidney and this is where the Dudley side of the family enters the frame. John Dudley, father of Mary Dudley and grandfather of Mary Sidney and Philip, was the Duke of Northumberland and the most powerful man in the country dominating the government before the death of Edward. As the king lay dying Dudley plotted for the throne to pass to his son Guildford's wife, Lady Jane Grey, another Protestant. She was a cousin once removed from Edward. Jane was queen for nine days only, when the plot was overturned by forces loyal to the princess Mary. Mary Tudor became queen whilst Jane, her husband Guildford Dudley and John Dudley were all executed.

So, although Mary Sidney was born into a family with close associations with the monarchy and seat of power, events surrounding Jane Grey illustrate that the Dudley and Sidney clans had chequered fortunes in their attachment to the crown. Whilst they lived a privileged life style, the pursuit of power came at a price and prominent members of her family had suffered imprisonment and death when their politics did not suit or match that of the monarch. It is very likely that Mary Sidney will have been raised to be highly aware that this position in society in Tudor England was not without risk. Her maternal great grandfather had also been executed for treason by a young Henry VIII. Alongside the death of her grandfather John Dudley, all her Dudley uncles were placed under suspicion and imprisoned in the

1   Strycharski, A, 2011.

Tower. They were only to be released after pleadings from Mary Sidney's grandmother who had lost her husband, one son and daughter-in-law, due to what turned out to be the somewhat foolhardy venture placing Lady Jane Grey on the throne.

The distinctively reformed nature of the Sidney family outlook came under threat with the accession of Mary Tudor to the throne. When Henry VIII's eldest daughter began her attempt to reverse some of the changes made in the English church after she became queen in 1553, many supporters of Protestantism, such as the tutor John Cheke, fled the country for their safety. Queen Mary set about restoring the fortunes of Catholicism. It was at this time that Mary Sidney's brother Philip was born, and named after Philip of Spain, the Roman Catholic husband of the queen. The king of Spain became godfather to Philip Sidney. It is interesting to question whether this was the result of pragmatism creeping in to the Sidney household. It presents individuals negotiating their way through a minefield of somewhat conflicting ideas. Their contemporaries at court were likewise engaged in efforts to survive the religious preferences of the queen. History has recorded some prominent individuals who would not conform at any particular time, and as a result died particularly gruesome deaths, being burnt at the stake at the behest of Queen Mary. Bishops Latimer and Ridley are amongst the most famous of the martyrs during the reign of Mary. As indicated previously, it is known that some prominent individuals moved abroad to escape the difficulties of denying or dying for their faith, whilst others were willing to quietly change their allegiance in order to avoid imprisonment and death.

Reflecting on how far the Sidneys would go to accommodate the beliefs of the new queen is interesting but is necessarily inconclusive. There is a sense though, that their action taken in naming Philip after Mary Tudor's Spanish husband replicates what was happening in wider society. It is an illustration of the importance of uncovering the lives of individuals to gain more understanding of the complex nature of change. In recent times scholars have moved away from treating Mary's reign with a categorical mind set. In other words, the over simplified version of the narrative which describes Mary as imposing pre-Reformation Catholicism on an unwilling population is not entirely accurate. The reality was more nuanced with the retention of some of Henry and Edward's reforms. There is evidence of churches embracing the restoration of material items that had been treasured by communities and the return of ritual was welcomed. In a particularly detailed discussion of church reform Eamon Duffy writes that: 'There is, moreover, considerable evidence that the religious programme of the Marian church was widely accepted, and was establishing itself in the parishes'.[1] Perhaps the parents of Mary and Philip Sidney had 'read the writing on the wall' and taken the measure of what was happening and had decided to opt for the winning side. Religion and identity are closely associated and with the death of Mary Tudor the Sidney identity became unambiguous once more.

1   Duffy, E, 2005.

Elizabeth I and the Sidney fortunes

When the life of Edward Tudor was cut short at the age of sixteen there is a sense in which the baton of the intellectual notions and philosophies of a new era were passed to the Sidney family and the other noble families who had been his close allies. The reign of Mary Tudor was brief and then, with the beginning of the reign of Elizabeth I, conditions became considerably more favourable for those opposing Roman Catholicism at court. No doubt the Sidney-Dudley clan were amongst those who could breathe a sigh of relief that there was an easing of pressure to conform to the beliefs of the former queen – beliefs which they did not share. Philip Sidney was born at Penshurst Place, Kent, the Sidney family home, in the year 1554[1], whilst Mary was still monarch. Seven years later on 27 October, 1561 Mary Sidney was born at Tickenhill Manor House, near Bewdley situated on the borders of the counties of Shropshire and Worcestershire. Elizabeth had been queen for three years. Mary's christening took place within days of her birth with her future father-in-law the first Earl of Pembroke taking vows to be her godfather.

Old Tickenhill Palace

Whilst his children were growing up Henry Sidney worked as Lord Deputy of Ireland and then President of the Council of the Marches in Wales. When Mary and Philip were not with their father they spent time at their home Penshurst Place. The house was surrounded by an exceptionally good example

[1] Jonson, B, *To Penshurst*. See Appendix

of an Elizabethan garden and it continues to be a popular site to visit in current times. The house has partly been made famous by a poem about the Sidney home – *To Penshurst* – written by Ben Jonson, a contemporary of the Sidney siblings. The full poem is printed in the Appendix. Ben Jonson wrote a number of successful plays including *The Alchemist*. Among the attractions in the garden is an ancient oak tree, believed to be one thousand years old: it has

Tickenhill Palace interior

been named Philip Sidney's Oak, as a reminder that the great poet was born in the house. *To Penshurst* offers some detailed description of the house. It gives, for example, information about the materials that went into constructing the building but also enters into some speculative thinking relating to the supposed benefits and aspects which made him think of the house and its contents as a type of Utopia:

> That taller tree which of a nut was set
> At his great birth where all the muses met (*To Penshurst*)

Evidence from the accounts books from Penshurst indicates that the children played musical instruments, with Mary able to perform on the lute and the virginal. She shared a governess with her sister Ambrosia and, no doubt, they had the best available education for girls in that era, learning French, Italian, Latin and Greek. The girls practised needlecraft and all of the children had bows and arrows for exercise out of doors. On special occasions such as May Day and Midsummer's Day groups of players took part in festivities at the house. Time spent in Wales gave the Sidney children a respect for the Welsh culture and an ability to speak the language.

Mary Dudley and Henry Sidney took a close interest in their children's schooling, which aimed at the rigour of their own education. For Philip this included a period spent at Shrewsbury School followed by attendance at Christ's Church College, Oxford University in 1568. All of Mary's education took place at home. Opportunities for the daughters of nobility to be educated with nuns in an abbey, such as that at Wilton, had been destroyed with the demolition of those institutions; other organizations had yet to take their place. Whilst Mary was growing up her mother became one of Queen Elizabeth's closest aids. As a gentlewoman in the Privy Chamber she nursed Elizabeth through a severe bout of smallpox in 1562, which she then caught herself. Mary's mother had to live with facial disfigurement thereafter becoming convinced that the queen had not rewarded her enough for her sacrifice and loyalty. In Henry Sidney's performance of his duty to act as Elizabeth I's Lord Deputy of Ireland from 1565-71, and from 1575-1578, and President of the Council of the Marshes in

Wales during the final years of his life, his family had to adapt to living in different and often separate households. This meant that for much of his career he was away from home. As was usual for the day, the parents were looking for their daughter to enhance the family status and attain financial stability by marrying well. At the age of fourteen Mary was presented at court and Queen Elizabeth approved of a plan for the girl to marry one of the wealthiest landowners in the country, Henry Herbert, Earl of Pembroke. He was the son of her godfather and was already a middle aged man.

Why should Mary Sidney's place in history be acknowledged?

When a marriage was arranged for Mary into the Herbert family, her husband had already developed a reputation for brutality in putting down revolts in Wales and Cornwall, as well as closer to home. Yet out of this milieu of wealth, intrigue, power-play and violence emerged a woman who deserves to be more widely recognised for a number of reasons: not least of which is the role she mastered in encouraging and developing English literary traditions. It was the age of William Shakespeare, Ben Jonson, Christopher Marlowe and Edmund Spenser. The sonnet form in particular and poetry in general was flourishing. The production of drama at a variety of venues was on the ascendancy. There are very few women associated with the proliferation of art during this period but Mary Sidney was one of them. On the face of it she played a fairly small part in terms of the volume of writing but she was breaking new ground for women and forging a pathway in a male environment which empowered women to follow in her footsteps. It must not be forgotten that a primary reason for this account must also be the recognition of her talent for writing. It is apparent, for example, in her version of the tale of Antony (spelt Antonie and Antonius by Mary Sidney[1]) and Cleopatra. As Cleopatra disputes that she has betrayed Antony:

> Rather sharp lightning lighten on my head;
> Rather may I to deepest mischief fall;
> Rather the opened earth devour me;
> Rather fierce tiger feed them on my flesh;
> Rather, O rather let our Nilus send,
> To swallow me quick, some weeping crocodile.
> And didst thou then suppose my royal heart
> Had hatched, thee to ensnare, a faithless love?
> (*Antonius*, Act 2, Scene 2, 7-14)

A printed copy of Mary's play appeared in 1595. The first folio of Shakespeare's *Antony and Cleopatra* was circulated years later; this detail alone gives her an interesting position in the development of literature written in English, but there is more. The relationship with her brother Philip is explored

---

1   The name is usually translated as Antony in modern texts although exceptionally it is Anthony. Mary Sidney uses either Anthonie or Antonius when referring to the same person.

alongside some of his major works: *Astrophil and Stella, Sonnets, The Arcadia* and *The Defence of Poesy.* Furthermore, another family member was the poet George Herbert, and his work will form part of a discussion of a legacy in literature. Mary's youngest brother Robert also wrote poetry as did his daughter Mary Wroth. In recent times Mary Sidney's niece Mary has been rediscovered and her poetry is given some attention in the final chapter. The thread of the narrative begins at Wilton but by no means ends there. The Sidney influence infiltrated the literary scene in England and beyond, with the tentacles reaching out to the New World and an association with the prominent 17th century New England poet Anne Bradstreet.

Mary Sidney and her world: her writing, family, networks, beliefs and undertakings provide a special insight into social change and the history of ideas during this period. In addition there is a sense in which her story can be read as a tale for our times. The issues in which she was embroiled have not gone away. She was a prominent woman but her legacy is tucked away in the archives. Re-visiting her story does not involve looking at the past through the lens of an 'ordinary' citizen but the focus is not entirely on the action of monarchs either as her life was spent on the fringes of power. However, a careful reading of Mary's life does reflect on the attempts made by an affluent woman to negotiate the advantages and disadvantages of living in that time and place. Although, unfortunately at least one fire at her home destroyed some documents there is still a body of evidence associated with her and her family, including her extant writings. To gain a balanced understanding of the past it is essential to restore to the record all sorts of people brushed aside by the passage of time. Mary played an active part in the Reformation and literary Renaissance as it took place in Elizabethan England. Where so few women have been applauded in this sphere it is time for widespread recognition of her creativity. This narrative illustrates the possible extent of her influence and tells the story of her visible achievements as well as looking at the context of her life and how she inspired the work of others.

It was ten years after Mary Sidney's marriage that Philip died. His funeral was not just a display of extreme wealth. The loss of her brother was a devastating blow for Mary to absorb particularly as both of her parents died earlier the same year. At least they did not suffer the knowledge of the death of their son. The brother and sister had been exceptionally close. Philip was already a courtier poet of some renown. In a collection of his work dedicated to his sister *'The Countess of Pembroke's Arcadia'*, Philip wrote his clearest statement of his affection for her. A letter printed as the Foreword of the book is specifically addressed 'To My Dear Lady And Sister The Countess of Pembroke'. The work begins: 'Here now have you (most dear, and most worthy to be most dear, lady) this idle work of mine...' , it ends with the expressed hope 'you will continue to love the writer who doth exceedingly love you, and most heartily prays you may long live to be a principal ornament to the family of the Sidneys'.

There was a touch of the prophetic about the final words of this letter of dedication. Mary did live long, surviving her brother by thirty-five years. It is not possible to know the extent to which she was motivated by her brother's loving words but after the funeral and a period of mourning for her parents and

Philip, Mary did become the Sidney who would sustain the family name for learning and high arts. She edited Philip's writing, developed her patronage of some of the most famous writers of the day and translated French philosophical and religious works. As mentioned previously, Shakespeare had access to her account of the classical play *Antonius* when he wrote his production. Claims have been made that she did more than influence one of Shakespeare's plays. A society exists in America to advance the idea that she actually wrote the plays attributed to Shakespeare. Assertions relating to her relationship with Shakespeare will not be made here but it is a matter of fact that she translated many of the ancient Hebrew poems known as the psalms. In this area too her work has been under recognised and there is scant evidence about the use of her psalms by the establishment in churches and cathedrals. Mary Sidney was a key figure in a network with a role in the English Renaissance. Her name was associated with leading poets of her time. She was an inspiration to the generations who followed her, including her niece (and her son's lover), the poet Mary Wroth. This latter writer has attracted more attention than her aunt with her writings finding their way on to the curriculum of university departments of English. It is widely acknowledged though that Mary Sidney had a noteworthy impact on metaphysical poetry and in particular, on her kinsman, George Herbert. The Countess of Pembroke's literary network had a wide reach. The purpose of this book is to set the life of Mary Sidney in the framework of the era in which she lived and present her story to a wider readership in modern times.

2
The Wilton Set

Wilton

Henry VIII had rewarded William Herbert's loyal service to the monarch with nineteen manor houses in England and many more in Wales. William was the first earl of Pembroke, Mary's godfather and father-in-law. Several of the English houses were in the county of Wiltshire with vast tracts of land being part of the gift there, and across other counties in Southern England, and half of the land in Glamorganshire. In Wiltshire, for example, there was Ramsbury Manor House, situated on the River Kennet. It was built for Pembroke in 1560 but of the Elizabethan structure only the wood frame of the stable block survives, on the site where an eighteenth century house was erected in place of the earlier manor. Closer to Salisbury in the village of Alderbury, Pembroke converted Ivychurch Priory into a dwelling and it is recorded that the family stayed there from time to time. In later life Mary built Houghton House in Bedfordshire, the ruin of which still stands today. The land on which it was built was given to her by James I. It is a fascinating piece of material culture that emerged out of Mary Sidney's life time preoccupations. Constructed of Jacobean and classical designs in 1615, it was completed in 1621, the year of the death of the countess. It is said to be the inspiration for 'House Beautiful' in John Bunyan's *Pilgrims Progress*.

Mary, however, spent the significant proportion of her married life at Wilton House and it was there that she worked on her literary collaboration with her brother. Wilton lies three miles west of the cathedral city of Salisbury. Wilton had been the most important centre in the area until the thirteenth century but 1245 saw the building of three bridges over the river Avon at Harnham in Salisbury. From that point onwards traders began to flow into the cathedral city whilst by-passing Wilton, the former capital of Wessex. By the 15th century the decline in trade left its mark on the town. The local population had to wait another two centuries before their settlement was re-built but meanwhile they were dealt another major setback when, in the late 1530s the abbey at Wilton was included on the list of institutions to be destroyed by Henry. Wilton Abbey had been a house of Benedictine nuns and a place of elite female learning, appearing in records which date back to AD 934. The last abbess surrendered the abbey to the king's men on 25 March, 1539. The extent of Henry's destruction of girls' education has not been fully explored. At Wilton he wiped out centuries of tradition of women educating women and a large and precious library was dismantled.

Map of Salisbury area adjacent to and including Wilton 1640

The extensive lands and buildings associated with the abbey were given to William Herbert, and he was created first earl of Pembroke, in October, 1551. For Herbert it was payment for favours and for enforcing the rule of the king in the Marches of Wales. He was an earl of the 'second creation' which broadly means that he might have had some real connection to the earlier earls of Pembroke but sometimes the links were not continuous. The acquisition of land by Henry's 'fixers' does not make for comfortable reading. In William Herbert's case he benefitted from what could reasonably be referred to as brutal behaviour which was apparently his usual way of conducting his affairs. He was noticed by the king after he had returned to England from seven years' voluntary exile. As a young man he became involved in a fight with a group of men in Bristol. During the combat he murdered a man in the crowd who happened to be from a well-known and established Bristol family. After Herbert took flight his exact whereabouts were a secret but on his return he wasted no time in convincing the king that his skills in battle were a good reason for giving him the task of keeping order and enforcing Henry's rule in Wales. For many of the population of Wilton it proved to be a disaster.

The old abbey at Wilton was dismantled and the building of the new manor house, intended for occupation by Herbert, began in 1553 and necessitated the removal of some village houses. A field used by families in the village for growing crops was purloined. For the sake of the view from his new home, and in order for the design of his parkland to be enhanced, William Herbert enclosed the seven acre field and put up a fence to keep local people away from the land. The field had provided essential space for growing crops to feed families; without this amenity hunger became a greater reality for the people of Wilton. Having overseen the development of his vast estate Herbert then returned to Wales. Thinking he was safely out of the way, villagers took down fencing and reclaimed their land and began to reinstate their dwellings which had been destroyed. When Herbert heard about their actions he returned to Wilton with a number of his Welsh troops. It did not go well for members of the local community and many did not survive the confrontation with the earl. Nevertheless, his popularity with the king continued to rise. For one reason and another, a certain aspect of Henry's reign is frequently airbrushed. Historians often concentrate on his relationship with the other great characters of the age such as Thomas More, Cardinal Wolsey and Thomas Cromwell and his battle with a pope makes a compelling story. But the impact of the measures that he imposed on ordinary people's lives may not be discussed so frequently. In the case of the Earl of Pembroke, a man lacking in the usual education and refinements expected of a courtier, there emerged someone with the capability and the propensity to commit violence. This made him useful to the king, who rewarded him to the extent that he became one of the richest men in England. By the time Mary Sidney entered the frame at Wilton, in the reign of Queen Elizabeth, the earls of Pembroke had established a firm base there.

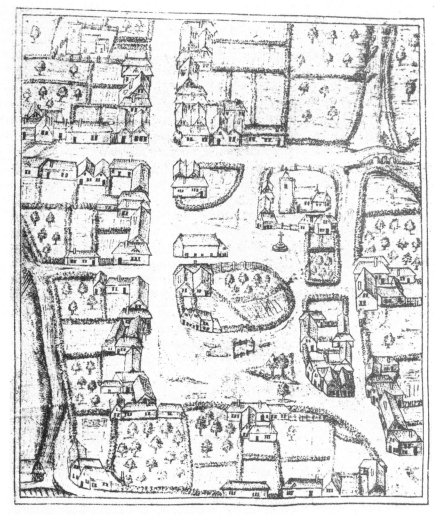

Map of Wilton c.1568

Wilton House

Mary, mistress of Wilton House

At fourteen years of age, Mary Sidney made a successful entrance into court life. With her parents and her brother Philip she accompanied the queen on a 'progress' through English counties which entailed being the guests of and being entertained by courtiers and land owners. A progress was a way that had been adopted by the monarchy to make sure they were visible to populations across the country. Whilst it was a great social honour to be chosen to accommodate the progress, at the same time the costs involved were enormous. The most noteworthy stop on this 1575 progress was on 9 July when the party reached Kenilworth Castle, Warwickshire, the home of Robert Dudley, Earl of Leicester, uncle to Mary Sidney. The queen and her entourage stayed at Kenilworth for nineteen days. No expense was spared in keeping the guests fed and entertained. As the queen entered the estate trumpets heralded her arrival at the gates and from then onwards the activities were apparently non-stop. Statues of mythological figures adorned the pathways whilst a concert played to welcome her. Over the next few weeks there was hunting, dancing, firework displays, bear-baiting and morris dancing, alongside drama productions for the entertainment of all. Dudley's efforts at Kenilworth were part of his charm offensive to win the hand of the monarch. But this was not the match that came to fruition at Kenilworth that year. Dudley had created the conditions for his niece, Mary Sidney, to attract the attention of Henry Herbert, the second Earl of Pembroke, son of William, who was also taking part in the festivities, and within the year she was married to him.

Mary Sidney took her place in adult society as the wife of the earl. It is speculated that the wedding ceremony was held at Penshurst Place. There is a very brief reference to the event in the family Bible, without mention of any details. Financial records do show that Herbert demanded a very large dowry of three thousand pounds from the bride's father, which the Sidneys had great difficulty paying. The transaction was completed after the marriage when Sidney was able to use some money borrowed from allies and friends. There was though no shortage of money at Herbert's disposal and Mary Sidney moved into the manor house at Wilton; it was still one of the most prominent estates in England at the time. For the forty-three year old earl it was his third marriage. It was a small world in aristocratic circles: Mary's new husband was the son of William Herbert and Anne Parr, sister of queen Katherine Parr. On 25 May 1553, whist he was still a child, Henry Herbert's father had agreed that his son should be married to Katherine Grey. This was arranged by John Dudley as part of his scheme to gain support for the accession of Lady Jane Grey to the throne. Jane was Katherine's eldest sister. Following the execution of John Dudley, Guildford and Jane Grey, the marriage between Henry and Katherine was annulled, for fear of association with the Protestant plot.

Penshurst Place

Henry's second marriage took place in 1563 when Katherine Talbot, daughter of the Earl of Shrewsbury became his wife. Katherine died thirteen years later while the couple were still childless. Henry had succeeded his father to the earldom in 1570 and was appointed Lord Lieutenant of Wiltshire. For the second earl of Pembroke the imperative was to secure a succession for the Pembroke estates: within a year the match had been made between himself and Mary Sidney. From a twenty-first century perspective knowing that this teenage girl was marrying a man previously married to the sister of her executed aunt, gives some insight into submission to duty which was necessary for survival in the Elizabethan world. Once Elizabeth I was monarch difficulties associated with religious identity diminished and the Herbert-Sidney alliance was regarded as being a joining of two Protestant families with strong links to the court of the queen, in that sense it seemed to be the ideal partnership. There are huge doubts though about the intellectual parity of the two. As mentioned before, Henry's father had not had an advanced education, there were rumours that he was illiterate. What a contrast to the Sidney level of learning.

The ageing earl was said to be overjoyed when Mary delivered her first child in 1580: a much longed for son and heir called William, after his paternal grandfather. Three more children followed in quick succession: Katherine in 1581, Anne in 1583 and Philip in 1584. The joy at the birth of the second son was severly muted as on that same day Katherine, the eldest of the daughters died of a childhood illness. The delivery of Mary's last child was said to be difficult and prolonged. The mother took many months to recover her physical strength and her grief for the loss of her daughter compounded the complications standing in the way of her recovery. At the age of twenty-three Mary had brought her fourth and final child into the world. Although there is evidence of one further pregnancy, Mary did not give birth to any more surviving children after the baby that she named after her brother.

Extant sources do not reveal Mary Sidney's view of her husband and tradition dictated that as a female it is most unlikely that her views would have been considered as being of any consequence. It is well attested that her education was in advance of that of her husband's. Perhaps the close relationship between the Sidney siblings reflected a lack of shared interests between Mary and her husband? It is very clear the reputation that Wilton House developed was due to the efforts and creativity of the mistress of the house and not the master. Historians reflecting on developments at Wilton in the sixteenth century use the diary of a 16th century citizen of Wiltshire, John Aubrey, as a source of primary evidence. He described the house during the Sidney era as being like a college. Part of this reputation rested on the foundation of an extensive library, assembled by Mary. Additionally, alongside the many royal and courtly officials attracted to the household, prominent artists of the day were guests of Mary Sidney: men such as the poet Edmund Spenser, the Salisbury playwright Philip Massinger and the writer Samuel Daniel. This has led some historians of literature to refer to the Wilton Set or Wilton Circle. It refers to the people surrounding the brother and sister: those who shared their interests in the pursuit of poetry and the arts.

As Mary was young when her child bearing years stopped somewhat abruptly, there is speculation that a difficult birth had physically damaged the countess. Perhaps it was this that led to her ability to focus on wider interests. With Wilton House becoming known for being a centre for encouragement of the written arts, Mary was at the centre of this circle, with the key figures in the literary and scientific worlds meeting there. The luxury of the lifestyle available to her and also the constraints upon her, are part of the narrative. Mary emerges as a noble woman who used the written word to make a stand for her causes, in an age when women other than the monarch were without a forum in which to speak openly. That said, the evidence is that Mary Sidney remained cautious as she was painfully aware of the realities of a life close to the powerful. Her early years were overshadowed by the recent history of the deaths of a number of close relatives who were found guilty of treason; perhaps this family tragedy, and the beliefs and events which surrounded it, did much to define Mary's own circumstances.

There is evidence that Mary and her brother Philip were able to offer each other mutual solace. Their shared past and family history shaped their outlook and reinforced their identity, and their relationship was close, to the extent that even in their own time there was an assumption their connection had sexual overtones. Philip stayed for prolonged periods in his sister's family home, most notably when he fell out of favour at court and he retreated to the countryside following particularly difficult episodes in his relationship with the queen. With a stable home life Mary could offer refuge to Philip. He could match her intellectual ability and they both shared their love of poetry. The companionship of her brother is likely to have filled a void for Mary. Philip is a constant presence in accounts of his sister's life as much of their work was inextricably linked.

Mary Sidney had advanced the family fortunes by marrying Herbert but Philip was expected to advance himself at court in the traditions of the courtier. In this Philip lacked consistent success. He exhibited a certain confidence and expectation that he could influence the queen which was not always appropriate. Perhaps this assurance lay in the shared education that his parents had with Elizabeth as a princess and with her half-brother Edward Tudor. It gave the Sidney siblings a certain outlook which served to set them apart. There was something enigmatic about Philip and Mary that a number of writers have described. There is a touch of mystery in their relationship: a hint of their being not quite wedded to the circumstances in which they found themselves; in being men and women thoroughly attached to the beauty and perfection of the natural world but finding disappointment and thwarted aspiration in the world of politics. This was especially true of Philip and it seemed to find force and to motivate his escape into the fantasy of the realm he created in the *Countess of Pembroke's Arcadia*. But these were entitled people, used to mixing with the most powerful men and women in the land. They were just one generation from Herbert's land and property grab but there does not seem to be any evidence that this was something that they regretted as they enjoyed the idyllic landscape with which they were surrounded.

Furthermore, it can be argued that there was a two pronged effect of the special education that Mary and Philip received which had interesting implications for their creative output. The Renaissance revival of classical learning added a pre-Christian dimension to their thinking. It is possible that engagement with the writings of ancient Greek and Roman writers offered a safe space for courtier families. There was a sense in which it allowed for a more neutral discussion of philosophical and moral issues. The stories that emanated from Greece and Rome could be used to convey ideas and notions which did not have the strong religious connotations of biblical interpretation which might be laden with fears of igniting religious controversy. There could be analysis of what makes a hero? What are the duties of a ruler? How might populations behave in a republic? What might have led to the failure of monarchs to represent their people and what makes a tyrant? Questions such as these leapt out of the pages of classical writings. Steeped in Renaissance philosophy it is no coincidence that Philip's most famous work was called *Arcadia*. Evoking the Greek district of the same name the suggestion is of a sort of Utopia, a place without conflict. It is interesting to note that Philip Sidney's *Arcadia* veered towards the secular.

Philip and Europe: in support of a Protestant Alliance

Well into Elizabeth's reign the Sidneys and their circle continued to remain loyal to Edward VI's hopes for the direction of travel regarding religion in England and they consistently favoured the type of Protestantism which had advanced across Europe. Philip and some of his contemporaries continued to identify with Calvinism and to associate with reformists who were hoping for a transformation of the English church to be based along the lines of the thinking and teaching of one of the prominent European leaders such as Martin Luther, Ulrich Zwingli or John Calvin. It was a time when allegiance to the Protestant or Roman Catholic brand still had significance in terms of loyalty to the queen and court. Whilst the dreadful pogroms against religious dissenters had ended with Elizabeth's reign, the queen was still highly alert to revolt and danger from Catholic quarters. The Sidneys and like- minded Protestants were looking for opportunities to forge new links with European churches under the auspices of a Protestant alliance so that they could support each other against the Spanish threat. This imperative shaped Sidney thinking and behaviour and ultimately led to Philip's wounding on the battlefield and subsequent death.

Despite Philip being the godson of King Philip of Spain, the country over which his godfather ruled was identified as the one that was most destructive of the aims and objectives of the reformers. Philip Sidney campaigned for an alliance to be formed in an attempt to halt Spanish aggression and imperialism. He had reached the conclusion for such a necessity whilst he was spending time in Europe working on a commission for the queen. Following his years at Oxford University Philip did not gain a degree. His time there was cut short when he left due to an outbreak of the plague in the city. It left him free to go on his first trip to the continent with permission from Elizabeth. He accompanied Edward Fiennes de Clinton, Earl of Lincoln, who had been tasked to sign the treaty of Blois with the French. The treaty was an attempt to offer support to French Protestants by making France and England allies against Spain, For Philip it ignited his enthusiasm to carve out a role for himself in the service of Protestant unity in Europe. The English party arrived in France during early June 1572. The treaty was signed by mid-June, after which time Lincoln decided to leave Paris and make his way back to England. The two men knew that to be a Protestant in France carried an element of risk, but could they possibly have foreseen the extent of the horror about to be unleashed on the French followers of John Calvin, known since the 1560s as Huguenots?

Instead of returning home in June 1572 after the signing of the treaty, Sidney stayed with the English ambassador to France, who was then his future father-in-law Sir Francis Walsingham. It was during the stay in this household in Paris that Philip experienced events that were both formative and possibly the most traumatic he witnessed until his own participation in battle. On St Bartholomew's Day, 24 August 1572 Paris was teeming as crowds gathered for the royal wedding of Margaret de Valois, the king's sister, and Prince Henry of Navarre at Notre-Dame. Henry, a Protestant prince was taking centre stage among the large numbers of Huguenots who were in the city in order to celebrate the wedding. There was already a history of religious unrest in Paris and it was no surprise to find that denominational feelings were inflamed by provocative incidents on both sides of the religious divide, but what occurred next was entirely one-sided. An orgy of unchecked violence was visited upon the Huguenots across the city.

The Massacre of the Huguenots

The massacre was indiscriminate and any man, woman or child identified as belonging to the group was dispatched with brutality. The streets and rivers were said to be running with Huguenot blood. The slaughter lasted for three days. It is thought that an aspect of the nature of the killing spree that became a further cause of trauma was the way in which it was carried out in an atmosphere of carnival and entertainment on the side of those committing the atrocities. Laughter accompanied the murder of babies in their mothers' arms. Meanwhile Sidney and Walsingham were in hiding in the latter's residence in Paris, alongside fellow citizens who were lucky enough to find a place of refuge before the horror began. The chaos reigned on the streets outside Walsingham's home. The queen's spymaster was thus witness to this extreme communal violence but he did not write about it in his letters following the event. Perhaps he had to take care about what was said or, knowing what we know today about the impact of extreme anxiety, it is possible he was in a state of shock. The playwright Christopher Marlowe had a detailed knowledge of the attack when he wrote his play *The Massacre of Paris*. When Philip Sidney devoted his time to writing: his chosen genre was far more along the lines of escapism.

For three years after witnessing the massacre Philip remained in Europe ostensibly with the purpose of completing his education. He travelled to the cities which played a prominent part in Renaissance thinking such as Venice, Vienna, Frankfurt and Heidelberg, visiting religious and political thinkers

Kenilworth Castle

along the way. His movements were sanctioned by the Privy Council as at this stage there were high hopes that Sidney had the presence and ability to forge useful links across Europe; it would seem at this time that Sidney was on a trajectory that would lead him into a position of power. When he returned to England it was in time to take part in the progress of the monarch round the country. He was at Kenilworth Castle when the court visited there and when Mary Sidney met with her future husband. Between 1575 and 1577 Philip played the part of the successful courtier: attending to the queen, participating in the tilt (jousting tournaments) and even possibly writing poems for circulation amongst fellow courtiers. Popularity at court translated into a role for which Philip believed himself to be eminently suited. At last he was chosen to fulfil a function in his own name and one that he thought of as a top priority. In the name of the queen, Philip was sent to Prague where he was to offer condolences at the death of king Maximillian II. The mission was accomplished but did not attract the attention that Philip Sidney might have desired. Once again his political ambitions were thwarted and visible outcomes resulting from this trip did not materialise. The notion of a league fizzled. Nor was he rewarded with the usual titles or honours given for work achieved by Elizabeth's allies.

Retreat to Wilton

It was a highly disgruntled brother who retreated to the Wilton estate at the end of the 1570s. Disappointment over the response to his European tour was compounded by two incidents which were said to move the queen to act against Philip. The first was a consequence of a letter that he sent to Elizabeth I in 1580, expressing his disapproval of the proposed marriage between her and the French Duke of Anjou. The monarch was not impressed with the interference from one of her courtiers and it was in Philip's interest to leave London for the countryside. What follows here is a very short extract from the lengthy epistle. It gives a flavour of the contents of the letter and gives some indication as to why Elizabeth may not have appreciated the advice from a young courtier:

> Now the agent party, which is Monsieur: whether he be not apt to work on the disadvantage of your estate, he is to be judged by his will and power; his will to be as full of light ambition as is possible; besides the French disposition, and his own education; his inconstant temper against his brother; his thrusting himself into the Low Country matters; his sometimes seeking the king of Spain's daughter; sometimes your Majesty; are evident testimonies of his being carried away with every wind of hope; taught to love greatness any way gotten; and having for the motioners and ministers of mind, only such young men, as have showed they think evil contentment a ground for any rebellion; who have…defiled their hands in odious murders: …in truth, it were strange that he cannot be contented to be the second person in France, and heir apparent, should be content to come to be a second person, where he should pretend no way to sovereignty[1]

The possibility that the duke may have been oscillating between two women in his marriage proposals must have made difficult reading for the monarch but the fundamental message that Elizabeth had not understood the character of the man was a step too far. Philip continued in this vein for almost one thousand words. Elizabeth's response to the advice was such that it was wise for Philip to remove his presence from court and seek the relative seclusion of his sister's Wilton home. The second offence was acted out on the tennis courts at Greenwich Palace where Philip broke etiquette, trading insults with the Earl of Oxford. Sidney had been moved to defend his father's reputation which had been somewhat trashed by the rival earl. It was not what was said but rather that Sidney had ignored the importance of rank, insulting a courtier higher in the food chain than himself. From this point Sidney believed he had been ostracized by the queen.

Philip's unwanted advice as regards the French suitor was likely to be especially offensive on a number of levels. He was engaging in a type of role reversal: it was the queen who was responsible for overseeing the marital plans of her courtiers not the other way round. Elizabeth acted in loco parentis ensuring that the young generation, surrounding her at court, acted with dignity and did not behave in such a way that would bring shame on their families. Courtiers and their families worked in the service of a queen.

---

1   Sidney, P, extract from a letter to Queen Elizabeth I in Kuin, R. (ed) (2012) Philip Sidney. The Correspondence of Sir Philip Sidney, Oxford: Oxford University Press.

Greenwich Palace

As marriages were part of the power politics of the day she would either approve or disapprove of matches. We know, for example, that Elizabeth had favoured and actively encouraged the Mary Sidney, Henry Herbert match. When her wishes regarding marriage were either disobeyed or unsought she was known to act decisively and with severity. Punishments were incurred by those who married in secret. What might be of particular relevance here is that Robert Dudley, Earl of Leicester, was her great favourite. He happened also to be uncle to Mary Sidney and Philip, being their mother's brother. After the death of his first wife Amy Robsart, in 1560, historians believe that he sought Elizabeth's hand in marriage but her refusal of him was partly based on the scandal surrounding that death, and the part which could have been played by Leicester. The earl was forced to look elsewhere and eighteen years later, in 1578, he married in secret. His bride was the dowager Countess of Essex. There were rumours that the couple had plotted to kill her husband in order to allow the marriage to take place. When the queen heard about the event she was furious and threatened to send Leicester to the tower. Within two years the nephew of the man who committed such a misdemeanour, Philip Sidney, was attempting to deliver a lecture to the queen about her own marital preferences. It is interesting to speculate, given the history of her family, if Elizabeth was especially sensitive about the propriety of sexual relationships within and outside marriage; remembering that her own father had her mother executed on charges of adultery and incest.

During the following decade the number of courtiers disregarding the monarch's wishes over marriage plans has been cited, in recent times, as evidence of Elizabeth losing her grip during the final years of her reign. In 1590 Leicester's stepson and her new favourite, the Earl of Essex, incurred Elizabeth's wrath when he married the widow of Philip Sidney, Frances (née Walsingham). In the latter part of 1592, Walter Ralegh (also spelt Raleigh) denied that he had married one of the lady attendants of the queen, Elizabeth Throckmorton; he was hiding the fact that in reality he had married her the previous year. The couple were both sent to the Tower and Ralegh was banished from court indefinitely. It is interesting that both parties received punishment so women were regarded as being complicit in the deception. When in 1601 Mary Fitton, a maid of honour to the queen, became pregnant, William Pembroke was named as the father. William was Mary Sidney's eldest son and the scandal caused by his misdemeanour rocked the family. After his refusal to marry the young lady he was banished from court; hence another descendant of the Sidney line, the generation after Mary and Philip, felt thwarted by the crown. There is a sense in which it was a concern which haunted the generations.

As a member of the Sidney family Philip had not been alone in believing that his efforts were not adequately acknowledged or rewarded. Both of his parents felt that they had been taken advantage of at court, towards the end of their lives. What is particularly interesting is the belief that is reinforced of the Sidney family as a group set apart. There was a hint of the anti- establishment about their beliefs. As Calvinist sympathizers they understood ideas taught by persons influenced by the religious leaders and their political theory. Calvinists believed in the submission of individual citizens to legitimate authority but preferred the idea of a republic rather than a monarchy. Some writers argue that they can detect anti-monarchical feelings in some of Sidney's works. At Wilton Philip began to cultivate his writing in earnest. On the fringes of court life this highly educated and able man turned to his life's work. He took his place in the literary empire fostered by Mary, beginning with the 'Arcadia'. It was in the house of his sister, where disillusionment with his public life had led him, that he wrote some of the great fictional and philosophical pieces for which he is now famous. There is a real sense that it was in this Wiltshire estate that Philip was most at home and felt the comfort of being understood. The shared past and antecedents of the brother and sister gave them both an outlook which was similar but their activity was, on the surface, divided by gender. Mary had insight into the conflict wrought by the drive to become soldier and poet and how these notions were not resolved by her brother within his life span. It was not Philip who made his works known as they were all printed posthumously. It was his sister who took upon herself the task of creating the Sidney legend as part of the literary scene in Elizabethan England.

The Literary Scene in the Second half of the 16th Century.

If Wilton House found a place in the literary life of England during the Elizabethan era what did it tap into and what did the world of literature look like in the country at that time? It is regarded as being the period when the English Renaissance was at its height. There was a proliferation of poetry and dramatic productions written in the vernacular language. There are multiple reasons given why this occurred. The Reformation encouraged moving away from reliance on Latin for written texts. The court of Elizabeth I had created a sense of stability which allowed for the development of creative thinking; the printing press enabled the production of texts and middle class males educated

Gray's Inn Hall

at grammar schools looked to developing a profession in the literary business: both Edmund Spenser and William Shakespeare fall into this category. When Spenser's *The Faerie Queene* appeared in print in 1590 his name was on the title page. It illustrated how the notion of the respectable professional author had entered the world of English literature. New texts such as *The Faerie Queene* had to be entered into a record book referred to as The Stationers' Register and operated by the Stationers' Company. Receiving a Royal Charter in 1557 the Company was tasked with regulating the production of printed material as it entered the public domain.

There was a long tradition of dramatic performance in Britain. In medieval England miracle plays and pageants had taken place under the auspices of local churches. Alongside the deliberate creation of works for public consumption there was a rich, more or less informal popular oral tradition of ballads, songs and stories circulating amongst the population. Performances took place in domestic settings, inns and taverns. The circumstances of the 16th century also allowed for the building of dedicated theatres. The Rose theatre was built in 1587 with the Globe appearing nearby on London's south bank a few years later. The Inns of Court in London on The Strand also provided an important venue for the performance of plays, probably for the more well-to-do when seeking amusement. The Inns of Court were four law schools in London which operated like a university for the sons of wealthy Londoners. They were the Inner Temple, the Middle Temple, Gray's Inn and Lincoln's Inn. For example, on 28 December 1594, it is known that a production of Shakespeare's *A Comedy of Errors* took place at Gray's Inn Hall and *Twelfth Night* at Middle Temple Hall in 1601-1602. Recent research indicates that the Inns of Court tended to put on revels and masques rather than academic plays as they had a tendency to imitate the programme of entertainment at palaces but there was a preference for using professional companies rather than the members of the Inns of Court[1]. The movement between there and the palaces is illustrated by the performance history of *Gorboduc* the play mentioned by Philip Sidney in his *Defence of Poesy*. During the 1561 -1562 Christmas season it was performed in the Inner Temple for the first performance and then moved to the court on 18 January. The variety of provision of venues for the production of plays appealed to a wide cross-section of Elizabethan society.

At another level of society literary pieces were shared and circulated amongst country house, aristocratic and courtly circles. There was some overlap; for example, Edmund Spenser has already been referred to as a visitor at Wilton House and under the patronage of Mary Sidney. He also published in print for the purposes of reaching a wide audience. So interacting with, but distanced from, the public enjoyment of verse and theatre was the intricate and convention laden production of literature in the form of verse and plays, circulated in manuscript form, within the setting of courtly society. As manuscripts were circulated they could be added to by multiple authors and so productions could be a collaborative process. Two categories of poets can be distinguished at court. There were those who were not from the upper echelons of society, in other words they were employees rather than having the status of companionship for the queen. They wrote poetry for the entertainment of Elizabeth and her courtiers. The other group, of whom Philip Sidney was a member, wrote poetry for the queen to display their wit and learning. They were from aristocratic families seeking favour from the monarch. Much of their

1   Nelson, A, 2009.

verse was personal and referred to everyday matters, including personalities and politics of court life. The key to the abundant production of verse and drama at court was patronage which was dependent upon the goodwill of the monarch.

Elizabethan acting companies had a huge role to play in the writing and presentation of new plays. There were a number of companies mainly active in London such as the Admiral's Men, the Queen's Men, the King's Men and the Chamberlain's Men. Plays were either written by an actor within the group or purchased by the company. The companies took on the major financial responsibility for the dramas performed and the cost of production. Many of the playwrights and all of the production managers were actors. Each man, upon being admitted to a company became a 'sharer', that meant that they had to invest a certain sum of money in the company. The companies were based on democratic principles in terms of responsibilities and rewards. Each 'sharer' participated in decisions about the productions with the person with the highest share being the business manager. Large amounts of money were needed for the costumes for new plays and for the playwright fees. Permissions also had to be granted from the Master of the Revels, a functionary based at court; this also came with a charge for which the companies were responsible. During the Elizabethan era costs incurred by the venues were separate from the companies so that so-called housekeepers were in charge of venues. This may have been more complicated though where certain companies were associated with specific venues, for example The Globe or Rose.

Recent studies have shown that there was interaction between the various mechanisms responsible for planning and staging performances. In his book *Shakespeare: Court Dramatist*[1] Richard Dutton puts forward the view that the function of the Master of the Revels played a key role in the process. Each Master of the Revels throughout the duration of the Tudor period was an individual with a high status at court and member of the Privy Council. Dutton argues that their task was not just one of censorship, although this was essential to an understanding of their purpose. From 1581 plays were scrutinized by the Master of the Revels before productions at court. According to Dutton their activity also covered rehearsing, calling for script changes, organising the making of props and costume design. In other words, they were engaged in the whole business of producing plays. The direct link between public and private theatre occurred as a result of the fact that elite companies of players, such as the Lord Chamberlain's Men and the Admiral's Men dominated performances at court but their public performances counted as practice for the events at court. In other words plays were presented to the public before being fine-tuned, adapted and made suitable for performance in front of elite audiences. There is no doubt whatsoever that the Sidney family were intimately acquainted with this world, as during the final decade of the 16th century Mary's husband sponsored a group referred to as Pembroke's Men. Furthermore, a member of the next generation in the Herbert family, Henry Herbert (not Mary's husband but a contemporary of their son, William) was Master of the Revels for fifty years.

1   Dutton, R, 2002.

So where did Mary Sidney fit into this picture? The wealth and influence that she was able to assume when she became the Countess of Pembroke on the day of her marriage enabled her to become a patron of the arts in her own right and she encouraged and supported the work of contemporary male writers. During the early part of the Elizabethan era patronage was an important part of the system of control of literary output. Even though Sidney fulfilled this function, there is some irony in the fact that an infrastructure for the encouragement of female writers simply did not exist. Current evidence points towards a paucity of women who were able to write at anything other than a rudimentary level in the 16th century. Education for Tudor girls was, in the main, differentiated from that of boys, with the former being specifically prepared for a life of domesticity. Mary Sidney was an exception: she had received an outstanding opportunity for schooling and this serves to illustrate female education was dependent upon parental attitudes. As adults Mary and her brother wrote on manuscripts which were circulated within their family and social circle. It has been argued that there was initially a certain vulgarity attached to rushing to print. This viewpoint would regard the Sidneys amongst those who valued the exclusivity of the hand written manuscript. But in this respect England was on the cusp of change and by the end of the century the widespread use of printing had transformed such thinking and Mary lived to see her work in print. The idea that Mary was actually instrumental in advancing this change of emphasis will be explored in a later chapter.

Whether or not writers of manuscripts ever intended their literary pieces to enter the public arena has been a matter of intense debate. The term 'closet drama' has sometimes been used in relation to Mary's *Antonious* but there is not always agreement over the exact meaning of the phrase. 'Closet drama' is sometimes used to refer specifically to drama produced in the 18th century which was deliberately written to be read rather than performed. It is not certain whether or not Mary Sidney hoped for a wide audience for her play. There is a widespread assumption that because she was female she did not intend the public performance of her play. Some writers believe the term 'closet drama' exists as a term in order to put plays back into the closet![1] However, Elizabeth Shafer states that there is no evidence that women did not want their plays to be performed and read aloud. Some interesting comparison can be made here in relation to translations of psalms. It is definitely most likely that the intention was that Mary's psalms would reach a wider public as women were taking tentative steps into the realm of religious writings. It was in this area that they began to breach the male stronghold over the written word.

The Reformation and Women Writers

It would be an inappropriate over simplification to associate the Protestant Reformation directly with more freedom for women to express their views. One of the foremost leaders of European style Protestantism in Britain, John Knox, was responsible for writing *The First Blast of the Trumpet Against the*

1   Schafer, E, 2015.

Monstrous Regiment of Women. Written in 1558 the aim was to contest the right of Queen Mary to the throne in the belief that the leadership of women was against biblical teaching. However, the new Puritanism did preach a doctrine of spiritual equality between the sexes. Despite this it is hardly necessary to emphasise that, apart from the queen, females were directed to stay absent from public life. Any women who had views which they made known necessarily put themselves at risk. However in a more or less indirect way Protestantism opened up a way in for female authorship that Mary Sidney was able to use to her advantage. It was the new wave of translation brought about by the release of religion from a discourse in Latin and Greek. In the need for translation those women in a position to translate opened a new world for women. They were necessarily amongst the privileged in the land as they had received a precious and scarce education. Mary's influence cannot be acknowledged fully without an understanding of the integral role of translation in the transformation and development of ideas.

Whilst translation of the Bible into vernacular languages was critical across Europe to the spread of new ways of thinking about religious belief and practice, there was also a thirst for translations of many kinds. The translator provided more than the alteration of a manuscript from one language to another. To begin with there was the translator's choice of text. An example to illustrate this is provided by the young Princess Elizabeth when Katherine Parr was queen and married to Elizabeth's father, Henry VIII. In 1545 the princess presented the couple with a gift each, of translations written in her hand. To Katherine she gave a translated copy of the works of John Calvin and to her father she gave some of Katherine's original writing translated into Latin, French and Italian. The motivation behind these choices hardly needs to be spelt out: they were to reflect the interests of the recipients and imply shared values. The manuscripts which were highly ornate and carefully prepared, reflected on the abilities of the translator and their interest in, and maybe adherence to, what was originally written. More than that though, the translator was not regarded as being subordinate to the original writer but in some way shared the authority of the text. There was most likely an assumption that the views and interpretation of the text were influenced by the intermediary action of the translator's voice. The evidence is strong which points towards Mary Sidney framing translations in this way.

The text translated by Princess Elizabeth was Katherine Parr's *Prayers and Meditation* written in 1545. It was the first work written by a queen and was followed two years later, after Henry's death, with *Lamentations of a Sinner*. Katherine and Elizabeth were leading by example. By putting their names on these publications they were clearing a pathway for other women. It was the precedent set by them that enabled other noble women to enter the fray and produce works using their own identity. It is particularly interesting that Mary Sidney as a countess was amongst the next layer of female writers in the political hierarchy and she felt the necessity to merge her identity with that of her brother in the presentation of her translations. In the 21st century it would be so easy for us to underestimate how brave these early women publishers were and what a task they were undertaking in making their views public. They had to tread warily. Katherine Parr's evangelical stance has been alluded to in an earlier chapter. The more religiously conservative bishop of Winchester, Stephen Gardiner, was vehement in his plotting against Katherine. During 1546 he had tortured a self-confessed heretic, Anne Askew, in the hope of her offering incriminating evidence against Katherine. Askew went to her death without offering Gardiner what he wanted and so he looked elsewhere. When his spies uncovered Katherine's secret library of Protestant books which Gardiner judged to be seditious, he issued a warrant for her arrest. It is surely likely that Katherine would have suffered the fate of previous wives of Henry had she not feigned illness and in her fear persuaded her husband that she had disagreed with him on religious affairs in order to take his mind away from his own illness. However, whilst he lived she did submit to his authority in matters to do with faith and practice. Despite obstacles, Katherine Parr and Queen Elizabeth did much to create an environment where the creativity of women could begin to prosper.

A consideration of the context of the lives of these Elizabethan royal and noble women renders it abundantly clear that, in their hands, translation became a creative process allowing for their voices to be heard in public. As part of her political awareness and modus operandi Mary Sidney deliberately composed manuscript translation in order to convey her understanding of the issues of the day.[1] In this way she expressed her views whilst avoiding controversy which would undermine her position in society by openly disrupting convention. In other words, when considering translations in current times there is an expectation that the best translations will represent the original writer with accuracy, both in the wording and spirit of the text. It was not so in the early modern era. When manuscript translations were circulated the translator's preface could point towards the authority of the translator and stress their ability to put their own slant on the text. The idea is that Elizabethan women translating texts, especially those of religious origin, provided a stepping stone in the direction of the acceptance of female authorship. They were engaged in the task of infusing their translations with contemporary wisdom.

In order for female publication to be regarded as being acceptable there was firstly the task of convincing the readership of the virtue of the writer. This was more readily convincing when the text was of religious origin. Women writers were trapped in the conundrum of how to appear to be squeaky clean in terms of virtue; thus spirituality and religion were regarded as being suitable subjects for their attention. But at the same time, religious beliefs were subject to scrutiny and care had to be taken to observe the conventions of the day. Mary Sidney used the name of brother Philip to justify her writing. The fact that she was able to do this helped to give her legitimacy as a writer. It was still safer for her to stay within the realm of religious writing despite the fact it could also arouse controversy. The Elizabethan and Mary Sidney legacy, however, cleared the way for the next generation of women to write in a secular medium as seen in the writings of Mary Wroth, the daughter of Sidney's younger brother Robert.

1   Goodrich, J, 2014.

3
The Sidney Family Philosophy

The 16th century ushered into western Europe massive upheavals in the way that people thought. Exploring the ideas represented in the writings of the members of the Sidney family gives an opportunity to gain insights into the processes of adapting traditions and forging change that occurred during the era, in the domains of literature and philosophy. It is the breadth of the Sidney enterprise which is so intriguing for the development of literary history. Mary Sidney's translation, from the French, of Phillippe du Plessis Mornay's *A Discourse on Life and Death,* was a deliberate choice to set out her stall in her campaign to promote the values which had been adopted by her brand of Protestantism. In so many ways the impact of Renaissance thinking made its way into the Sidney world view. For the educated citizen in the 16th century the ability to translate from the classical languages had opened up access to the full range of Greek and Roman philosophers. The wisdom of certain thinkers from antiquity was drafted in to support and inspire the expansion of ideas amongst Europeans with an intellectual outlook. One of the most popular classical writers during the Renaissance was the Roman, Lucius Seneca and he had inspired some of the thinking behind the original *Discourse,* written in French by Mornay. Seneca was regarded as being a particularly reliable source; he was a Roman whose writings were judged to be compatible with Christian doctrine. Thus Sidney was employed in the task of importing ideas from ancient Rome (1st century CE) via the medium of a contemporary French writer. Although she probably completed the work sometime earlier, Mary's *Discourse* was printed in 1592 and appeared alongside her play *Antonie* as a pair of translations. It was issued again the following year as a single volume.

Philip's *Defence of Poesy* drew on the ideas of the Greek philosopher Aristotle as a key source. From the pages of the *Defence* Philip, the individual, emerges with hopes, fears, sensitivities, prejudices and aspirations. It provides a wonderful source for understanding the thinking of how this man perceived the value of poetry. In writing this extraordinary volume he was striking a chord which resonated with the ages before the early modern era and continues to this day: an attempt to uncover what it is about framing words within verse which seems to be such a vital aspect of the human psyche. It provided a spur for a host of other writers to engage in the discussion, and evidence has emerged of one such very individual debate. Jean Cavanaugh has brought to light a letter written in 1627 by one Lady Anne Southwell to her friend Lady Ridgway. The letter was discovered in a common-place book which had belonged to the author of the letter and was evidently written as a

A
Diſcourſe of Life
and Death.

Written in French by *Ph.*
Mornay.

Antonius,
A Tragœdie written alſo in French
by *Ro.Garnier.*

Both done in Engliſh by the
Counteſſe of Pembroke.

AT LONDON,
Printed for *William Ponſonby.*
1 5 9 2.

The Frontispiece of the printed edition of the Countess of Pembroke's Translation of
'A Discourse of Life and Death'.

response to her friend (Lady Ridgway) saying that she had become 'a sworne enemye to Poetrie'. In her defence of poetry Anne Southwell agrees with her friend that it is an art which is frequently 'abstruce' but believes that this does not detract from the position of poetry as 'The mere Herald of all ideas.' [1]

It is likely that Mary Sidney chose Mornay's work to translate because he was a Huguenot thinker and philosopher, greatly admired by Philip. The two men met when Philip was residing in Europe. In translating the work of

---

1   *Lady Southwell's Defence of Poesy,* in Farrell,Hageman, and Kinney, 1988.

a French philosopher Mary Sidney was expressing ideas with which she was in agreement. It was a way of spreading Mornay's beliefs and presenting them as her own. For that reason the narrative here will refer to Mary Sidney as the author of the translated work. Mary's *Discourse*[1] begins with a reference to one of the most ancient of poems: Homer's *Odyssey*. She starts by comparing the end of a voyage with the end of life but questions why the traveller can greet the end of a sea trip with jubilation whilst the end of life always provokes fear and dread. The allusion to 'Penelope's webbe' refers to the story line in the Greek text *The Odyssey* which depicts Penelope, wife of Odysseus, repeatedly weaving and unpicking the cloth on her loom. It is a device that she uses for keeping the suitors at bay whilst she faithfully waits for the return of her husband from fighting in the Trojan war:

> This life is but a Penelope's webbe, wherein we are always doing & undoing: a sea open to all winds, which sometime within, sometime without never cease to torment us: a wearie journey through extream heats, & colds, over high mountains, steep rocks, & thievish deserts. And so wee tearme it, in weaving this web, in rowing at this oar, in passing this miserable way: yet lo when death comes to end our work, when shee stretcheth out her armes to pull us into the port, when after so many dangerous passages, and loathsome lodgings she would conduct us to our true home and resting place instead of rejoicing we would againe hoise saile to the winde, and willingly undertake our journey anew.

Mary Sidney is no doubt speaking from experience when she likens this predicament to a person who observes a barber approaching to pull out a tooth and they forget their pain, and a child complaining all day about illness feeling better when unpalatable medicine is offered. She asks the question: what good is there in life that we should pursue it so much? No one in the world, rich or poor can claim immunity from the condition of life which imposes suffering and death.

It is somewhat surprising that considering the phases of life that are passed through, she writes that the first years of life give no pleasure to the baby or infant and offer nothing but annoyance and displeasure to those around them. For those surviving infancy they fall directly into the 'subjection of some schoolmaster' and wish only to be free and finished with that part of their life. With youth and liberty come the choice between virtue and vice and at this stage, continues Mary, few are not beguiled. As a parent Mary Sidney faced the ultimate pain of losing a child through fatal illness. She must have watched over all of her four children through sickness. As her eldest son, William, heir to the Pembroke estate, became an adult it is known that she fell out with him when he incurred the displeasure of Queen Elizabeth after causing the pregnancy of one of her maids-in-waiting but stubbornly refusing to marry her. He had to make a hasty exit from court and lie low for a while. In her translation Mary expresses the duality of the options which lie before

---

[1] All quotations taken from Mary Sidney's translation, Early English Books, British Library.

a young man on the verge of independence. For the son abandoning himself to the life of liberty dictated by his own passions, it is as if he is possessed by an 'uncleane spirit'. However, if the newly independent young man makes the choice to follow reason, then he has another set of obstacles thrown up in his way: 'He must resolve to fight in every parte of the field, at every step to be in conflict'. For Mary Sidney, as for the French philosopher writing these words in the original text, it is recourse to God that can offer the individual help in the battle of good against wrong doing: 'God only and none other can make him choose this way: God only can hold him in it to the end: God only can make him victorious in all his combates. And well wee see how fewe they are that enter into it, and of those few how many that retire againe'. Again and again when describing the difficulties faced in life Sidney (and Mornay) turn the story back to an explicitly religious message.

The great wealth of the Pembroke empire did not shield any of the family from harm and misery, although, of course, they were completely spared the hardships brought about by poverty. In this consideration of how best to equip the individual to face the demands of life this treatise reflects the Renaissance revival in ancient Roman and Greek influence and in this case, how to make it compatible with the thinking of John Calvin. Deliberate and sustained attempts were made to reconcile the beliefs of pagan stoics with the beliefs of Christianity during the 16th century. Calvin referred to the process as producing a neo-stoicism for which he held reservations. Stoicism shunned the emotional response of humans to believe in external forces thought to be greater than humans, such as concepts of God. For Calvin the emotions were part of the whole character of a human and were to be sanctified rather than eliminated, as proposed by stoics. In stoicism reason as the highest quality could work at its best when emotions are supressed. The stoic was to be self-reliant; there was no notion of a God who was made man to set the human on the path towards virtue by means of grace. The stoic argued that virtue was necessarily the outcome of a person acting upon reason. Christians believed that only the right relationship with God could enable a restoration of moral order and that was achieved through the acceptance of God's grace, as expressed here by Sidney.

As part of the translation Mary Sidney launches a scathing attack on court ambition and the motivation of some princes:

> Of those that give themselves to court ambition, some are greate about Princes, others commaunders of Armies: both sortes, according to their degree you see saluted, reverenced, and adored of those under them. You see them apparelled in purple, in scarlet, and in cloth of golde: it seems, at first sight, there is no contentment in the world but theirs. But men knowe not, how heavie an ounce of that vaine honour weighes, what those reverences cost them, and how dearely they paye for all of those rich stuffs: who knewe them well, would never buy them at the price.

Sidney continues in this trajectory saying that men at the 'pleasure' of a prince often lose an arm or a leg for some trivial requirement of their leader.

From the world of religious values Sidney has moved to the uncertain domain of politics. A man is foolish to serve a prince who treats him without regard for his worth:

> Others growe up by flattering a Prince, and long submitting their tongues and hands to say and do without difference whatsoever they will have them: whereunto a good minde can never command it selfe. They shall have indured a thousand injuries, received a thousand disgraces; and as neare as they seem about the Prince, they are neverthelesse always as the Lyons keeper ....When a Prince after song breathing hath raised a man to greate height, he makes it his pastime, at whet time he seems to be at the top of his travel, to cast him downe at an instant : when hee hath filled him with all wealth, hee wrings him after as a sponge; loving none but himself, and thinking everie one made, but to serve, and please him

In an extraordinary debunking of the system of courtiers and monarchy Sidney says that the 'blind courtiers' are deluded in thinking that they have friends. Their superiors look upon them with disdain, whilst those who are below them in the hierarchy feign good feeling and comradeship because they need them; and amongst their equals contentment does not exist as they envy and distrust each other continually. The position of kings is even worse for they are able to trust no one, as a consequence of which, although their beds are soft and comfortable, they are not able to sleep but toss from side to side because of the anxiety created by their situation. According to the *Discourse* corruption then grows when men have to compete in an environment where they have to look for favours rather than act with virtue as their motivation. Moral decay results from corruption within political systems.

This anti court narrative raises compelling questions about the text being a reflection of Mary Sidney's own views. There is something deeply subversive about aspects of the content of the *Discourse*. This was translated in the final decade of the 16th century. Within twenty years of its publication the queen had been replaced by a man, James I, who assumed that the notion of the divine right of kings was entirely legitimate and not to be challenged. This points towards a certain attitude of absolutism and yet here is the member of the household of an influential courtier appearing to undermine the perceived value of a key part of the system of government within the realm. The question might be asked, was Mary Sidney intending to set out these views or was it just an inadvertently rebellious piece of writing? In view of the arguments set out about translation in the early modern era it would seem to be unthinkable that Mary Sidney was not writing this with purpose and deliberation with an eye on the reception of her work. The original writer was a French Huguenot and this religious group suffered extreme violence at the hands of the French monarchy. Did this provide a 'keep out of danger' clause for Mary? Could she resort to a claim that this addressed the French court if challenged regarding her meaning? The most likely argument would seem to rest on Sidney's close association with the English monarch and members of the Privy Council. She was known as a woman to be trusted.

Attempts to ground the account in France and relate the storyline entirely to the French situation don't appear to be plausible in the face of the broad sweep of generalisations made by Sidney:

> The prisoner drawes his fetters after him, the courtier wears his upon him. The prisoners minde sometimes comforts the paine of his body, and sings in the midst of his miseries: the Courtier tormented in mind, wearieth incessantly his body, & can never give it a rest. And as for the contentment you imagine they have, you are there in yet more deceived. You judge and esteeme them greate, because they are raised high: but as fondly, as who should judge a dwarf great, for being set on a Tower, or on the toppe of a mountain. You measure (so good a Geometrician you are) the image with his base, which were convenient (to knowe his true height) to bee measur'd by itself: whereas you regard not the height of the image, but the height of the place it standes upon.

However, if the political interpretation is minimized in favour of the religious then the piece can be seen to emphasize another message. Sidney continues in the critical analysis of the character of courtiers stressing that her readers misinterpret the elevation of the ground for the character of courtiers, for if they could see inside their minds they would judge them to be slaves to vain greatness. What is more, courtiers are never content with their lot but are perpetually seeking a level of promotion which their accomplishments fail to justify. The problem that arises for the courtier is in constantly regarding a competitor higher in the pecking order; this has such a damaging effect on the upwardly mobile courtier who feels himself trapped. There are plenty of examples from history, continues Sidney, to alert the courtier to the dangerous pitfalls such a life entails and the storms, lightning and thunder at the top of the Alps commonly dashes them from a high pinnacle into 'powder'. But how does this compare with the destiny of kings? Sidney anticipates the question raised by readers:

> But say you, such at least whom nature hath sent into the world with crownes on their heads, and scepters in their hands: such as from their birth she hath set in that height, as they neede take no pain to ascende: seeme without controversie exempt from all these injuries, and by consequence may call themselves happie.

Even those born into kingship cannot be guaranteed contentment and peace for they get their comeuppance when lightning blasts their crowns and shatters their sceptres. Grief continually 'blindeth their wit and understanding'. The emperor Augustus, his successor Tiberius and even the great Greek conqueror Alexander all sought to satisfy foolish ambition and tread under foot God's kingdom. Indeed, Mary Sidney's translation here depicts a God who laughs at the 'vaine purposes' of such men. The thrust of the remainder of the *Discourse* is to convince the reader of the need for service to the all-powerful God and, in so doing, to prepare to meet death without fear. The *Discourse* concludes 'It is enough that we constantly and continually waite for her coming, that she may never finde unprovided. For as there is nothing more certaine then death, so is ther nothing more uncertain then the houre of death, knowne onely to God, the onely author of life & death, to whom wee all ought endeavour both to live & die.' In this final section of the discourse is to be found a combination of the ideas of the stoics and the Christians. Humans need an emotional attachment to God whilst being able to face the prospect of death with an attitude of acceptance and peace.

Ultimately then this text has a theological message. Sidney has used this Huguenot source to reinforce the message of the Calvinists in relation to earthly kingdoms. Calvinists were particularly taken with the image of the city of God with a spiritual ruler, rather than one who gained authority by way of birth holding a sceptre and crown. It is an astonishing piece of translation by someone who had lived within the orbit of one of Europe's most influential monarchs who was on the verge of empire building. It must be acknowledged that Sidney deliberately placed this translation in a manuscript side by side with her translation of *Antonie*, the play based on the re-telling of the Antony and Cleopatra story: two monarchs who were so self-absorbed that they led their nations into a battle which they had no hope of winning and set aside the needs of their countrymen in the pursuit of their own agendas. Despite the clear religious content of the *Discourse*, it is difficult to ignore the politics and even harder to brush the sentiments aside as if they apply only to countries and rulers other than those in the British Isles. The combination of the two translations by Mary Sidney, of the *Discourse* alongside *Antonie*, would seem to support the argument that there was a distinct group amongst 16th century intellectuals with leanings towards the creation of a republic. Perhaps the reason why Mary Sidney was able to write what might be considered to be challenging in other contexts was, as hinted at earlier, because she developed a reputation for extreme piety so that this was seen entirely as a work of religious faith. It was widely read in her lifetime and three editions were published. Sidney was breaking new ground; the frontispiece of her printed version named the text and the original writer but underneath there was an outstanding and rare sentence 'Done in English by the Countesse of Pembroke'. It was a translation but women were making their way into the world of authorship through the printed word.

A Poem written for the queen: *A Dialogue between two shepheards, Thenot, and Piers, in praise of Astrea.*

Caution needs to be exercised when making judgements in relation to the Sidneys and the monarch. Philip had made several mistakes which impaired his relationship with the queen. He found himself distanced from the inner circle at court and frustrated about his career prospects in the political domain as a result of his detachment. There is no evidence to suggest that Mary had similar difficulties with the queen. Mary Sidney upheld her positive relationship with the monarchy throughout Elizabeth's reign and later in the era of the kingship of James 1. It is apparent that she was a woman skilled in the art of diplomacy. Nothing illustrates this more than an intriguing poem that Mary wrote when expecting a visit from Elizabeth to her home. The most likely date for the production of the poem was July 1599 as the progress, or visit from the Elizabeth and her entourage, was due to arrive at Wilton the following month. *A Dialogue between two shepheards, Thenot, and Piers, in praise of Astrea, made by the excellent Lady, the Lady Mary Countesse of Pembrook, at the Queens Majesties being at her house at Anno 15.* [1] associates Elizabeth with Astrea the mythological symbol of female justice whose anticipated return to earth would usher in a golden age of justice and peace.

The poem is written in ten six line stanzas (verses) in which Thenot praises the divine attributes of Astrea in the first three lines of each whilst Piers responds with comments on the inadequacy of words to portray the extent of the praiseworthy nature of Astrea:

Thenot	I sing divine ASTREAS praise
	O Muses! Help my wittes to raise,
	And heave my Verses higher.
Piers	Thou needst the truth, but plainly tell,
	Which much I doubt thou canst not well,
	Thou art so oft a lier.

Despite the serious subject of the poem, the notion of divine truth and the ability of Elizabeth to represent it, there is a lightness and degree of wittiness and comedy in the piece. It continues in this tone:

Thenot	Soone as ASTREA showes her face
	Strait every ill avoids the place,
	And every good aboundeth.
Piers	Nay long before her face doth showe,
	The last doth come, the first doth goe,
	How loud this lie resoundeth!

The subtlety of this piece is such that with the use of two male voices it is easy to overlook the fact that it is a poem addressing a female: 'ASTREA sees with Wisdoms sight, Astrea works by Vertues might'. The word 'Wisdoms' is almost interchangeable with Astrea. Astrea has classical connotations while Wisdom is deeply embedded in Hebrew biblical literature. In Hebrew and Greek tradition wisdom is a feminine voice. These are striking thoughts when it is considered that hundreds of years were to pass before notions of feminist theology emerged as a discipline.

Finally, in the poem Piers concludes that whatever attempts are made to describe the character and virtues of the queen they fall short as ultimately her 'honour' is beyond words:

Thenot	Then Piers, of friendship tell me why,
	My meaning true, my words should ly,
	And strive in vain to raise her.
Piers	Words from conceit do only rise,

---

1 Quotations from Clarke, D, (2000)

> Above conceit her honour flies,
> But silence, nought can praise her.

Using the voices of shepherds as a device in Elizabethan poetry was not unusual. Real shepherds populated the fields and hillsides around Wilton, with the rearing of sheep being a major industry in the area. Shepherds also appeared in the mythological worlds of the ancient Greeks and Romans where they are frequently associated with the idea of an ideal countryside, reflecting the bounty of nature. It is the language of the rural existence of the Sidneys where 'Wisdoms' and 'Vertues' are associated with a notion of natural order where:

> Thenot   A field in flowry Roabe arrayed,
>   In season freshly springing.

One of the very refreshing aspects of Mary Sidney's writing is that despite her religiosity it is clear that her life was rooted in the natural environment and it is to this that she turns when she looks for ways of expressing the wisdom of the queen.

1595 *The Defence of Poesy* or *An Apology for Poetry*

A decade before Mary Sidney printed her translation of the *Discourse* Philip Sidney was retreating from his life at court, staying at his sister's home in Wilton. He did not have a home of his own and his career as a courtier had stalled. It seems that Philip was at a loss in terms of the direction his life would take. It was in this context that he wrote the first major work of literary criticism in English during the Elizabethan age: *The Defence of Poesy*. The idea was not original. The Greek philosopher Aristotle had written the *Poetics* in the fourth century BCE which included debate about the nature of tragedy and comedy, and the distinctions between history and poetry. Sidney would have been very familiar with this work and it furnished him with ideas and arguments which he could examine in his own writing.

This long treatise, *The Defence of Poesy*, is a clever defence of poetry and it is worth looking closely at how he argues in its favour. From the outset his tone is wry and spirited and we glean much about his character and intellect by the way he expresses himself. At the beginning he modestly says he has 'slipped into the title of poet' and asks for our patience so that he can explain and justify his rationale for defending poetry. In a self-deprecating way he asks the reader to bear with him as he attempts to justify his 'unelected vocation.' He speaks directly to us and from the outset we are aware of his speaking voice, debating issues and letting us into his inner thoughts. He is concerned about how poetry has 'fallen to be the laughing-stock of children' and he is determined to show us its history and importance:

> ...in the noblest nations and languages that are known, [poetry] hath been the first light-giver to ignorance, and first nurse, whose milk by little and little enabled them to feed afterwards of tougher knowledges.

Sidney champions the impact and purpose of poetry by referring to how important it was for classical writers such as Homer, and later writers such as Dante and Chaucer. The early philosophers saw the value of poetry too, such as Empedocles or Thales who 'sang their natural philosophy in verses' and 'though the inside and strength were philosophy, the skin, as it were, and beauty depended most of poetry.'

He praises the poet further, by comparing a poet to other professions such as the historian who can explain 'what men have done', but:

> Only the poet [...] lifted up with the vigour of his own invention, doth grow, in effect, into another nature; in making things either better than nature bringeth forth, or quite anew; forms such as never were in nature, as the heroes, demi-gods, Cyclops, chimeras, furies, and such like; [...]. Nature never set forth the earth in so rich a tapestry as divers poets have done; neither with so pleasant rivers, fruitful trees, sweet-smelling flowers, nor whatsoever else may make the too-much-loved earth more lovely; her world is brazen, the poets only deliver a golden.

Poetry transforms nature into something amazing, something 'golden'. He later says that it is like 'a speaking picture, with this end to teach and delight.' In other words poetry can create an enthralling imaginary world, which gives us pleasure but it can open our eyes and teach us too.

Sidney's style of writing mixes long, elaborate sentences with some pithy comments too. And it demands our concentration! We have become used to short sound bursts. But it is worth persisting and he draws us in cleverly. He is methodical, leaving no stone unturned he categorises all different kinds of poetry: from tragic to comic, to religious and philosophical. But he is adamant about one point - that verse (meaning here use of rhyming) is ornamental and that:

> there have been many most excellent poets that never versified, and now swarm   many versifiers that need never answer to the name of poets.[...] it is not rhyming and versing that maketh a poet (no more than a long gown maketh an advocate...)

This is an interesting section. If we ask someone today to define a poem they will often say that it must rhyme, but here is Sidney saying that rhyming is not the be-all and end-all. He then elaborates a little more about how learning should lead to virtuous action and that poetry is best placed to enable this. He sets out his stall in a key sentence:

> So that the ending end of all earthly learning being virtuous action, those skills that most serve to bring forth that have a most just title to be princes over all the rest; wherein if we can show it rightly, the poet is worthy to have it before any other competitors.

He looks closely at these competitors. For example, he questions if moral philosophers can challenge poets and he refers critically to their 'sullen gravity', complaining that they are difficult to understand. The historian is not accorded any compliments either – being referred to as 'laden with old mouse-eaten records [....] whose greatest authorities are built upon the notable foundation of hearsay.' The lawyer is treated with gentle scorn too because he does not really try to make men good, but to ensure that 'their evil hurt not others'.

Of course the poet is praised: '..the peerless poet' who can create a 'perfect picture.' He clinches the argument against the philosopher who 'bestoweth but a wordish description, which doth neither strike, pierce, nor possess the sight of the soul, so much as that other [poetry] doth.' He stresses that the creation of imaginary places and people allows the poet to give insights into virtues, vices and passions and concludes that:

> the philosopher teacheth, but he teaches obscurely, so as the learned only can understand him; that is to say, he teacheth them that are already taught. But the poet is the food for the tenderest stomachs; the poet is indeed the right popular philosopher.

Sidney is determined to hammer home the virtues of the poet and we are cornered into agreeing with him.

The essay is full of detailed examples which we are skimming over here. But one interesting section is a further exploration of his views about the limitations of a historian, who depends upon what actually happened – the past which he calls the WAS:

> But history being captive to the truth of a foolish world, in many times a terror from well-doing, and an encouragement to unbridled wickedness.

He concludes that the poet 'excelleth history'. The advantages of poetry are that it is not tied to the WAS, but can feign situations and events and move the reader. He stresses the importance of 'moving' the reader or listener; in doing so poetry creates delight and effectively teaches. He convincingly defends the imaginary world created by the poet and gives the poet a high accolade, referring to 'our poet the monarch' who will lead the way and entice us into this imaginary world:

> As virtue is the most excellent resting-place for all worldly learning to make his end of, so poetry, being the most familiar to teach it, and most princely to move towards it, in the most excellent work is the most excellent workman.

We can only agree with him, swept along by his fervent arguments. He may repeat himself a little and backtrack but it is all in the cause of explaining why poetry matters so much, and to convince us of its value.

Sidney asserts that poetry 'is of all human learnings the most ancient' and 'universal' and he points out that no nation has despised it. He says that Romans and Greeks gave it divine names: one links poetry to prophesying and the other to the idea of a 'maker'.

Objections to Poetry

Ever the politician, Sidney makes room to deal with those who object to poesy and to examine their arguments. He comments on those who scoff, who do 'prodigally spend a great many wandering words in quips and scoffs' and reminds us that 'scoffing cometh not of wisdom' and our best reaction is 'to laugh at the jester'. In particular people scorn 'rhyming and versing' but Sidney has already indicated that 'one may be a poet without versing, and a versifier without poetry.'

He makes a positive point though, and strongly declares that 'verse far exceedeth prose in the knitting up of the memory.' What a memorable phrase! The value of rhyme and versifying can be simply that it acts as an aide-memoire. He mentions that rules in mathematics are often remembered through verse. Also, he cites the value of learning verse such as that of Virgil or Horace, 'which in his youth he learned, and even to his old age serve him for hourly lessons'. But of course he is also implying that it is not just rhyme which makes poetry memorable, it is the way poetry creates images and evokes ideas in such a concentrated, rhythmical form.

His brief is to defend 'poesy' so he delves into further criticism. For example he quotes a common criticism (and still true today) that many think there are better ways of using time than writing imaginary verse, but he asserts again that no learning

> is so good as that which teacheth and moveth to virtue, and that none can both teach and move thereto as much as poesy, then is the conclusion manifest that ink and paper cannot be to a more profitable purpose employed.

This sentiment has often been echoed by modern poets such as Seamus Heaney in the 20th century who in his poem 'Digging' compares his father's and grandfather's ability to work the land, to his chosen profession of writing. He ends the poem in a quietly triumphant way, asserting that he will achieve much through writing:

> Between my finger and thumb
> The squat pen rests,
> I'll dig with it.

He, like Sidney, 'digs' very deftly and convincingly.

Why has England become 'so hard a step-mother to poets'?

Sidney bewails the fact that poesy seems to be embraced by many countries but that in England it gets a 'hard welcome', so hard that England can now 'scarce endure the pain of a pen' which has meant that 'base men with servile wits undertake it, who think it enough if they can be rewarded of the printer.' He is not at all complimentary about his contemporary poets. He complains that some writing is 'a confused mass of words, with a tinkling sound of rhyme, barely accompanied with reason.'

Concerning comedies there is a fascinating section where he criticises the comedic writers who:

> think there is no delight without laughter, which is very wrong; for though laughter may come with delight, yet cometh it not of delight, as though delight should be the cause of laughter; but well may one thing breed both together.

He gives examples such as 'we are ravished with delight to see a fair woman, and yet are far from being moved to laughter;' but he admits that there are some situations where we take delight and also laugh such as Hercules in a woman's attire 'spinning at Omphale's commandment' which 'breeds both delight and laughter; for the representing of so strange a power in love procures delight, and the scornfulness of the action stirreth laughter.' In his view the purpose of all comical writing is to provide 'delightful teaching which is the end of poesy.'

Throughout the essay Sidney frequently apologises for being verbose: 'I have lavished out too many words of this play matter.' The direct addresses to the reader make us aware of him as a self-conscious, endearing commentator but one who is determined to press home his arguments.

Further Criticisms of other poets and orators

Sidney is not shy in criticising other writers and speakers for being too pretentious or in straining for effect. For example, he criticises those who attempt to write love poetry, which in his view would never persuade anyone they were in love because 'so coldly they apply fiery speeches' and he complains about their 'certain swelling phrases' which read like factual lists. He refers to their word choice as 'honey-flowing matron eloquence[...] disguised in 'a courtesan-like painted affectation'. In 'printed discourses' he rails against the excessive use of figurative language ('similitudes') and much 'tedious prattling'.

Sidney states that some orators and preachers only 'cast sugar and spice' everywhere or they use too many figures of speech without the skill to persuade or the subtlety employed by the best orators. In the past the classical orators, he suggests, used 'these knacks very sparingly' and he says that today 'I have found in divers small courtiers a more sound style than in some professors of learning.' He declares that this is because they do not use such excessive artfulness whereas the professor is self-consciously artful and in doing this 'flieth from nature and indeed abuseth art.'

In today's sound-bite world, Sidney's sentences seem long and elaborate, but they often contain brief, witty phrases that very cleverly sum up his objections (' sugar and spice'). Language and its possibilities excite him and he often gets carried away and floods his prose with colourful examples to underpin an argument. But he is very conscious of this excess and apparently self-critical too, although we sense that, in fact, he relishes his own creation of vivid images.

Sidney justifies why he has digressed into 'wordish considerations' and speaks of how wonderful English is as a means of expression. It may not have elaborate grammar but this is a positive point - 'no cumbersome differences of cases, genders, moods and tenses.':

> But for the uttering sweetly and properly the conceit of the mind, which is the end of speech, that hath it equally with any other tongue in the world,..

Versifying (the arrangement of verses and the use of poetic techniques such as rhythm and rhyme and sound play)

Sidney is clear and convincing in his discussion of types of versifying. He distinguishes briefly between ancient and modern systems. In a nutshell the ancient (or classical system) uses the 'quantity' of each syllable (its length) to provide a framework for the poem[1]. In contrast, the modern system uses the number of syllables to provide a framework (for example, 10 syllables to a line) but also with 'some regard to the accent' or the emphasis to create a rhythm, but it is also particularly dependent on the sounds of words and the use of rhyme[2].

Sidney praises the ancient system and suggests that it was 'no doubt more fit for music, both words and time observing quantity; and more fit lively to express divers passions, by the low or lofty sound of the well-weighed syllable.' But also, he affirms, that the modern system 'striketh a certain music to the ear' and that English above other languages is well suited to poetry and to both the ancient and modern systems. He talks of Italian having so many vowels that their poetry must always be full of elisions; in contrast Dutch has so many consonants that they 'cannot yield the sweet sliding fit for a verse'. French has no accent on the final syllable and Spanish has few: so, according to Sidney, they cannot gracefully produce some poetic rhythms.

Sidney also gives examples of how rhyming in English can be so much more varied than in other languages. For example, he states that in Italian a rhyme cannot be put on the final syllable. As usual he digresses in an interesting way and bombards us with his praise and love for the English language and its amazing flexibility. He then calls himself back to the main argument. He sums up finally with a self-deprecating, none too serious apology:

> I conjure you all that have had the evil luck to read this ink-wasting toy of mine, even in the name of the Nine Muses, no more to scorn the sacred mysteries of poesy; no more to laugh at the name of poets, as though they were next inheritors to fools; no more to jest at the reverend title of a 'rhymer'; but to believe with Aristotle, that they were the ancient

---

[1] For example – the first syllable of season (sea) would be long and the second syllable (on) is short.
[2] 'Warm well thy wits if thou wilt win her will'- is a line spoken by Therion in 'The Lady of May'.There are ten syllables here and we can feel a rhythm which is the well-used heart beat ' iambic' rhythm: a quiet beat followed by a stronger one.

treasurers of the Grecians' divinity;[...]to believe[..] that they are so
beloved of the gods that whatsoever they write proceeds of a divine
fury. Lastly, to believe themselves, when they tell you they will make
you immortal by their verses.

He ends this praise of poetry and poets with rhetorical flourishes of repetition,
building to a climax:

Thus doing, your names shall flourish in the printers' shops[...]thus
doing you shall be most fair, most rich, most wise, most all [..]

His final paragraph is an amusing, yet serious warning, that if you 'cannot
hear the planet-like music of poetry; if you have so earth-creeping a mind,
that it cannot lift itself up to look to the sky of poetry' he will finally curse you
that 'when you die, your memory die from the earth for want of an epitaph.'
Strong stuff, reminiscent of the way Shakespeare often ends his sonnets – don't
you dare argue with me! In Shakespeare's sonnet 116 he talks of love lasting
forever: 'Love's not Time's fool' and he clinches his discussion in the final
couplet:

If this be error and upon me prov'd,
I never writ nor no man ever lov'd.

Here we are - reading and writing about these poets, proving the point that
words last and have power.

Sidney takes us on a wordy journey and entertains us with so many
examples and convincing arguments. Much of his detailed discussion has
had to be omitted (the original text is more than 20,000 words) but the focus
here has been to summarise the main thrust of his defence. And he defends
poetry with such passion and commitment. The essay reveals much about his
commitment to 'poesy' and his strong belief in its value.

Looking at these early texts written by the Sidney siblings highlights the
way that gender influenced the way the writers set about their task. Mary's
document is a translation but Philip writes in his own name using sources such
as Aristotle, woven into a narration of his own construction. An important
contribution to this discussion is offered by F. O Matthiessen, commenting
that 'A Study of Elizabethan translation is a study of the means by which
the Renaissance came to England'[1]. Both parties were engaged in the task
which imported and interpreted ideas in the movement of cultural exchange
taking place across Europe. It is worth emphasising that scholars argue that
translations from the Elizabethan era can be regarded as 'original' texts by
the translators. That translation is part of a constant process which includes
original composition. Key to understanding the status of Mary's and of Philip's
text is the understanding of how Elizabethans viewed these works, rather than
how that might be interpreted today: 'In a culture in which literary excellence

1 Matthiessen F, 2013.

is as likely to be defined by successful assimilation as by originality, almost all texts have to be understood as a dialogue with their sources'. In other words during the Renaissance, the proliferation of new texts presented in English whether they were 'translations' or what we might more readily regard as 'original' today, were regarded by contemporaries as providing unique and individual voices[1].

The likelihood is that Philip wrote his *Defence* during the years 1579 – 1580 whilst he was ensconced at Wilton House nursing his wounded pride after being rejected for service to the state in the arena of his choice. Once he had the option of taking part in action on the international stage, that was the route which he took and he turned to the life of a soldier. The *Defence*, in part, seemed to be his attempt to make the alternative life as a poet more palatable if his ambition as statesman and soldier was permanently excluded from the options. The idea that the goal of poetry is virtuous action chimes with his desire for virtuous action on the field of battle. It is possible that Mary Sidney's translation of the *Discourse* was written at about the same time. Although it was published in the last decade of the century the work might have been completed earlier. In both of these works presented by brother and sister there is a deep interest in the relationship between politics and ethics in personal and national life.

1   Rhodes, N, 2013.

4
The Poetry of Philip Sidney

Philip Sidney's short life of 31 years was undoubtedly packed with action and adventure. He was a courtier, a governor and a soldier but above all a prolific and talented writer of prose, dramatic plays, and verse: from sonnets to songs and psalms. Today he is mostly remembered for the fascinating essay *The Defence of Poesy* already discussed in the previous chapter, but a few of his sonnets are also well known and still appear in anthologies, especially his famous sonnet addressed to the moon. Here are the first four lines which muse on whether Cupid is at work in the moon's sphere:

> With how sad steps, O moon, thou climbs't the skies!
> How silently and with how wan a face!
> What, may it be that even in heavenly place
> That busy archer his sharp arrow tries?[1]

The Death of Sir Philip Sidney

1   Sonnet 31 from the sonnet sequence 'Astrophil and Stella'. See the appendix for the complete poem.

Sidney evokes a strikingly simple image of a pale, melancholy moon and asks a question; always a good technique to draw in the reader. It is an intriguing start to the sonnet. This is one of many which he wrote and circulated to a small, select audience in manuscript form and it was only after he died that printed collections were made.

In current anthologies he might appear sandwiched between other Elizabethan writers such as Spenser, Drayton and Surrey, but usually Shakespeare trounces them all! However, Sidney's sonnet sequences predate Shakespeare and he deserves to be read and enjoyed more, not just because he was influential and experimental in how he adapted the sonnet form (developed originally by Petrarch and Dante) but because he still speaks to us today with a freshness and originality. This is true also of *The Defence of Poesy* where he argues so effectively about the role of a poet, the value of poetry and the language of verse; or his play 'The Lady of May' which is full of humour and wordplay.

We will begin by looking at a selection of his poetry.

Certain Sonnets (the title of a collection published in 1598)

O fair, O sweet, when I do look on thee,
In whom all joys so well agree,
Heart and soul do sing in me.
  The opening of sonnet 7 – a song to be sung to the tune of a Spanish song

We hear the speaking voice: plain, direct but heartfelt. Sonnets are better heard, not just read quietly. The poet assumes a persona, a character or personality, who speaks directly to the listener. For example, Shakespeare's famous love sonnet begins with a dramatic question: ' Shall I compare thee to a summer's day?' Also, Wilfred Owen's sonnet about the first world war startles us with the question: ' What passing bells for those who die as cattle?' One of Dante Gabriel Rossetti's nineteenth century sonnets has a striking opening line which is a declaration rather than a question, but it neatly sums up the amazing impact a sonnet can have: 'A sonnet is a moment's monument.'

Originally a test of eloquence, the sonnet form is certainly a real test of the ability to compress and express thoughts and ideas in a short poem of usually twelve or fourteen lines. The rhyme scheme and the line length can vary, and poets enjoy playing with and adapting the poem's form, as Sidney does. Sonnets, however, usually use the classic heartbeat rhythm: lub-dub, lub-dub, lub-dub, lub-dub, lub-dub. The 'lub' is a not such a strong stress, whereas the 'dub' is a strong beat. This rhythmical framework (iambic pentameter to give it its metrical name) provides a structure for the poet within which they might vary the rhythm, perhaps by adding an extra beat for effect or surprising us with unexpected stress on a word. This can all become very technical and dry when we attempt analysis, but the best poets orchestrate the rhythm so effectively to convey the poem's sense that we are often unaware of all the skilful shaping of the poem. Sidney is a master of the traditional sonnet format, but he also takes liberties with it to avoid becoming too predictable or monotonous.[1]

The sonnet form probably originated in Italy in the 13th century and Petrarch is one of the most celebrated authors of love sonnets who became famous in the 14th century. Sidney must surely have read his verse and he clearly enjoyed writing sonnets – the collection 'Certain Sonnets' was probably put together by him before he died and then published posthumously in 1598 in *Arcadia*. There are some sonnets which follow the classic line length of ten syllables and the use of fourteen lines, such as *A Farewell* which begins:

> Oft have I mused, but now at length I find
> Why those that die, men say they do depart;
> 'Depart', a word so gentle to my mind,
> Weakly did seem to paint death's ugly dart.

But Sidney can be inventive and confidently playful with the form, as we see in song sonnet 7 quoted earlier. In that poem he skips from short to long lines but keeps the sound mellifluous, and the language simple and effective for a song. The whole song sonnet consists of four verses of ten lines each – quite a departure from the classic formula.

However, Sidney also displays all the tricks and fireworks of a poet who revels in playing with repetition and more complex imagery. The third poem in the collection groups two sonnets together: each of twelve lines but with varying line lengths. Sidney is never predictable. The poem was to be sung to music and is about a woman who is unsympathetic to his problems and according to the speaker 'My fall her glory maketh'. There is a hint of unrequited love, but the main thrust of the poem is that he is in her thrall but she does not value or sympathise with him. The second verse displays Sidney's powers as a poet: his ability to conjure up dynamic and sensuous images and to draw us into the poem. We have to listen as he catalogues the reactions of all the elements, and then finishes on a sad, simple note:

> Fire, burn me quite, till sense of burning leave me;
> Air, let me draw no more thy breath in anguish;
> Sea, drowned in thee, of tedious life bereave me;
> Earth, take this earth wherein my spirits languish.
> Fame, say I was not born;
> Time, haste my dying hour;
> Place, see my grave uptorn;
> Fire, air, sea, earth, fame, time, place, show your power.
>   Alas, from all their helps I am exiled;
>   For hers am I, and death fears her displeasure.
>   Fie, death, thou art beguiled;
>   Though I be hers, she makes of me no treasure.

---

1 See the appendix for more information on metre.

Stonehenge

One fascinating long poem, *The Seven Wonders of England*, is very experimental in form: short verses of four lines followed by a six line verse linked to the first in theme and rhyme, creating a ten lined sonnet. Each verse has the rhythm and line length of a sonnet and the topic is the Seven Wonders of England, the final wonder being the Queen herself. So it is still a love poem with recognisable sonnet features. He opens with reference to Stonehenge:

> Near Wilton sweet, huge heaps of stone are found;
> But so confused, that neither any eye
> Can count them just, nor reason reason try
> What force brought them to so unlikely ground.

At that time many of the stones were not upright and the site would have been more haphazard: no clear concentric circles. Its origin and purpose clearly puzzled Sidney but he recognises its immense significance.

He then conjures up an image of a magical lake and uses the description to hint at his 'Long drowned hopes' in connection with his love (the Queen?). The watery theme continues with reference to a pike and the analogy that he is like this strange fish who is 'rapt with beauty's hook' and has given his heart away . The next wonder is a cave at Buxton in Derbyshire; he uses this image to talk about his mind, like a 'roomy cave' and like the cave in the Peak District full of mist and rain, of 'sorrow's drops'. There follows a description of the strange land around a monastery near Bath. A stake pushed into the ground there is said to turn to stone. Sidney links this image with his love whose ears are said to be like the earth and he is the stake thrusting into it. The implication is that his supplications and requests are met with no response. Then in a dramatic verse using sea and ship imagery he speaks of shipwrecks around the English coast: rotting timbers but from which the goose flies and finds life (the barnacle goose was supposedly born from the barnacles clinging to ships). There follows a heartfelt description of his own desire, akin to a ship, and how that is wrecked by the hardness of chastity:

> My ship, desire, with wind of lust long tossed,
> Brake on fair cleeves of constant chastity;
> Where, plagued for rash attempt, gives up his ghost,
> So deep in seas of virtue beauties lie.

The final, the seventh wonder, is the Queen and he openly extols her wisdom, grace and chastity, and credits her with being his main motivator. The reader tends to retrospectively link his other images with love for the Queen, but they are probably references to an imaginary lover or to someone he desires and the whole poem is an exercise in wit and the ability to use analogies cleverly. We think that he assembled all the 'Certain Sonnets' himself and we assume he had an audience for them at the time, but the extent of that audience, and whether or not the Queen would ever have heard this poem or read it, is not known. It would seem risky to openly express his lust for her; but the ambiguity in the whole poem, the veiling of feelings through the imagery, would allow him to cleverly explore his feelings. The final verses would surely reap favour with the Queen who appears as both angelic and strong. Such praise indeed:

> These wonders England breeds; the last remains,
> A lady, in despite of nature chaste,
> On whom all love, in whom no love is placed,
> Where fairness yields to wisdom's shortest reins.
>
> An humble pride, a scorn that favour stains;
> A woman's mould, but like an angel graced;
> An angel's mind, but in a woman cast;
> A heaven on earth, or earth that heaven contains;
>   Now thus this wonder to myself I frame;
>   She is the cause that all the rest I am.

The poem builds to this climax which depicts a very flattering image of a woman whom he raises to angelic heights and credits with giving him 'cause' - a raison d'être. But there are also some ambiguous moments. 'In whom no love is placed' could refer to her necessarily distant and aloof stance and her apparent rejection of favourites, but it also creates an image of a woman who has been unfortunate in love and one to whom few dare to commit. If we understand fairness to be beauty, rather than the modern sense of fair play, then the implication is that her wisdom is the stronger force. It is not always easy to be sure of the main thrust of Sidney's verses, but that makes them all the more fascinating. We are certain of the tone though: this is a strong woman whom he admires.

Sidney is the consummate courtier but he is also the action man and a multi-talented writer who is not afraid to take a form like the sonnet and play with it.

Astrophil & Stella- a sonnet sequence

This is the first published sonnet sequence in English, predating Shakespeare's collection. It was published in 1591, although the sonnets would have been written earlier, probably between 1581 and 1582. Sidney married Frances Walsingham in 1583 and it is thought that the sequence was finished well before then. What stimulated him to gather a collection of love sonnets in this way? Penelope Devereux was probably his inspiration for Stella, although she married Robert, Lord Rich, in November 1581. The name Astrophil is Greek in origin but has echoes of Sidney's first name – Philip. So the main protagonists are scarcely disguised. Was Sidney suffering from a rebuff, from disappointment at Penelope's marriage? The sequence is certainly a powerful collection of poems reflecting on love: moving, witty and not dusty and predictable. We can hear the voice of Astrophil, the voice of Sidney, and we are drawn into the lively debates about love.

For example, in one of the earlier sonnets (14) he reacts to criticisms about his desire and argues that if it is sinful to desire someone (Stella) and be faithful to them :

Then love is sin, and let me sinful be.

In Sonnet 22 Sidney is amazed at her beauty and strength. She shines likes the sun and does not seek the shade like other women. Such is her power and magnetism that the sun can't hurt her – but it caresses her:

The sun, which others burned, did her but kiss.

The vocabulary is simple (often monosyllabic) and the message clear.

Throughout the collection Sidney speaks of the power of love: the torment, the joy, the beauty and attraction of Stella, and his own ambition and perceived inadequacy. He can be biting and scarcely veiled in his criticisms, for example of Lord Rich and in his reference to Penelope's forced marriage. He speaks of a 'nymph' (Penelope) who is:

Rich in all beauties which man's eye can see;

And later:

Rich in the treasure of deserved renown;
Rich in the riches of a royal heart;
Rich in those gifts which give the eternal crown;
  Who though most rich in these, and every part
  Which makes the patents of true worldly bliss,
  Hath no misfortune, but that Rich she is.
                              Sonnet 37

There are some beautiful, heartfelt poems such as sonnet 74 where he praises Stella as his muse, his inspiration, and he marvels at how easily his words flow when speaking of her. In the second half of the poem he says:

> I am no pick-purse of another's wit.
>   How falls it then, that with so smooth an ease
> My thoughts I speak, and what I speak doth flow
> In verse, and that my verse best wit doth please?
> Guess we the cause: 'What, is it thus?' Fie, no;
>   ' Or so?' Much less. 'How then?' Sure, thus it is:
>   My lips are sweet inspired with Stella's kiss.

In sonnet 90 he conjures up a simple image of how she compels him to write:

And love doth hold my hand, and makes me write.

The lover's curiosity and desire to know everything is captured in sonnet 92:

> I would know whether she did sit or walk,
> How clothed, how waited on? Sighed she or smiled?
> Whereof, with whom, how often did she talk?

She is everything to him and in sonnet 68 Astrophil says:

> Stella, the only planet of my light,
>   Light of my life, and life of my desire,

These could be words from a modern song: simple, direct and beautifully conveying how much he loves her.

In the collection Sidney writes several sonnets about tormented sleepless nights. In sonnet 39, for example, he addresses Sleep:

> Come sleep, O sleep, the certain knot of peace,
> The baiting place of wit, the balm of woe,
> The poor man's wealth, the prisoner's release,

Some phrases and ideas are echoed in the later romantic poetry of John Keats. In his sonnet he speaks to Sleep: 'O soft embalmer of the still midnight' and he describes the torture of lying awake and reflecting on troubles: 'my pillow breeding many woes'. Had he read Sidney's poem? Probably!
Sidney also gives a brilliant depiction of lying awake in sonnet 98. He addresses his bed – 'Ah bed' and describes how his bed invites him to rest, but it is like a field of war:

> With sweet soft shades thou oft invitest me
>   To steal some rest; but, wretch, I am constrained
> (Spurned with love's spur, though galled and shortly reined
> With care's hard hand) to turn and toss in thee.

There is no Stella to keep him company or allay his fears and the poem ends with a plea for the dawn to come. The sun wakes up nature but he wants his 'sun', Stella, to give him life. He expresses this so simply and effectively:

> [...] worms should have their sun, and I want mine.

In these love poems Sidney uses a wide range of imagery including references to war, to diplomacy, to his ambition and to people he knows, or writers he is familiar with. Sonnet 37 is cleverly riddling with a play on the word 'rich' as shown earlier. In sonnet 30 he speaks of his diplomatic activities and mentions a range of countries and people: Turks, Poles, the Dutch and references to his work in answering political questions:

> These questions busy wits to me do frame.
>   I, cumbered with good manners, answer do,
>   But know not how, for still I think of you.

A wonderfully simple ending which shows Astrophil's preoccupation. Amidst all the political turmoil he can only focus on her.

Images of war and fighting are used effectively in several sonnets. For example, in sonnet 36 he speaks of an 'assault 'arising from Stella, of a 'ransacked heart' and 'battered eyes':

> Stella, whence doth this new assault arise
> A conquered, yielding, ransacked heart to win?
> Whereto long since, through my long battered eyes
> Whole armies of thy beauties entered in;
>   And there, long since, thy lieutenant lies,
> My forces razed, thy banners raised within.

Sidney /Astrophil is touchingly self-aware about his own weaknesses and inclinations. In sonnet 27 he admits to neglecting his friends whilst focusing on Stella. This has made him seem aloof and proud but his defence is that his only ambition has been to woo Stella. The sonnet begins with his tongue-tied reactions, leading to rumours about his pride and stand-offishness and then he offers us an explanation. Here is the full fourteen line sonnet:

> Because I oft, in dark abstracted guise,
>   Seem most alone in greatest company,
>   With dearth of words, or answers quite awry,
> To them that would make speech of speech arise,
> They deem, and of that doom the rumour flies,
>   That poison foul of bubbling pride doth lie
>   So in my swelling breast, that only I
> Fawn on myself, and others do despise.
>   Yet pride, I think, doth not my soul possess,
> Which looks too oft in his unflatt'ring glass;

But one worse fault, ambition, I confess,
That makes me oft my best friends overpass,
   Unseen, unheard, while thought to highest place
   Bends all his powers, even unto Stella's grace.

The whole collection contains 108 sonnets and eleven songs: a prolific output. In the very first sonnet he had lamented his ability to find just the right words to describe his feelings - but he concludes that sonnet by calling himself a 'Fool', a fool who only needs to 'look in thy heart, and write'. This is what he does so effectively and produces witty, moving, inventive poetry. *Astrophil and Stella* is a collection well worth reading in its entirety.

The Lady of May – presented to Elizabeth 1 in May 1578 at the Earl of Leicester's house in Wanstead

Welcoming in the spring is an ancient tradition and today we still celebrate May Day with fêtes and maypole dancing. However, our celebrations are probably nowhere near as raucous as in the past, when May Day was seen to be a time like Twelfth Night when all rules could be abandoned and the 'lord of misrule' would be centre stage. Robin Hood was often the symbolic figure who orchestrated the games: dashing, irreverent and rebellious, and full of vitality. There might be organised combat, singing, archery and feasting. The events were popular and not just in the villages and towns but with the court too.

Sidney's *The Lady of May* was presented to Elizabeth on one of her progresses around the country – when the court visited other stately houses. Sidney was not alone in presenting a drama to the queen. She was entertained at numerous country houses including Kenilworth, Cowdray (Lord Montagu) and Elvetham. But Sidney's script (which would have been written up after the performance) is full of humour and fascinating detail and it is interesting to speculate on his purpose: to impress the queen and Leicester; to further his ambition; to further Leicester's pursuit of Elizabeth? The story itself is simple: two men, one a forester and one a shepherd, love the Lady of May, but she cannot decide between them. The Lady's mother begins the pageant by asking the queen for her help about which suitor her daughter should choose. The queen then listens to the characters wooing the daughter. Each suitor briefly sings and Sidney effectively shows how different they are. There is the outspoken Therion:

Warm well thy wits, if thou wilt win her will,
For water cold did never promise fire:

And the more conventional Epsilus:

Two thousand sheep I have as white as milk,
Though not so white as is thy lovely face;

Sidney gives the good lines to the one he favours!

The detailed case for each suitor is presented by an older shepherd, Dorcas, and an older forester Rixus. The forester Therion is called 'a wild fool' by Dorcas and Rixus labels the shepherd Epsilus 'a sheepish dolt'. Therion is painted with more vitality and it seems clear that Sidney wanted the queen to choose the less conventional 'action' man. When she selects Epsilus, Sidney writes a non-commital paragraph which states: '..what words, what reasons she used for it, this paper, which carrieth so base names, is not worthy to contain.'

There is much humour in the drama especially in the person of the hilarious pedant, Master Rombus. He attempts to flatter the queen and to give advice to the suitors on how to argue their point. But he is verbose and peppers his speech with grandiose vocabulary- usually misused - and many Latin phrases. Rombus reminds us of people who use long words wrongly in trying to sound clever. In his first speech he announces his credentials:

> I am *Potentissima Domina*, a schoolmaster; that is to say, a pedagogue; one not a little versed in the disciplinating of the juvental fry, wherein (to my laud I say it) I use such geometrical proportion, as neither wanteth mansuetude nor correction,

He rambles on, overdoing the adjectives and calls the two suitors:

> two, a brace, a couple, a cast of young men, to whom the crafty coward Cupid had *inquam* delivered his dire doleful digging dignifying dart.

Mocking those who are not concise and clear often provides for good comedy. Shakespeare's plodding constable Dogberry who appears in *Much Ado about Nothing* gets his words wrong when he tries to 'up' his vocabulary: vitigant instead of vigilant, or senseless instead of sensible. But the most celebrated example is Mrs Malaprop in Sheridan's *The Rivals*. Perhaps Sheridan had read *The Lady of May*? Certainly he exploits pretentious mistakes with language to great comic effect. For example, Mrs Malaprop refers to 'the pineapple of excellence' instead of the pinnacle!

Sidney's festive drama for the queen shows what a good entertainer he is, but it also reminds us of his wish to be in the queen's favour. Her reaction to the presentation indicates that she was not swayed by the more dashing suitor which must have disappointed Sidney and Leicester.

Philip's writing of a *Defence of Poesy* and analysis of this court drama alongside his poetry provides a unique opportunity to observe the theory and practice of poetry produced by him. Although opinions about him are divided it has often been said that *Astrophil and Stella* is the finest sonnet sequence in the English language and his literary achievements and outlook have been credited as having influenced writers of subsequent generations, although he is far from being a household name. Until recent decades volumes have been written about Philip Sidney without a mention of his sister Mary. Her role in the propagation of the Sidney image and the fashioning of Philip's authorship is actually vital to the narrative.

5
Mary Sidney Herbert Takes Charge

The life of a countess

As the final decade of the 16th century approached, the Countess of Pembroke was mistress of Wilton House, Ramsbury Manor, Ivychurch, Cardiff Castle and Ludlow Castle. The family residence whilst in London was Baynard's Castle on the north bank of the River Thames. She did not leave a personal account of her daily activities but information about how her time was spent can be gleaned from what is known about running a manor house in Elizabethan England. In addition there are useful, albeit brief, references to her undertakings in a variety of sources, such as family letters. Her husband was frequently away from home, involved with duties to do with his court roles, and during these times Mary would have been in charge of running the principal home at Wilton, and the oversight of some two hundred servants responsible for the upkeep of the house and grounds. Preparation for trips to stay in their various homes, such as the London residence during winter, would have involved a great deal of organisation. Of course another mammoth task would have been preparing for a visit from the queen, which occurred from time to time. It is known, for example, that Elizabeth visited Ramsbury and stayed with her own retinue for a few days, but there is no record of her staying at Wilton whilst Mary was in residence. Queen Elizabeth had visited Wilton when Henry Herbert's second wife Katherine was alive but a proposed visit in the late 1690s, when Mary Sidney was in charge, did not happen.

In addition to administrative duties there is likely to have been a structure to the day based around organising tutors for the education of her children and dealing with responsibilities for her own and her servants' spiritual welfare. There would have been public and private prayer alongside the singing of psalms. It is known that she continued to play the lute and Mary also had a particular reputation for her skills in needlework. There must have been visits from surrounding noble families. It is known that Mary Sidney spent time supporting her extended family. In particular she had a very close relationship with her sister-in-law, the wife of Robert, Barbara Gamage (Sidney). The two women and their children spent much time together during Robert's frequent trips abroad. Besides her duties and social contacts Mary Sidney would have set aside a considerable amount of time for her translations and writing. In common with a number of women in charge of Elizabethan manor houses she took an interest in medical knowledge; there were books on herbs and 'phisick' in her library and she was known within her Wilton household and beyond for her attention to those who might benefit from her remedies. One or two of the recipes used in order to alleviate the symptoms of various ailments still exist in written form.

At the beginning of 1588, while Sidney was at her Wiltshire estate engaged in household and family duties as well as coming to terms with the loss of her brother, there was disquiet and insecurity across the country: fear of a Spanish invasion had increased. During this significant year Mary Sidney deliberately stepped forward to enter into public life. She emerged from years of mourning following the

Ramsbury Manor

deaths of her little daughter, eldest brother and both parents. She had been stalked by earlier tragedies too: her sister Ambrosia, and closest companion during her teenage years, had died when Mary was thirteen. Another sister, Elizabeth, had died in childhood. It is not entirely certain why she chose to face the world again at this stage, after all the personal tragedies she had suffered; but what is certain is that her political and religious interests were inextricably linked to the crises which faced the country: monarch, government and people could not ignore the growing sense of threat that gripped the nation.

The Spanish Armada

Tensions ran high across England from May until the autumn of 1588. As knowledge of the fleet of ships gathering at Lisbon spread, preparations to defeat the Armada were put in place. Walsingham, in charge of the defence of the country, had proof of the Spanish intention to attempt the invasion of England in April, two months before the ships left Lisbon harbour. Whilst there were predictions that the Armada would aim for counties along the south coast with Hampshire, Sussex and Kent being regarded as the most vulnerable, Walsingham was convinced that the Spanish leadership had set their sights on London. The task of protecting the country was formidable and there were varying assessments of the number of enemy ships, which did not help matters. Rivers were deliberately blocked; harbours were fortified as fighting forces gathered. The country was placed on a war footing. Across England there was planning over how to keep safe and what to do once the Spanish arrived on the shores. Pembroke mustered three hundred horse and foot soldiers and made them available in the service of the queen. Mary's preparations included keeping her three children William, Anne and Philip safe at Wilton as well as looking after her youngest brother Thomas. In addition, the countess had taken her sister-in-law Barbara and her little niece under her wing. Robert relied on his older sister to support his family in England. Their close relationship led to the decision, taken by Robert and Barbara, to name their first child Mary after her aunt from the Sidney line. As

The Armada

the eldest surviving male Robert was frequently away from the family home in Penshurst on duties associated with the court. For Mary the turmoil brought about by the dread of a possible Spanish invasion is likely to have appeared to be a complete vindication of her own and her family's beliefs. Had Philip gathered more support for a European wide Protestant alliance, would his godfather have attempted the invasion of England? Part of the motivation in sending the Armada though was to end English interference in the Low Countries where Philip Sidney had been part of the fighting force.

Opinions differ between historians regarding the readiness of the Elizabethan state to face the crisis. England did not have a standing army trained in the tactics of warfare. The structures for such an organisation did not exist except for the troops on active service in the Low Countries and in Ireland and Scotland. Even so, historians point towards definite evidence that strategic military preparation had been active and relatively effective during the years of Elizabeth's reign. In planning the defence of the country the government had to call upon the county militias. These groups had been encouraged to form since the 1570s in each of the counties across England. The intention was that a group of men in each militia should be trained in the use of weapons and equipment. Response to this initiative varied across the counties but the Privy Council, responsible for decisions involving the protection of the monarch and state, were persistent in pressing for this to happen. In addition to the militia a key development occurred with the appointment of lord lieutenants. The office of Lord Lieutenant had been created when Elizabeth's father was king but they became an effective force after 1585 when they were appointed in every county in England and given direct responsibility for the militias.

There is no doubt that, under the circumstances, defending the long south coast of England was a challenge. Without insider knowledge of where the enemy would land it was uncertain where the troops could most usefully be deployed. Militias in the coastal regions were needed in their own counties. Moving large numbers of men to one district was problematic for financial reasons, with the costs involved in providing food and shelter. Those historians who argue that troops were ill prepared and in the wrong position find that their case is difficult to support since those men were not actually put to the test: the Armada did not land. By 1588 the Privy Council could call on companies of men from every county, some of whom were trained in the use of weapons. With fears for the safety of Elizabeth in London, a larger force collected in Essex ready to move rapidly up the Thames to back up the soldiers in the capital, should the need arise. It is of great interest to note that two of Sidney's close relatives or associates were in positions of the highest command during preparations to repel the invasion. On 23 July Robert Dudley, Earl of Leicester was made commander in chief by royal commission although in reality the Privy Council headed by Walsingham was in control.[1] However, it

was Dudley who gathered the men based at Tilbury and he was with Elizabeth when she made the rousing speech which included the famous words: 'I know I have the body of a weak and feeble woman but I have the heart and stomach of a king....' It was Dudley's last appearance by her side; he fell ill and died in early September. By the first week in August though, it was clear that at this stage the Spanish would not invade England. The weather was not favourable for the invaders and the English navy, the strongest arm in the defence of the nation, was successful in using fire ships against the Spanish galleons as they gathered at Calais.

Robert Dudley, Earl of Leicester

1   Younger, N, 2008.

Accession Day, November 1588

The anniversary of Elizabeth's accession to the throne was 17 November. In 1588 the day began with a series of festivities held in the capital. However, it was 24 November in particular which turned out to be another remarkable day for Mary Sidney and the city of London, but this time the event was to do with joy and pleasure. It was the day chosen by Elizabeth and the Privy Council to celebrate the defeat of the Armada. Celebrations had been delayed partly because there were still fears that Elizabeth's life might be in some danger. Once festivities were arranged the citizens of London were forbidden from watching from the upper floors of their homes as that might have provided a vantage point for an attack on Elizabeth. The Armada celebration was obviously a singular and important event but the tradition of celebrating accession was well established. From early on in her reign the day had been recognised as a time to give thanks for her leadership, and to express some gratitude for the suppression of Roman Catholicism under her rule. There was a tradition to mark the day with special tilts put on at court, and across the nation church services were held. Bonfires were lit and public feasts were part of the display of national pride. The practice of bell ringing had also become a feature of the day, even though this had been looked down upon as an activity for papists in the early years of her reign. The practice began to be included in the Protestant ceremonies in Lambeth in 1567 and one of the first churches to follow the lead was St Thomas's Church in Salisbury where the bells were rung from 1569 and St.Edmund's, Saiisbury, which started ringing in 1572. In 1558 the exercise was extended so that bells were also rung on the birthday of the queen[1]. After 1588, 17 November was designated a day of national thanksgiving and it was in Salisbury where this continued to be commemorated as a triumphal day in a way that was not generally observed outside London.

In 1588 Elizabeth had been on the throne for thirty years. The Privy Council ensured that this was to be a celebration to rival her coronation three decades before. Arrangements were made for her to process from Somerset House to St. Paul's cathedral. All of the London Guilds were told to assemble in full livery. The monarch was carried in her chariot throne surrounded by the officers of the crown and key members of her household. They made their way through the jubilant crowds. At the cathedral she was met by church dignitaries including the Bishop of London and Dean of St. Paul's. John Piers, Bishop of Salisbury preached a sermon of thanksgiving for the reign of the queen and deliverance from the Armada. Amongst the crowd of onlookers were artists and musicians who composed ballads describing the event. It is known that there were at least twenty- seven of these songs associated with the commemoration and four of the ballads survive in printed form. They provide eye witness accounts of the procession and give a fascinating insight into the interest and observations of participants on the day. The following is an example of a verse from one of the ballads, ballad two, which is composed of twenty two verses:

1   Strong, R, 1958.

Me thought yt was a heavenlye syght
To se hyr lyke an angeli bryght
Yt made my heavye hart so Lyght
To see hyr Ryde to London
Amydest hyr Lordes and ladyes fayre
A statlye trayne and troupe they were.
I never sawe non suche I sweare
Before that Daye in London
God blesse I praye, owre sovereigne Quene[1] (Lines 56-64).

Amongst the lords and ladies was Mary Sidney. It was the time selected
by Mary Sidney to mark her entrance back into society at large. She arrived in
the city prepared for the rejoicing in a horse drawn carriage which followed
forty gentlemen on horseback, all wearing the blue and gold Sidney colours.
Carriages for more of her lady companions followed with another carriage
for the children. To the rear of the carriages were another fifty or so servants:
again, all dressed in blue cloth made into matching cassocks. It must have
been an incredible sight to behold. The display signalled active presence
and participation in the political agenda of the day. It was not just the queen
engaging in an act of self-assertion; Sidney was proclaiming her power
before the people of London, the court, and the nobility and church leaders: a
profoundly political statement. Robert Dudley had not lived to see the occasion:
there was a sense in which Mary Sidney was replacing him in representing
the great Sidney-Dudley clan. There was just one more year ahead before the
final decade of the 16th century. Sidney intended to use those years to ensure
that Sidney family values were upheld and acknowledged. During the next
eleven years Mary consolidated her brother's reputation as one of the greatest
writers of the age and the translations, edited works, original manuscripts as
well as the printed word flowed from the hand of the Countess of Pembroke in
abundance.

The existence of the ballads points towards a deeply interesting aspect
of the national life on these islands of Great Britain. When the Privy Council
and Elizabeth created the pageant and ritualistic procession they were not
just evoking Elizabeth's coronation. There was a tradition beyond these
shores to which they were reaching out. The triumphal procession had its
roots in Roman military processions. The work of Petrarch describing such
rituals was well known to Elizabeth and Mary Sidney as both women had
translated sections of his work. In his *Arcadia* Philip Sidney wrote about the
notion of an annual feast held in honour of the queen. It is a motif used by
Edmund Spenser in *The Fairie Queene*. In November 1588, during the national
celebration of the defeat of the Armada, pomp, religion, ritual, drama,
literary allusions, musical performance and display all met in an expression
of relief, as war had been averted and there was pride in those who had made
it possible.

---

1   Marroti , A and May, S, 2011.

Epitaphs to 'The Wonder of Our Age'

The concepts of patronage and literary dedications, so familiar to 21st century thinking, really came into their own with the spread of printed documents and the burgeoning of writing in all sorts of genres in the 16th century. Authors producing a piece of writing such as a poem, religious tract, or work of prose, would choose an appropriately influential leader in their field of writing to whom they could dedicate their work, with the aim of achieving their patronage and endorsement of their productions. For example, Robert Dudley, uncle to Mary and Philip, recognised as Elizabeth's favourite, was also regarded as being instrumental in working towards a more puritan style of church organization. As a consequence of his fame Dudley was considered to be an important religious patron with no fewer than ninety eight books dedicated to him. As chancellor of Oxford University he had a say in the appointment of bishops and there is a school of thought that argues he deliberately encouraged the selection of weak men in order to undermine the office. Those who adopt this view may also attribute his motives to a desire to weaken the church in order to acquire land still held by that institution. Whether or not there is any truth in these assertions it is known for sure that Dudley was the man who led Philip into his last battle and he provided a conduit for praise directed towards the heroic action of his nephew. When Dudley died suddenly on 4 September in 1588 the responsibility was passed to Mary Sidney and it became very clear, as Mary became visible on the national platform, that praise and dedications directed towards the life and work of her brother would be likely to win her patronage. The list of those seeking such patronage was extensive. Others honoured Sidney's memory in different ways. The universities of Oxford and Cambridge produced volumes of elegies in his memory. At Leiden university in the Netherlands, another collection was composed in his honour. Poems or elegies were written by some of the famous names of the day: Sir Walter Raleigh (also spelt Ralegh), Matthew Roydon, Nicholas Breton, George Peele, Michael Drayton and Ben Jonson.

Following the celebrations of the defeat of the Spanish it was Mary Sidney who became the recipient of the formal memorialization of her brother. This took the form of epitaphs, elegies and dedications. Philip was so highly regarded by his close friend Fulke Greville, later to become his biographer, that he wrote Philip was: 'The wonder of our age'. On Greville's gravestone were the words 'Servant to Queen Elizabeth...friend to Sir Philip Sidney'. Such thoughts about her brother were encouraged by Mary and it became known that in order to win the patronage of the Countess of Pembrokeshire fulsome praise of her deceased brother was required. Amongst the group responding to this opportunity were Edmund Spenser, Samuel Daniel and Abraham Fraunce. Mary also wrote her own epitaph for Philip: *The Doleful Lay of Clorinda*. The style is later echoed in her translations of the psalms. *Clorinda* was a poem written in sixteen stanzas. Five of those stanzas are reproduced here:

Woods, hills, and rivers are now desolate,
Sith he is gone the which them all did grace:
And all the fields do wail their widow state,
Sith death their fairest flow'r did late deface.
   The fairest flow'r in field that ever grew,
   Was Astrophel; (Philip) that was, we all may rue.

What cruel hand of cursed foe unknown,
Hath cropped the stalk which bore so fair a flow'r?
Untimely cropped, before it well were grown,
And clean defaced in untimely hour.
   Great loss to all that ever him did see,
   Great loss to all, but greatest loss to me.

Break now your garlands, O ye sheperds' lasses,
Sith the fair flow'r which them adorned, is gone:
The flow'r which them adorned is gone to ashes,
Never again let lass put garland on.
   Instead of garland, wear sad cypress now,
   And bitter elder, broken from the bough.

O Death, that hast us of such riches reft,
Tell us at least, what has thou with it done?
What is become of him whose flow'r here left
Is but the shadow of his likeness gone:
   Scarce like a shadow of that which he was,
   Naught like, but that he like a shade did pass.

But that immortal spirit, which was decked
With all the dowries of celestial grace:
By sovereign choice from th'heavenly choirs select,
And lineally derived from angels' race,
   Oh, what is now become, aread.
   Ay me, can so divine a thing be dead?

The message of the poem is clear and it is a moving expression of a sense of loss, especially of a young life. In the plea to death to say what has happened to the richness it has taken away: 'Tell us at least, what has thou with it done?' there is a manifestation of the disbelief and puzzlement of those left to grieve; how could one with such energy and ambition be no more? There is one line in particular reflecting the special relationship between this brother and sister: 'Great loss to all, but greatest loss to me'.

Whilst this poem had been attributed to Mary for centuries, during the twentieth century a debate arose as to whether she was the actual author. There is a hint of misogyny and a full dose of sexism in the denial that this could be the work of the sister of the Protestant hero and the claim has been made that *The Doleful Lay of Clorinda* was written by Edmund Spenser as aspects of the poem reflect his other works. In addition those adopting this outlook believe that the poem is just too good to have been written by a woman. However, as misconceptions associated with female authorship peeled away and a greater understanding has emerged in relation to how women circumvented the conventions that were imposed upon them, the recognition of Mary as the source is secure. The point about Mary Sidney was that she had to use her craft in exceptional ways. As a woman in the 16th century she was not at liberty to publish a collection of poems with which to compare this poem; unlike Spenser. A poem based on mourning for a member of her family was acceptable as was the translation of specifically religious poems: the psalms. Arguments that the poem was the product of a more advanced education than Mary received are undermined by the actual historical evidence of her learning. Mary Sidney's biographer, Margaret Hannay[1], has also presented external evidence to support Mary as writer which includes reference to Edmund Spenser's own acknowledgement of the fact.

An array of followers

In 1588 Mary was twenty seven years of age and she must have appeared to be mistress of all she surveyed. She could enjoy the new found confidence that, at least for the time being, the Spanish enemy would not be landing on England's shores. She entered a highly creative period of her life. There has been a great deal of discussion over the years about the names and numbers of Mary's followers and some doubts have been cast as to whether she really took an interest in all of those associated with her name. The debate about whether she deliberately set out to impose a certain rigid European ideal on the art of writing in England has been outlined earlier and is largely dismissed. However, one author in particular, amongst the prominent literary figures in Mary's circle appears to have perceived that indeed this is precisely what the Sidneys wanted. Abraham Fraunce was one of those poets, some scholars believe, whose long term reputation was hampered by their association with the Sidney cause. There is a notion that the Sidney alliance cramped his style. Philip Sidney had originally sponsored Fraunce making him a beneficiary of his patronage by paying for his attendance at St John's College, Cambridge, followed by membership at Gray's Inn, London, where Fraunce received legal training. Steven May argues that in English literary history Fraunce survives as a mere 'curiosity'[2] because of his adherence to an outdated form of verse in pursuit of his patronage. This was manifested by writing all of his verse in hexameters, giving it a stilted style which even some of his contemporaries treated with derision. It was the standard metre with six accents or 'feet' of which the classical epics such as *The Iliad* and *The Aeneid* were composed. Although it must be said it was not a style adhered to by the Sidneys in their own writing.

In 1590 it is known that Henry Herbert contacted Lord Burghley, adviser to the queen, on behalf of Fraunce, to endorse his aspiration for the office solicitor in the Court of the Marches. After 1590 Fraunce shifted

1   Hannay, M, 1990.
2   May, S, 2011.

the focus of his dedications from Mary's brothers, both Philip and Robert, to the countess. The first work was a religious piece: *The countesse of Pembrokes Emanuel*. This was followed by *The countesse of Pembrokes Ivychurch* and then *The third part of the countesse of Pembrokes Ivychurch. Entituled, Amintas Dale, wherein are the most conceited tales of the pagan gods in English hexameters, together with their auncient descriptions and philisophicall explications, 1592.* All of these works were written in hexameter. The second and third of the titles were re-workings of classical mythology featuring Mary Sidney as a character.

Ivychurch Priory ruins

Perhaps the most ardent of Mary's followers were those who might have enhanced their political or social standing through her patronage. The likelihood though is that the authors living alongside her at Wilton House wrote because she simply encouraged them and created an environment where the texts of various genres were valued. One of the Wilton circle who was pursued and persuaded to join the Sidney orbit by the family, rather than being chosen because of paying homage to the earl and countess, was the family doctor Thomas Moffett. Born in Shoreditch in 1553 Moffett was of Scottish descent. In 1576 he graduated MA from Trinity College Cambridge, where he had also studied medicine. He travelled to Basle, continuing with his medical studies there and in 1578 received the MD. He travelled to Spain and Italy in the following year and made a careful study of the silkworm. This became important later in connection with Mary Sidney. Before his association with Wilton however, he published medical books in Frankfurt. By 1585 he was working as a doctor in London and in the year of the defeat of the Armada, 1588, he became a fellow and a censor of the Royal College of Physicians.

In his London practice Moffett was in contact with some of the figures in the court of Elizabeth. In 1590 he treated Francis Walsingham during his final illness, and one year later was appointed as physician to the soldiers based in Normandy under the leadership of the Earl of Essex. On his return to London he was noticed by Henry Herbert and within a short period of time Mary Sidney persuaded him to move to Wilton House, where he lived for a time as a member of the household. Later he was given the manor house at Bulbridge as a residence for his family. In 1597 he became MP for Wilton. His wife died in Wilton and was buried in the church there in 1600. Just as the lady of Wilton House was a woman with wide ranging interests so was the family doctor. In the year before the death of his wife, whilst resident in Wilton, Moffett wrote a poem *The Silkewormes and their Flies* based on the subject of his studies in Europe. The poem was dedicated to and inspired by the countess. A modern

T H E
Silkewormes, and
their Flies:

Liuely defcribed in verfe, by **T. M.**
a *Countrie Farmar, and an ap-*
prentice in Phyficke.

For the great benefit and enriching of England.

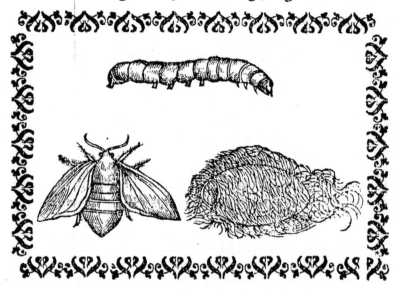

Printed at London by V. S. for Nicholas Ling, and
arc to be fold at his fhop at the Weft ende of
Paules. 1 5 9 9.

The frontispiece of the printed version of Thomas Moffett's 'The Silkewormes and their Flies'

version of the poem does not exist but it is an extraordinary piece, forty two pages long in the printed version. It covers the life cycle of the silk worm in the context of the natural world and provides great insights into the thoughts of a 16th century man grappling with new ways of thinking about the world during the Renaissance. Because of similarities in the use of language there has been some debate between scholars as to whether this poem was the source for the Pyramus and Thisbe episode in Shakespeare's *A Midsummer Night's Dream*. Those against the idea claim that there is no evidence to suggest that Shakespeare would have access to a manuscript circulating privately amongst the Wilton circle. Some of Moffett's most interesting works were his studies undertaken in the field of entomology. Amongst his interests in Wiltshire was his concern with the population of spiders. He wrote impressive illustrated books which were completed by 1590 but not published until 1634, after his death. They included *The Theater of Insects* and a book devoted to the study of beetles.

Linked to Sidney's interest in medicine was a fascination with alchemy which was the proto science of modern chemistry. The 17th century Wiltshire scribe, John Aubrey, responsible for providing information and, quite possibly, misinformation in regards to the local population, was most likely correct when he wrote that: 'she was a great Chymist, and spent yearly a great deal in that study'[1] Within the laboratory at Wilton Mary made space for the half-brother of Sir Walter Raleigh, Adrian Gilbert, who lived at Wilton, as he had also shown some aptitude for the study of this science. Mary was apparently tolerant of this character who, again according to Aubrey, was somewhat eccentric: '[he] was a great Chymist in those dayes and a Man of excellent natural Parts; but very Sarcastic, and the greatest Buffoon in the Nation; cared not what he said to man or woman of what quality soever'. If what Aubrey states here was true and Gilbert spoke freely to the countess it paints a picture of this man working in the laboratory at Wilton providing a complete contrast to the effusive praise that she was used to receiving from other quarters, in the form of dedications from hopeful poets and writers.

Whilst some able and gifted individuals, such as Moffett and Gilbert, became associated with the Wilton household Mary Sidney also attracted followers whose work would not be considered noteworthy. Mary Ellen Lamb takes the view that Mary's patronage has been exaggerated as many of the writers dedicating poetry or prose to her were actually presenting work of inferior quality which would neither have impressed her or have been successful in gaining her sponsorship. Lamb sees this process as being a part of the mythology which grew up around Mary Sidney. Another aspect of the myth involved praising the virtue of Sidney: she was awarded an unrealistic religious status which is evident in some of the dedications written for her. Nicholas Breton pursued her patronage but seemed to embrace a rather strange and possibly ambivalent representation of Mary Sidney.

Breton was not one of the 'also ran' poets dismissed by Mary Ellen Lamb as presenting sub-standard works targeting a female readership. He was a highly praised poet in his own day. The worth of his poetry was recognised after he contributed to a collection of poems: *The Phoenix Nest* in 1593. He requested sponsorship from many members of the nobility and from other prominent and wealthy London families so his attachment to Sidney was not exclusive but he did appear to develop a fixation on her which we might consider to be strange and not necessarily flattering today. Amongst

---

1 Aubrey, J. 2014.

his dedications and in his writings he constructed images of her which consistently associated her with Mary Magdalene. As in this book, the New Testament contains more than one notable female with the name Mary. Mary Magdalene is thought to have come from the district of Magdala near the shores of Lake Galilee; hence her name. She is a mysterious figure. It is thought that Breton was emphasizing a possible mystical side to Mary Sidney's nature in his linking her with Magdalene. A belief was prevalent that Magdalene had experienced a sinful life until Jesus had cast out the demons which haunted her, so she was thought to represent the ideal of the penitential woman. She was regarded in some quarters as being an independent and particularly wise woman but it is not certain which was the view influencing Breton. In any case, it seems to be judgemental and presumptuous to identify Mary Sidney in this way. As part of this inappropriate attempt to control the image of his hoped for patron, Breton overstepped the mark. In his poem *The Countess of Pembrokes Love* he ventriloquizes or appropriates the voice of Mary Sidney and 'she' speaks to God thus:

> Not that my wits can touch the smallest worth
>   Of that high wonder worthiness of thine
>   For, from a sinner, what can issue forth?
>   And who more sinner than this soule of mine?

If Sidney read this poem surely she would have been offended by the implications of Breton's words. In the world of religious belief it is not uncommon for women to be seen as particularly 'sinful' but even so, this sort of rhetoric is unlikely to have pleased Mary Sidney. In her translations of the psalms the 'I' was a seriously penitential figure, quick to recognise personal failings so there is a possibility that Breton was reinforcing this message here. However, there is quite a difference between the voice Sidney used in the psalms and Breton's projections of these thoughts onto the countess. Perhaps this was the last straw for Mary but for one reason or another Breton found himself out in the cold and without the patron he had worked hard to impress.

The Arcadia, Mary Sidney and the history of the book

Philip Sidney's writing derived in part from the Greek mythological world called to mind by the name Arcadia. The Greek world mattered to this courtier in ways that it might be hard to imagine. Learning in the classics, both Greek and Latin provided access to a world set apart from the real and every day. It was a place to which only those who had had an advanced education had access. When translations into the vernacular were just gathering pace there must have been excitement attached to the ability to transform the Greek and transplant some of the ideas therewith, onto English soil. For the Greeks Arcadia represented a rural idyll, a place of perfection and a utopian delight. Sidney adopted this place of escape and was one of the artists who established the concept of Arcadia in the English Renaissance context. Another aspect of Sidney's Arcadian retreat was provided by the environment of Wilton, where he did so much of his writing. Sidney's Arcadia had much in common with the Greek forerunner. It was a place of hills, valleys and rich pastureland where shepherds and (supposedly) simple people lived alongside princes and nobles. There were the tropes which became familiar: of quarrelling lovers and musical delights. Moving away from the strictures of Puritan thinking, which Sidney himself was doing much to advance, Arcadia allowed for a kind of 'speak easy' environment for Philip, permitting his imagination to express ideas of love, sexuality and freedoms which the religious conventions of the time might have disallowed in his public life. The massacre of Protestants was set aside and the looming fear of absence of power and influence, plus his desire for political recognition, could be forgotten temporarily in Arcadia.

In a post Shakespeare world it can be hard to perceive that a text which is not widely known today had great authority in late Elizabethan England in the realm of English literary culture. Philip Sidney's *Arcadia* was such a text. Whilst in exile from the court, staying in Wilton at the persuasion of his sister, Philip wrote his story in manuscript form. Caxton's printing press had begun operating in 1476, so manuscripts and printing had coexisted for one hundred years. There is no evidence to suggest that Philip intended his work for public consumption, except for *The Defence of Poesy*. There is every appearance that Philip was indifferent to the print culture in relation to his work and, as a consequence of this, it is important to stress that his writing was not published whilst he lived. After his death the *Arcadia* was printed. Once in print it was amongst the most popular texts of its day and since then it has taken a prominent place in the history of the book. How did this happen? Enter Mary Sidney. Writing for *Studies in English Literature* Patricia Pender shows the extent of Mary's role in constructing Philip Sidney's authorship. She argues that it was through her intervention and due to the arrangement of her own and her brother's writing that the Sidney corpus was modelled in a form which contributed to the development of English literature and provided a legacy which had direct consequences for writers, their peers and future generations. Pender has pointed out the irony that Mary was so effective at her task of creating a poetic mythology round her brother that she obscured her own pivotal role in the achievement[1]. Following Accession Day 1588, Mary acted in the public arena as Philip's literary heir and editor. Previous to this date it cannot be certain how far Mary influenced her brother's work. Given their proximity whilst he was engaged in his writing and the collaborative nature of manuscript production there is a strong likelihood that she had already contributed to his work.

Understanding how *Arcadia* came to be a notable Elizabethan text and linking this to the developing notions of authorship, as well as its place in the history of English literature, is an essential part of uncovering the whys and wherefores of the processes that have led to perceptions that have not been entirely accurate. For centuries Philip Sidney has been lauded as a foremost poet of his age but assumptions about gender and the consistent tendency to cover up women's lives and agency has led to a massive underestimation of Mary Sidney's role, which is only now being put right. A detailed look at the publication history of *Arcadia* provides a fascinating example; illustrating

1   Pender, P, 2011.

the reasoning behind the sea change in attitudes. One of the issues which complicated the discussion is that there are several versions of what has been referred to here as *Arcadia*. There is Philip's original copy, lost until 1907, known as *The Old Arcadia;* Philip had completed this account in 1581. He later revised and added to the work which became known as *The New Arcadia*. This remained in manuscript form until the 'New' version of the story was printed by Fulke Greville in 1590. Greville claimed Philip had left the manuscript with him when he went to war. In 1593 Mary instigated the printing of an edition entitled *The Countess of Pembroke's Arcadia* . It was this latter version on which the popularity of the book was based and it was republished three times during her lifetime. To her printed version of *Arcadia* the countess had added the last two books of *The Old Arcadia*. In 1598 she published a collection of her brother's work including the 1593 *Arcadia.*

During recent decades scholars have come to realise that the task of the translator and the remit of the editor, in Elizabethan England, were different from what we expect of people in those positions today. A previous chapter introduced discussion of the way translations were used to reinforce the views and the voice of the translator. Joel Davis[1] has carried out a fascinating and important study on the voice of the editor in the printed productions of *Arcadia*. He challenges the assumption that Sidney's contemporaries would make every effort to convey the purposes of his authorship in their edited productions of his work. Davis puts forward detailed and convincing arguments to illustrate this in showing that there was a profound disagreement over the interpretation of Philip's *Arcadia* between Mary Sidney and Greville; this is supported by evidence within the text and external evidence. The arguments rest, in part, on changing fashions in allegiance to philosophical ideas. Davis postulates that Philip and his associates in the anti-Spanish group who sought alliances with the Huguenots and European Protestants, men such as Robert Dudley and Walsingham, had adopted a Christian form of Roman ideas associated with Stoicism which encouraged them to look towards establishing a greater role for the English aristocracy within Europe, with greater freedom from the monarch. However, their failure to achieve this and the deaths of these men led to subtle changes in outlook over subsequent years, with the next generation of courtiers adopting less optimistic and more cynical approaches. This was particularly thought to be the case amongst men attaching themselves to the circle of Robert Devereux, 2nd earl of Essex, a courtier who had married the widow of Philip Sidney, Frances Walsingham. Devereux increasingly regarded himself as the right person to inherit his wife's former husband's legacy. In addition to Devereux's ambition, Fulke Greville happened to look towards Devereux for patronage.

Fulke Greville had claimed close friendship with Sidney in his lifetime and within a year of his death he wrote to Walsingham saying that Philip had left a copy of *Arcadia* with him, authorizing his friend to make use of the text. The argument is that Greville did not share Sidney's political and philosophical views in their entirety by the time he came to adapt *Arcadia* for print, but that he made use of his copy to promote his own views which happened to be an

1   Davis, J, 2004.

outlook which Devereaux also shared. Davis points towards the heavy editing of the text for which Greville was responsible. As internal evidence, within the text, Davis highlights Greville including chapter divisions and summaries of chapters in his version that were not in *The Old Arcadia*, the purpose of which was to influence readers in the direction of Greville's own reading of the text and to then read Philip's work in the manner of a moral and political history.

Davis includes a detailed example of Greville's edits in his discussion. A letter written by Greville to 'The Honourable Lady' chimes with ideas expressed in his *The New Arcadia*. In this thirty six page letter of advice Greville expresses his belief in the view that unlimited sexual passion is the root cause of wrong thinking in the arena of morality and politics. It is not surprising that a parallel thought in the *Letter* outlines what Greville believes to be the logical outcome and necessary cure, which looks to the duty of wives to submit passively to male sexual expression, with virtue governing the behaviour of the ideal wife who would necessarily not inflame the desire of their partners. Not only does Greville's *Letter* draw out similarities with *Arcadia*, he also uses his chapter summaries to nod towards where he believes the piece reflects the same thinking in relation to the ideal of the submissive woman. In the section of *Arcadia* referred to as the 'captivity' scenario by Davis he states that the response of two princesses, Pamela and Philoclea, to their imprisonment and psychological and physical torture provide an example of passive female stoicism that Greville argues for in his letter. The chapter summaries then provide an effective means of conveying the 'right' interpretation and of associating this with Philip Sidney; thus Greville was using the *Arcadia* to advance his own thinking rather than that of the original author.

Davis argues that part of the purpose of *The Countess of Pembroke's Arcadia* was to refute this re-fashioning of Sidney along Greville lines. In other words it was written as a direct response to Greville's efforts.A portion of this endeavour entailed reaffirming the view held by Philip that immoderate sexual passion arose out of corruption at court where greed and self interest was rewarded rather than the rewarding of virtuous behaviour. Mary discarded the notion that Greville had expounded which placed the blame for moral decay in society at the feet of the women who failed to yield to male demands. After the printing of the 1590 edition Mary set about the task of undermining the philosophical assumptions on which Greville based his version. Her husband's secretary Hugh Sanford began the process by writing a scornful attack on Greville's efforts in the Preface of the edition produced by the countess. Sanford referred to the earlier edition as a 'disfigured face' which once and for all exposed Greville to the charge of misappropriation of the Sidney legacy. Chapters and chapter summaries were removed in order to exclude Greville's commentary and the pastoral elements of the narrative, minimised by Greville, were restored. In this way the 1593 edition was a direct response to the 1590 publication. From 1593 it was the countess's version which superseded the earlier version.

With the 1598 printed collection of the works of Philip Sidney, Mary made a leap forward in the presentation of work of literary merit. For in this volume could be found a precursor to the English novel, *The Countess of Pembroke's Arcadia*, and a sonnet sequence which set a precedent for other writers to follow as a single author collection. It also contained *Lady of May*, *Astrophil and Stella* and *Defence of Poesy*. As England morphed from reliance on a manuscript culture to the widespread use of print Mary Sidney had observed at first hand a problematic consequence of the change. Whilst manuscripts circulated amongst groups of people, friends and family, the message conveyed could be understood through means other than the written word. Political, social and religious influences that underpinned a text would be understood. With the dissemination of the written word through print the field opened for the appropriation of texts to begin on a scale hitherto not possible. Mary put the Sidney stamp on her brother's work and made certain that it reflected the Sidney family outlook. The frontispiece contained a bold statement of joint authorship *The Countess of Pembroke's Arcadia: Written by Sir Philip Sidney* and a picture of the family crest. At this stage Philip had been dead for twelve years. It was this powerful collaboration that placed the Sidney family name in literary history and raised the status of the printed word in fiction.

6
Translating Antony and Cleopatra

Antonius

When the 20th century novelist Virginia Woolf set out to write *A Room of One's Own*, she was attempting to convince readers that in order to express themselves women needed to be financially secure and have a space where their writing was not impinged upon and disrupted by the needs of other people. Woolf imagines that if Shakespeare had a sister what would have happened if she had tried to write plays of her own: she would have been ridiculed, exploited, made pregnant and eventually, it is speculated, she would have committed suicide. Whilst this might seem to be an overstatement it does point towards some of the difficulties faced by women wanting to write. First and foremost they needed the material circumstances allowing them space and freedom to put pen to paper. It is not surprising to learn that the small number of women who wrote a play during the Elizabethan era were from materially wealthy families. Sidney was amongst that very small group. The other names which appear next to that of Mary Sidney are Jane Lumley, the first person to translate *Euripides* and Elizabeth Carey, the first woman to write an original play. Of the three women, two wrote translations of plays and one, Elizabeth Carey, wrote a play that was not based on a previously existing piece. All three women were from aristocratic backgrounds as they had received that all too rare phenomenon for females: an education.

Mary Sidney was responsible for the first version of a play written in English based on the classic story of Antony and Cleopatra. It should be emphasized that Sidney was not writing her drama from scratch. Similarly, when Shakespeare wrote *Antony and Cleopatra* he used North's translation of Plutarch's *Lives* as his principal source, which he used extensively. He relied upon writing by different authors to construct dramas for a cast of players prepared for the public presentation of the plays. There were multiple characters, with dynamic action taking place both on and off the stage. Chapter two of this book contains a discussion of how the task of translation taken on by a few Elizabethan women from the nobility and royal circles was used as a means of self-expression in which they developed their own voice as authors. In this way translators were propagating the work of the original writer and sometimes tweaking scripts to give a slightly different emphasis or added meaning; in other words it was a means whereby the voices of the translator could emerge in translated script. It follows that what was considered as being a 'good' translation differed in relation to how this judgement might be made today. In the 21st century there is an expectation that a translation must be faithful to the original text. As manuscripts circulated and changed hands during the early modern era there was more fluidity in terms of authorship. Texts were altered and changed as they were passed from person to person. It was once printing became established as the norm that concerns grew over the control and ownership of the written word.

Sidney's play *Antonius* was translated from *The Tragedie of Antonie* by Robert Garnier. The translation was printed in 1592 as *Antonius* and reprinted in 1595 as *Antonie*. The drama was written some sixteen years before Shakespeare wrote his version and it is highly likely that he had access to this copy. When the play emerged again from obscurity during the 20th century expansion of literary scholarship Virginia Woolf's guesswork regarding Shakespeare's sister strikes a chord. It is perplexing that some prominent 20th century figures from the world of literature wrote off the text in one fell swoop, in a frenzy of narrow mindedness. Amongst a range of defects identified, the countess has been accused of using her aristocratic background, and knowledge of classical languages to attempt the halt of popular plays written in the vernacular. According to this view her play and the companion play written by Samuel Daniel were an attempt to set the tone and recommended structure for any new plays written in English, with emphasis on retaining the classical model. This argument claims that by trying to establish a convention for drama in the style of the ancient Greeks and Romans, Mary Sidney was attempting to stifle the English style made popular by Shakespeare, Marlow and others. Daniel's play *Cleopatra* was published two years later than Mary Sidney's version and came about as a direct result of her patronage and sponsorship. Even the more reasoned responses have not been sufficient to promote Mary Sidney's play either as a production, or even as reading material. The failure to appreciate the text written by her, in its own right, has led to a gap in the historical record and to the neglect of some striking, interesting and impressive writing.

There has been some consideration of the closet drama label attached to Mary's *Antonius,* in a previous chapter. Looking at literary criticism since the second world war it would appear that it has been a useful description for those plays which continue to be neglected in relation to the literary canon. A somewhat false analogy has been used which then involves a leap which is not logical. There is a frequently used argument that because women were not allowed to act on the Elizabethan stage therefore they would not write a play intended for reading outside their small circle. Women were not allowed a voice in Elizabethan churches either but Mary Sidney still translated psalms. If she did not want her play to be performed or to be widely read some explaining needs to be done as to why she oversaw the printed version in 1595 by her favoured publisher, William Ponsonby. *Antonius* is one of the great stories from the classical world in which Elizabethans displayed a profound interest. It is a story which has also inspired huge interest from the 19th century through to the present day. The narrative surrounding the character Antony is uniquely entwined with the last queen of Egypt from the Ptolemy dynasty, Cleopatra. Of all the translations surely this one prepared by Mary Sidney must rate as being of great interest because it offers an insight into perceptions of Cleopatra by an English woman in the early modern era.

Roman perceptions of Antony and Cleopatra

The historical sources concerning Antony and Cleopatra, most familiar to Elizabethans, emanated from Rome. The narrative was written from the viewpoint of the victors following the battle of Actium; it was during this sea battle that Octavian inflicted a massive defeat on the Roman and Egyptian allies, so it is no surprise to find that both parties are portrayed with negativity. The Egyptian queen's details were conveyed via Roman commentators who were notoriously prejudiced in their perceptions of Cleopatra. In Roman thought she was the serpent who had lured away an upright Roman leader, emasculated him and undermined his sense of duty to his homeland. Furthermore, it was believed that Antony adopted some of the superstitious and, what Romans believed to be, inferior Egyptian cultural practices. However, even his countrymen most admired Cleopatra for the manner of her death. To a certain degree it redeemed her in their eyes. In this, Sidney and her associates were in agreement with Roman writers. The manner in which an individual faced death was a critical element of Protestant thinking and was a feature in their adoption of the stoic outlook. This echoes some of the thought in *The Discourse on Life and Death*, the translation which Sidney printed in the same volume as this play. The Roman perception of Cleopatra is encapsulated in this Ode written by the Roman poet Horace; he lived from 65-8 BCE, a contemporary of Octavian, Antony and Cleopatra:

The Fall of Cleopatra
Nunc est bibendum
By Horace[1]

Now we must drink, now we must
beat the earth with unfettered feet, now,
    my friends, is the time to load the couches
      of the gods with Salian feasts.

Before this it was a sin to take the Caecuban
down from its ancient racks, while the mad queen
    with her contaminated flock of men
      diseased by vice was preparing

the ruin of the Capitol and the destruction
of our power, crazed with hope
    unlimited and drunk
      with sweet fortune. But her madness

decreased when scarce a ship escaped the flames
and her mind, deranged by Mareotic wine,
    was made to face real fears
      as she flew from Italy, and Caesar

---

[1] This translation is by David West, Oxford World's Classics.

pressed on the oars (like a hawk
　　after gentle doves or a swift hunter
　　　　after a hare on the snowy plains
　　　　　　of Thrace) to put in chains

this monster sent by fate. But she looked
for a nobler death. She did not have a woman's fear
　　of the sword, nor did she make
　　　　for secret shores with her swift fleet.

Daring to gaze with face serene upon her ruined palace,
And brave enough to take deadly serpents
　　in her hand, and let her body
　　　　drink their black poison,

fiercer she was in the death she chose, as though
she did not wish to cease to be a queen, taken to Rome
　　on the galleys of savage Liburnians,
　　　　to be a humble woman in a proud triumph.

The events recorded in the play *Antonius* take place after the battle of Actium. This was an incredibly important conflict which marked the destruction of the Roman republic and the beginning of the Roman empire. The battle took place at sea off the coast of Greece. Octavian's fleet sent both Antony and Cleopatra into flight in different directions with Octavian in pursuit. In 30 BCE in Egypt Octavian slaughtered Caesarion, the child of Cleopatra and Julius Caesar, and the children of Cleopatra and Antony. Thus Octavian made sure that claims to succession would not come from that quarter. Octavian was making plans to ensure he cleared the pathway to becoming Augustus, Emperor of Rome.

Mary Sidney's *Antonius* text

In the opening scene of Act 1 Sidney has Antony reflecting on his defeat at the hands of Caesar in the recently fought Battle of Actium and his relationship with Cleopatra:

It's meet I die. For her have I forgone
My country, Caesar unto war provoked
(For just revenge of sister's wrong, my wife,
Who moved my queen (ay me!) to jealousy)
For love of her, in her allurements caught
Abandoned life; I honour have despised,
Disdained my friends, and of the stately Rome
Despoiled the empire of her best attire,
Contemned that power that made me so much feared,
A slave become unto her feeble face. (Lines 7-16)

In the original French text Garnier used a different metre and line arrangement: the traditional French 'alexandrine'.[1] Sidney, however, chooses the familiar iambic pentameter: a shorter line of ten syllables with usually five stresses to the line, the heartbeat rhythm. She is at home with a rhythm used in much of her verse and it has the advantage, perhaps, of being more concise and compressed.

In the above extract Antony has accepted the recurrent portrayal of him as a man besotted with the allurements of a woman who has deliberately set out to make him captive to her charm. But he is resolute about the fact that he will not allow Caesar the pleasure of celebrating the imprisonment of his foe. He will not allow his person to be part of any triumphal procession in Rome or anywhere else:

> Thou only Cleopatra triumph hast,
> Thou only hast my freedom servile made,
> Thou only hast me vanquished; not by force
> (For forced I cannot be) but by sweet baits
> Of thy eyes' graces, which did gain so fast
> Upon my liberty, that naught remained.
> None else henceforth, but thou my dearest queen,
> Shall glory in commanding Antony. (Lines 31-38)

Sidney, the poet, is at work in these passages, using the range of techniques displayed throughout her writing. The insistent repetition of 'Thou only' emphasises Cleopatra's power but it is followed by the clever undercutting of this image of a conquered warrior: 'not by force' but by her mesmerising eyes.

The determination expressed by Antony, and later by Cleopatra, that they should not suffer the humiliation of being paraded in a triumphal procession is based on the content of early Roman sources. At this early stage in the play there is a foreshadowing of the dramatic ending when Cleopatra takes her own life in order to prevent such degradation. Of course Mary Sidney had taken part in a spectacular procession marking the defeat of the Spanish only a short period of time before she printed her play. She had first hand recent experience of being a victor in such a pageant and is likely to have been able to imagine what it might be like for those not on the winning side. The Roman general reveals his ambivalence towards his homeland, as later in this long speech Antonious admonishes himself for his lack of duty to Rome and he joins those regarding Cleopatra in the light of having unusual, perhaps supernatural charms:

> Thou threw'st thy cuirass off, and fearful helm,
> With coward courage unto Egypt's queen
> In haste to run, about her neck to hang,
> Languishing in her arms thy idol made:
> In sum, giv'n up to Cleopatra's eyes.

---

1 Twelve syllables to each line, and a break or 'caesura' in the middle.

Thou break'st at length from thence, as one encharmed
Breaks from th'enchanter that him strongly held. (Lines 74-80)

Antonius admits that he became enchanted by her spell.

Antony then recalls leaving the side of the Egyptian queen to go once more to face the battle field making the enemy tremble as the Roman forces:

Breathe horror, rage, and with a threat'ning eye
In mighty squadrons cross his swelling streams.
Nought seen but horse, and fire-sparkling arms;
Nought heard but hideous noise of mutt'ring troops (Lines 87-90)

Here Antony sees the onward march of the Roman troops from the perspective of those communities assaulted by them. Sidney is creative in her translation and often strikingly original in her choice of phrases. For example 'fire-sparkling' is an interesting word: delicate sounding yet so apt to convey an image of fire lighting up the sky in all its beauty and terror. She also skilfully uses repetition of form: ' threat'ning', ' swelling', 'sparkling' and ' mutt'ring' to give cohesion to the passage and emphasis on movement and action. The use of language helps to make the point that even with battlefield mayhem going on around him the picture of Cleopatra follows Antony.

For of thy queen the looks, the grace, the words,
Sweetness, allurements, amorous delights,
Entered again thy soul, and day and night,
In watch, in sleep, her image followed thee;
Not dreaming but of her, repenting still
That thou for war hadst such a goddess left. (Lines 101-106).

It is worth pointing out that these lines were written by a woman who was close to male relatives with experience of battle, both as defenders and aggressors, if that distinction can be drawn. Not only her brother Philip but her father, uncles, younger brother and husband engaged in armed conflict. In Europe it was a religious war, bloody but easily justified according to the religious principles of the Protestant elite in England.

Some of Sidney's 20th century critics particularly disliked her use of the structure of the Greek plays and central to this is the device of a chorus, but in this she is following Garnier's format. Traditionally the chorus was a group of actors present on stage in order to describe and comment upon the main action, sometimes with singing, dancing and recitation. In this play Sidney is keeping to the original structure but adapting the verse form and putting her own slant on the action and characterisation. *Antonius* is unusual in that there is a Roman chorus and a separate Egyptian chorus. After Antony's speech in Act 1 the chorus of Egyptians enter and reinforce the message about war:

War and war's bitter cheer
Now long time with us stay,
And fear of hated foe

Still, still increaseth sore;
Our harms worse daily grow,
Less yesterday they were
Than now, and will be more
Tomorrow than to day. (Lines 229-236)

In the choruses Sidney keeps to the traditionally short line, but she experiments with different rhythms and rhyming patterns, and use of repetition, such as 'Still, still'which emphasises how hatred is always increasing. Similarly, in the first line she repeats 'war' whereas Garnier says it once in his line: 'War and its bitter effect'. Sidney's changes seem small but they subtly alter the sense: the broad concept of war is evoked and then the more reflective second mention of war stresses its ghastly impact. Scene 2 opens with Cleopatra's lament at her loss of Antony, with a clear denial of her betrayal of her lover:

...Oh too cruel hap!
And did not I sufficient loss sustain,
Losing my realm, losing my liberty,
My tender offspring, and the joyful light
Of beamy sun, and yet, yet losing more,
Thee, Antony, my care, if I lose not
What yet remained? Thy love, alas! Thy love,
More dear than sceptre, children, freedom, light. (Lines 17-24)

The final line here is a good example of Sidney's ability to simply and emphatically sum up the quality of their love with a clear list, beginning with the concrete image of the crown (sceptre) , then children, and thirdly the more abstract notion of freedom. She finishes with the ethereal: 'light', the light of the world; the light which sustains life itself.

Thoughts such as these expressed by Cleopatra have also led some scholars to conclude that Mary Sidney was reflecting on the duty of a monarch to place the country at the forefront of decision making over and above their own personal lives. Sidney is conveying to the reader the effects and the dangers of such overwhelming passion and love. The timing of this does not seem to be quite right for Elizabeth though, as when this drama was printed the queen was heading towards the final years of her reign. She was past the usual age for both marriage and child bearing. This tends to support a view that Sidney was processing ideas about leadership in general terms rather than being critical of Elizabeth.

Sidney's play consistently returns to the theme of death. Cleopatra expresses the hopelessness of her life without Antony, should they continue to be forced apart:

Sooner shining light
Shall leave the day, and darkness leave the night,
Sooner moist currents of tempestuous seas
Shall wave in heaven, and the nightly troops

Of stars shall shine within the foaming waves,
Than I thee, Antony, leave in deep distress.
I am with thee, be it thy worthy soul
Lodge in thy breast, or from that lodging part
Crossing the joyless lake to take her place
In place preparèd for men demi-gods.
Live, if thee please, if life be loathsome die:
Dead and alive, Antony, thou shalt see
Thy princess follow thee, follow, and lament,
Thy wrack, no less her own than was thy weal (Lines 147-160).

Charmion, Cleopatra's lady in waiting tries to persuade her against this twinning of her destiny with that of Antony: 'Ill done to lose yourself, and to no end' (line 163). Cleopatra rejects Charmion's plea for her to live for her sons 'Nay, for their father die' (line 169). Unable to convince Cleopatra that 'Our first affection to ourself is due' (line 200) Charmion changes tack, adapting her argument in an attempt to persuade her to honour Antony by bringing up his children as the wife of Caesar, thereby ensuring that they could inherit the heritage which was their birth right. Charmion to Cleopatra:

Breed and bring up the children of you both
In Caesar's grace, who as a noble prince
Will leave them lords of this most glorious realm. (lines 230-232)

Cleopatra responds with more moral integrity than Charmion has anticipated:

What shame were that? Ah, gods! What infamy!
With Antony in his good haps to share,
And overlive him dead; deeming enough
To shed some tears upon a widow tomb?
The after-livers justly might report
That I him only for his empire loved,
And high estate; and that in hard estate
I for another did him lewdly leave.
Like to those birds wafted with wand'ring wings
From foreign lands in spring-time here arrive,
And live with us so long as summer's heat,
And their food lasts, then seek another soil;
And as we see with ceaseless fluttering
Flocking of seely flies a brownish cloud
To vintaged wine yet working in the tun,
Not parting thence while they sweet liquor taste,
After, as smoke, all vanish in the air,
And of the swarm not one so much appear. (lines 233-250)

In these lines Sidney follows a trend in classical writing begun in the *Iliad*; expressing human actions and thought using imagery from the natural world:

'Like to those birds wafted with wand'ring wings'. In other ways Sidney's Cleopatra was departing from the ideal in her disregard of her reputation after death. Another of her women Eras asks her 'What praise shall you of after-ages get?' In response Cleopatra says that she wants neither 'glory' nor 'praise'. Again, in terms of Greek and Roman classical thinking there is something anti-heroic about such a stance; seeking honour and glory after death was a crucial aspect of behaviour of the leaders and their mythological forerunners. When Eras challenges Cleopatra's statement that her only priority rests upon carrying out her duty the discussion turns on the concept of 'virtue':

> Eras: Your duty must upon some good be founded!
> Cleopatra: On virtue it, the only good, is grounded.
> Eras: What is that virtue?
> Cleopatra: That which us beseems.
> Eras: Outrage ourselves? Who that beseeming deems?
> Cleopatra: Finish I will my sorrows, dying thus.
> Eras: Minish you will your glories doing thus. (Lines 256-262)

These fast exchanges are traditional in plays following the Greek structure. They provide contrast with the lengthy speeches and add pace to the narrative. Called 'stichomythia' they are short sharp exchanges and each exchange is a rhyming couplet. It is no mean feat to translate from the French and create such convincing, rhyming dialogue.

Cleopatra's notion of virtue is ambiguous and once more the focus turns on her imminent death. She has not predicted the impact that her death wish has on her women servants:

> And think you, madam, we from you will part?
> Think you alone to feel death's ugly dart?
> Think you to leave us? And that the same sun
> Shall see at once you dead, and us alive?
> We'll die with you, and Clotho, pitiless
> Shall us with you in hellish boat embark (Lines 273-278).

In Act 2 Cleopatra has tried to insist that her servants should not be affected by the misfortune that has led to her downfall. Her fear is not to do with defeat in battle but has everything to do with the belief that Antony suspects her of infidelity and inconstancy and of betraying him with Caesar:

> Ah, live, I pray you. This disastered woe
> Which racks my heart, alone to me belongs;
> My lot longs not to you; servants to be
> No shame, no harm to you as is to me. (Lines 279-282)

The servants are then sent on an errand to find Antony and report back to Cleopatra if he is less angry with her so that she can '...Depart this world...' in a more contented frame of mind. In her translation Sidney has made numerous adjustments to the speeches of the main characters. According to Coburn

Freer[1] Sidney worked on each voice of the speaker to make the language and
tone reflect the mental state of each character. Act 3 opens with Antony who
is exhibiting quite a different frame of mind from that of Cleopatra. He is in
despair at his fate and lamenting his treatment at the hands of the Egyptian
queen. Apparently he has not inspired loyalty from his associates:

> Lucil, sole comfort of my bitter case,
> The only trust, the only hope I have [....]
> All leave me, fly me; none, no, not of them
> Which of my greatness greatest good received,
> Stands with my fall: they see me as now ashamed
> That heretofore they did me ought regard;
> They draw them back, showing they followed me,
> Not to partake my harms, but cozen me (Lines 1-12)

Antony scorns the attempts that Lucilius makes to restore Cleopatra's
character as he claims that she has 'too high a heart' and 'Too princely thoughts'.
For the audience or reader who has heard Cleopatra reject any future without
the love of Antony his words have more than a touch of irony:

> Too wise a head she wears
> Too much inflamed with greatness, evermore
> Gaping for our great empire's government. (lines 21-23)

For proof of her treachery he points towards the battles which he has
lost:

> Pelusium lost, and Actium overthrown,
> Both by her fraud; my well appointed fleet,
> And trusty soldiers in my quarrel armed,
> Whom she, false she, instead of my defence,
> Came to persuade to yield them to my foe. (lines 26-30).

Despite his belief in Cleopatra's treachery, Antony still has to face up to
his obsession with her:

> Well, be her love to me or false or true,
> Once in my soul a cureless wound I feel.
> I love, nay, burn in fire of her love:
> Each day, each night her image haunts my mind,
> Herself my dreams; and still I tired am,
> And still I am with burning pincers nipped. (lines 45-53)

In Act III of *Antonius* Antony contemplates how his life has reached the
stage where a hasty death provides the best option for him. Sidney follows
Garnier in inserting warnings about exhibiting an extreme ambition for power.

---

1   Freer, C 1971.

Blood and alliance nothing do prevail
To cool the thirst of hot ambitious breasts:
The son his father hardly can endure,
Brother his brother, in one common realm.
So fervent this desire to command,
Such jealousy it kindleth in our hearts,
Sooner will men permit another should
Love her they love, than wear the crown they wear.
All laws it breaks, turns all things upside down:
Amity, kindred, nought so holy is
But it defiles. A monarchy to gain
None cares which way, so he may it obtain. (lines 147-158).

Knowing the Sidney family history, how poignant these two last lines were for Mary. The plot to place Lady Jane Grey on the throne had led to the imprisonment and execution of her grandfather, two uncles and her aunt Jane. The Sidney siblings had very personal insights into the impact of unsuccessful attempts to gain control of the monarchy.

Lucilius, Antony's loyal companion counsels him to leave public life and become a philosopher in a remote place in order to live a peaceable life. However, Antony has already decided that this is not an option as Caesar would never leave him in obscurity:

Never will he his empire think assured
While in this world Mark Antony shall live.
Sleepless suspicion, pale distrust, cold fear
Always to princes company do bear
Bred of reports, reports which night and day
Perpetual guests from court go not away. (lines 167-172)

Whilst written in language denoting male leaders and princes this dialogue could not more closely refer to Elizabeth I's situation with Mary Stuart: lurking in the wings, an ever present threat to the security of the realm and a reminder of England's religious past. The greater the monarch the more persistent the menace:

This poison deadly is alike to all,
But on great kings does greatest outrage work.
Taking the royal sceptres from their hands... (lines 317-319)

Sidney leaves no room for doubt in convincing the reader that civil war and the enemy 'within' is as destructive as any other force. Caesar makes this point clear in a later Act:

Nay, never Rome more injuries received,
Since thou, O Romulus, by flight of birds
With happy hand the Roman walls didst build,
Than Antony's fond loves to it hath done. (Act 4 lines 96-99)

Queen Elizabeth I

Both Antony and Cleopatra have to face up to the fact of their failure as leaders, the former a commander and the latter a monarch. Throughout the play Sidney stresses the duty of leaders towards the people that are led. This is represented through the traditional device of the Chorus which represents the voice of the common people: Roman and Egyptian. Once the main protagonists accept the inevitability of their deaths the chorus of Egyptians enter at the end of Act 3 with a commentary on the self-pity that engulfed the couple:

> Alas, with what tormenting fire
> Us martyreth this blind desire
> To stay our life from flying!
> How ceaselessly our minds doth rack,
> How heavy lies upon our back
> This dastard fear of dying!
> Death rather healthful succour gives,
> Death rather all mishaps relieves,
> That life upon us throweth;
> And ever to us death unclose
> The death whereby from cureless woes
> Our weary soul out goeth. (Act 3 lines 387-398)

As the play nears its climax the chorus here keep the focus grounded in the real world of ordinary existence as they note that even the mighty have a fear of their death as it approaches, when they should be contemplating the relief that it will bring. The chorus go some way towards representing the notion in stoic philosophy that freeing oneself from the fear of death is the soundest form of liberation. During the last scene of Sidney's play Cleopatra takes centre stage and the drama ends with her death. (Samuel Daniel, a member of the Wilton household and tutor to Mary's son William, takes up the story in his own translation of *Cleopatra*.)

There are one or two features worth noting in relation to gender in Sidney's text. A question arises as to how far Sidney was overturning gender expectations in pointing towards the regret felt by Antony for leaving his loved one to go to war. There are repeated reminders in the text that he is a descendant of the hero Hercules and yet he has shunned the glory of war for the sake of his embroilment with a woman. There is a sense in which he plays the part of the anti-hero. In *The Iliad*, the account of the Trojan war which dates back to antiquity and is said to be written by Homer, Andromache, the wife of Hector, one of the main protagonists, begs her husband not to re-enter the conflict against Achilles which he has little chance of winning. Roman sources show contempt for Antony because of the way they believed that Cleopatra 'unmanned' him. Is Sidney following that convention or is she pointing towards the possibility that strict definitions relating to the behaviour and thinking of the sexes are not appropriate? In *The Iliad* Andromache takes on the part of the anti-hero in countenancing that there could be an alternative to seeking glory on the battlefield: that Hector's priority is misguided for he is about to leave his wife and son without protection in a dangerous environment. In Sidney's play it is a man, Antony, who perhaps plays the role of anti-hero. There are many questions of course, which cannot be answered in hindsight but what a fascinating opportunity this drama presents in the insights it gives into the world of an Elizabethan woman living adjacent to courtly circles, whose life had been turned upside down by grief at the loss of a sibling in war.

On a very different and more domestic note, but a relevant one, Mary had an exceptional reputation for her needlecraft – a skill which formed an essential part of the training of girls for womanhood. Imagery linked with this skill, and with spinning and weaving is used by Mary in her poetry and touched on here in the following important speech from her play, when Lucilius talks with Antony. He refers to Hercules as suffering from the same affliction as Antony did: pursuing pleasure and passion. Lucilius describes how Hercules fell in love with the queen of Maeonia; she captivated him and made him 'spin' for her and they exchanged clothes:

> Did he not under pleasure's burden bow?
> Did he not captive to this passion yield,
> When by his captive so he was inflamed,
> As now yourself in Cleopatra burn?
> Slept in her lap, her bosom kissed and kissed,
> With base unseemly service bought her love,
> Spinning at distaff, and with sinewy hand
> Winding on spindles' thread, in maid's attire?
> His con'quering club at rest on wall did hang;
> His bow unstrung he bent not as he used:

Upon his shafts the weaving spider spun;
And his hard cloak the fretting moths did pierce (lines 353-364)

Antony recognises the similarities between himself and Hercules and suggests that this proves his 'lineage': Hercules is his ancestor. Ironically the domestic details remind us about the everyday life of Antony and Cleopatra but also about its intensity and how Cleopatra, like the queen in the legend, has dominated Antony. There are aspects of Mary Sidney's writing in *Antonius* that chime with some of Philip's writing in *Arcadia* and in *The Defence of Poesy*: that gender lines should not be sharply drawn. It is in this play though that the women exhibit grave concerns for Cleopatra's children. When Euphron tells the queen that her children will be slaughtered she hands them over into her servant's care:

Ah, my heart breaks. By shady banks of hell,
By fields whereon the lonely ghosts do tread,
By my soul, and the soul of Antony,
I you beseech, Euphron, of them have care. (Act 5 lines 41-44}

At the close of the play Cleopatra concludes with a speech of seventy two lines which vividly display the queen of Egypt's emotional state:

Weep, my companions, weep, and from your eyes
Rain down on him of tears a brinish stream.
Mine can no more, consumèd by the coals
Which from my breast, as from a furnace, rise.
Martyr your breasts with multiplièd blows,
With violent hands tear off your hanging hair,
Outrage your face! Alas,why should we seek
(Since now we die) our beauties more to keep? (Act 5, lines 191-198)

Cleopatra is heartbroken to leave her children, but her determination and her resolution are never in doubt. This concluding speech (a further extract is given later) vividly displays her emotions. It also focuses on the transience of life. Her companions are exhorted to 'tear off your hanging hair'; beauty is no use in death: a salutary reminder of how short-lived everything is.

In this landmark play Sidney has placed a powerful woman at the centre of the stage. It has allowed her to explore the nature and ethics of leadership and lay bare the temptations placed in the pathway of those in power. In Garnier and Sidney's hands the queen of Egypt is critical of her own behaviour but stoical to the last. When Shakespeare wrote his version of the story some years later he ends his narrative with the somewhat clinical, matter-of-fact statement by Caesar after the drama of the suicide has subsided and he seeks a language which will detract from Cleopatra's bravery after being told by a guard that she is poisoned by the asp:

Most probable
That so she died, for her physician tells me

> She hath pursued conclusions infinite
> Of easy ways to die. Take up her bed,
> And bear her women from the monument;
> She shall be buried by her Anthony-
> No grave upon the earth shall clip in it
> A pair so famous. (Act 5 Scene 2 Lines 352-358)

The man in this extract from Shakespeare's play, has taken charge once more. The matter is closed and it is the task of Caesar and his men to cover over the traces of emotion brought about by conflict: good order and convention is required as the men clear away the bodies of Cleopatra and her ladies from the stage and make their exit. Shakespeare has Caesar say:

> Our army shall
> In solemn show attend this funeral-
> And then to Rome. Come, Dolabella, see
> High order in this great solemnity.
>> (Shakespeare's version, Act 5 Scene 2 Lines 561-564)

This final section of Shakespeare's play provides quite a contrast to Sidney's translation where Cleopatra's passion is sustained to the end. It is incredibly difficult to avoid linking Mary's personal experiences with how she shapes the moving ending to the play. She had experienced an arranged marriage and a lost love and, while working on the translation, was also in the midst of her last efforts to memorialise her brother in writing. Perhaps this accounts for the passionate and heartfelt sentiments which provide such a memorable concluding speech:

> I, spent in tears, not able more to spend,
> But kiss him now, what rests me more to do?
> Then let me kiss you, you fair eyes, my light,
> Front seat of honour, face most fierce, most fair!
> O neck, O arms, O hands, O breast where death
> (O mischief) comes to choke up vital breath!
> A thousand kisses, thousand thousand more
> Let you my mouth for honours farewell give,
> That in this office weak my limbs may grow,
> Fainting on you, and forth my soul may flow.
>> (Mary Sidney's translation, Act 5 Lines 199-208)

Garnier's words quoted below go a long way towards showing how the slight tweaking of the translator makes subtle differences that may indicate significant meaning. For the final lines Garnier has Cleopatra say:

> And let my body thus growing weak
> Faint over you, spewing forth my soul.[1] (Garnier's translation)

---

1 Bell, M, 2017.

The contrasting imagery of the two versions speaks for itself. 'Spewing forth my soul' is visceral and not as gentle and affecting as 'forth my soul may flow'. The use of alliteration here and earlier in the speech, with the repetition of soft 'f' sounds (fainting, fair, farewell) and sibilants (kisses, tears) is very evocative. We sense her passion and desire. Some histories of English literature pinpoint Charlotte Brontë's heroine, Jane Eyre, as being one of the first female characters to effectively express the emotion of desire in the novel. Without detracting from Brontë's achievement in any way it has to be said that in her portrayal of Cleopatra, and especially in the final sections of the final act of the play, Sidney has done a remarkable job in adapting the language of Garnier to express female desire.

Why did Sidney choose to write *Antonius*?

Mary Sidney translated *Antonius* from an edition written by the French writer Robert Garnier. So her translation was from French into English. Garnier had used Roman sources for his play, including Plutarch's *Lives*, which had been written in Greek early in the 2nd century CE. In 1579 Sir Thomas North published the first copy of *Lives* in English. Notable playwrights, including Shakespeare, used this source extensively for their own writing. Debates about the play often focus on why Mary Sidney chose this particular story on which to base her writing. As well as exploring this question it is also pertinent to ask why she chose to translate Garnier's work? There are some strong arguments supporting the idea that it suited her political purposes in terms of sending more or less coded messages to Elizabeth which, presumably could be denied if they were misinterpreted or if the writer was thought to be out of order. It is argued that the play examines the idea of virtue and monarchy and that it is this which Sidney was presenting to the current English queen. There are some parallels between Elizabeth and Cleopatra: they upheld the virtue of constancy in leading their respective countries. Like Mary Sidney, Cleopatra was a noble mourning heroine and it is this feature which leads some writers to claim that the similarity led to Mary Sidney's choice of Cleopatra for her translation. In other words it was an elaborate ploy in her re-fashioning of her own image, in presenting herself as an influential presence capable of inheriting the Sidney legacy in the political, religious and literary spheres and adding to her authority as Philip's successor. Of course there cannot be certainty as to why Sidney chose this classic story but the arguments which are rooted in the historical background and publication history of the play are especially credible.

One such view has been expressed by Anne Lake Prescott in *Ambiguities in French History*. According to Prescott's perspective on Mary Sidney's motivation, her choice of subject was influenced by the historical parallels between Renaissance Europe and Rome at the end of the republic: the latter providing the backdrop to the story of Antony and Cleopatra. November 26 1590 is the date Mary gives for the completion of her translation of *Antonie*. At that stage both France and England had recent experience of severely difficult times with a potential threat to undermine the security of their nations: in

England the Armada with the possibility of resurgent Catholicism, in France the pernicious impact of religious wars. To fully appreciate this view it must be remembered that during Tudor times French and English history was deeply entwined. Furthermore, on a more personal level, the alliance between the Dudley and Sidney families with their influence at the heart of the monarchy, showed their great affinity with the cause of the French Huguenots. For Elizabethans looking across the sea to France, fear of civil war was a reality. In Sidney's play two Roman generals had been at loggerheads, fighting over the control of Rome. The Battle of Actium in 31 BCE where the forces of Mark Antony and Cleopatra were defeated by Octavian, was the final battle involving the Roman republic. Prescott believes that any play set at the time of the collapse of the Roman republic and the beginning of the empire could not avoid political overtones and that this underpinned Sidney's selection of this play for translation.

Sidney's biographer, Margaret Hannay, agrees with the assessment that political motivation did much to influence Sidney's choice of text. This view is especially persuasive bearing in mind that Robert Garnier knowingly used his drama to criticize the state. In particular, Garnier pointed out the similarities between the events he describes and the French civil wars. Hannay argues that the sympathetic attitude towards the poor in Garnier's play would also have been an attraction for Sidney who also stressed the role of the monarch in protecting their subjects; in her play a concern is shown for the impact of violence in war wrought on ordinary citizens:

> Come, you poor people tired with ceaseless plaints
> With tears and sighs make mournful sacrifice
> On Isis' altars (Act 2, Lines 35-37)

It is argued that by the time Shakespeare was at his most prolific as a writer it was accepted that by concentrating on a particular period of Roman history playwrights were able to explore constitutional and moral questions and their possible outcomes. So Roman history was used to address discussion of political scenarios. Hannay places Sidney at the centre of this important literary development: 'Her work was thus near the outset of the dramatic movement to comment on contemporary affairs by means of Roman historic allusions, parallel to the use of the Psalms as a privileged genre for political statement.'[1]

The comments in relation to the psalms are interesting and will be pursued in the following chapter. What is noteworthy here is that far from relegating Sidney's work to an elitist drama written for a côterie of the privileged, Hannay sees her work as being part of a movement to bring about a new tradition of reformist political drama. Mary Sidney was a pioneer, alongside other dramatists of her day, in the genre of historical drama in England, which Shakespeare and his contemporaries developed to full effect. For Hannay the key messages of the plays written on Antony and Cleopatra by both Sidney and Daniel were to illustrate what happens when lust is put before

---

1   Hannay, M. 1990.

duty to country by those in power, and the damaging impact of civil wars upon populations. Some scholars make the point that the common assumption made about Elizabethan drama is that Rome stands for England whereas in *Antonius* the analogy is between ancient Egypt and contemporary England. In other words an argument could be made that Mary Sidney is pointing towards the dangers of civil war in England in translating the Garnier play. Civil war was a spectre which haunted Elizabethans from time to time. Daniel then picks up on this theme and develops the notions in his presentation of *Cleopatra.*

The imperial ambition of Philip II of Spain is also regarded as being a victim of Mary Sidney's pen. This interpretation goes further than criticism of Cleopatra and Antony for indolence and failure to prioritise what was good for the people of their realms, brought about by their obsession with personal gratification. For the circles in which Sidney moved there was a literary habit of drawing parallels with the kingship of Philip II on which to base warnings for the edification of the English queen. Whilst the Roman empire had long been associated with a corrupt papacy, the Sidney tradition continued to highlight the potential for Spanish incursions into England. In the worst scenario there were fears that England might succumb to conquest by Roman Catholic Spain and, like Egypt, lose its independence, deteriorating into a province of the Spanish Empire. Paulina Kewes[1] supports the idea that the majority of Elizabethan plays about Rome cover the period of the downfall of the republic with both Sidney's and Daniel's writing drawing parallels between Rome, Philip II's Spain, Elizabeth's England and Egypt in relation to unsettled lines of succession. A list of the plays with the dates in which they were written shows an overwhelming interest in Octavian's (Caesar) rise to power as he transformed into the Emperor Augustus. The list begins with Sidney's *Antonius* (1592), followed by Samuel Daniel's *Cleopatra* (1594), Thomas Kyd's *Cornelia* (1594), Samuel Brandon's *Octavia* (1598) and William Shakespeare's *Julius Caesar* (1599). What is apparent is that the final decade of the 16th century saw the production of a number of plays which displayed ambivalence towards monarchy and empire.

The Book of Cleopatra, a missing resource

Images of Cleopatra in a series of iconic films created in America and Britain during the 20th century make it problematic to shift a certain image of the Egyptian queen in contemporary times. In particular the 1960s version, with Elizabeth Taylor and Richard Burton in the leading roles, set the tone for her image as a somewhat uneducated seductress. It is interesting that this has been the image of her propagated in the west whereas Arab sources have centuries of tradition looking upon Cleopatra as a scholar and philosopher. There is definitive evidence that Elizabethans were also aware of a document which upheld her reputation as a knowledgeable practitioner in the fields of medicine and astronomy. A book which no longer exists today, *The Book of Cleopatra*, was known to have circulated amongst Elizabethan readers as it is quoted from in records dating back to the period. Such early modern books which

1   Kewes, P, 2012.

quote from *The Book of Cleopatra* use it as a source for medical, gynaecological and alchemical authority. This resource no longer exists but we know about some of its contents because they are referred to in other documents written by Greek and Roman authors. Mary Sidney will have identified herself with this interest in medicine which Cleopatra had allegedly developed within Egypt, as it is a role which Sidney fulfilled in her own community in Wilton. In contrast then, in Arabic historical records she is a much more serious queen. Highly educated with a reputation as a philosopher, a great linguist and knowledgeable in the fields of medicine and astronomy. She was the eminent descendant of the Ptolemies and would be the last of the dynasty to rule Egypt. Interestingly, Sidney's and Daniel's Cleopatra brought out some of the thoughtful and intelligent aspects of her character which resulted in a portrait of the Egyptian, at the close of her life, full of regret over the consequences of her love for Antony:

> ......Alas! The wrath
> Of all the gods at once on us is fall'n.
> Unhappy queen! Oh, would I in this world
> The wand'ring light of day had never seen!
> Alas! Of mine the plague and poison I
> The crown have lost my ancestors me left,
> This realm I have to strangers subject made,
> And robbed my children of their heritage. (Act 5, lines 7-14).

More on the French context for Robert Garnier and Mary Sidney's translation of *Antonius*

The French wars of religion had political implications that crossed borders into Europe and across the sea into Britain. What happened in France in matters of religion had the potential to have an impact in Britain, not least because the French noblewoman, Mary of Guise, was mother of Mary Queen of Scots the possible rival to Elizabeth. In terms of the Sidneys' interest and involvement in the conflict, their sympathy for Calvinism, with its French associations, and Philip's witnessing of the massacre of the Huguenots in Paris contributed to their deep-seated concern for the events which unfolded there. Historians often point to the date 1562 when the Massacre of Wassy took place, as the actual beginning of the religious war. The Duke of Guise's men slaughtered dozens of men, women and children during a church service. The duke had taken up the cause of stamping out heretical Protestants. The Holy League was formed in 1576 to continue this work. It represented those Catholics wanting to protect an ultra-militant form of their faith.

For those who disliked Protestantism but feared the excesses of the League the way forward was uncertain. Four years later, in 1588, the year of the Armada, the League took control of Paris leading King Henry III to flee in fear of his life. On the 2 August of that year the king was stabbed to death by a monk who was said to be acting on instructions from the League and Pope Sixtus the Fifth. Historical accounts dating back to the period record the pope celebrating the death of the king. It was Mary's younger brother Sir Robert

Sidney who conveyed Queen Elizabeth I's response to the French in the form of an angry but restrained and pragmatic letter. Robert Sidney, acting in the capacity of ambassador for Elizabeth, in early 1594 visited King Henry IV of France. The king had converted to Catholicism and in so doing, had alarmed supporters of the Protestant movement in England. The more moderate approach of Henry IV undermined the power of the League and it appears that Robert Sidney, at this point, could return to England in the hope that the Protestant cause for which he stood, was not immediately under threat from that quarter.

Against this background it is entirely plausible to regard events on the continent as being a motivating force in Mary Sidney's writing. When Robert Sidney returned from France to report to the queen on the success of his ambassadorial role at the French court it was 1595, the year that Mary Sidney published her play for the second time with the title *Antonie*. Since the death of Philip, Robert had been the official head of the Sidney family and keeper of the family tradition to serve the cause. The ties with Europe remained strong. Like Philip, Robert had served under his uncle Robert Dudley, in the war in the Low Countries. Robert Sidney had been with his brother when he received his injury at Zutphen and present at his death. After which, witnesses say he shed copious tears. It appears to be wholly natural for Mary to turn to translating a text which was so relevant for her time and circumstances. The depiction of Antony and Cleopatra gave Mary Sidney the opportunity to explore issues relating to authority, power, gender and the abuse of leadership. Ideas associated with virtue and monarchy can also be detected amongst the pages of the play. It is likely that Mary Sidney chose to write about Antony and Cleopatra precisely because they were such flawed characters. In their story it was hard to distinguish between right and wrong amongst the actions of the key protagonists. There is ambiguity about how gender roles should be played out and there are issues surrounding succession and loyalty to both family and kingdom. In 1587 Elizabeth signed the death warrant of the former queen of Scotland. Mary was beheaded at the behest of Elizabeth in Fotheringhay Castle, one year before the Armada. She was a Catholic and member of the Guise family in France. Mary Sidney's family knew what it was to face the ire of a monarch and the death penalty had been inflicted on them in the previous generation. The links between Queen Elizabeth, Mary Stuart and the play *Antonius* can be taken a step further.

Mary Sidney, Mary Queen of Scots and the text of *Antonius*

One aspect of Elizabeth's reign that could have implications for this narrative is the execution of Mary queen of Scots. What could possibly be the overlap between Mary queen of Scots and Mary Sidney? In particular why might the death of the former queen at Fotheringhay have been noteworthy and significant for Sidney? The story of Mary Stuart had huge implications for the English Protestants with leanings towards Europe, Calvinism and with Huguenot sympathies. Mary Stuart was born in Scotland in 1542, the daughter of King James V of Scotland and Mary of Guise. During childhood Mary Stuart was sent to France in order to marry the French prince to form a Catholic alliance. At the age of eighteen she returned to Scotland, a widow after the death of her young husband. What happened next mirrors the indiscretions, scandal and poor judgement in the Antony and Cleopatra narrative. Mary Stuart married Henry, Lord Darnley, after apparently promising to let him rule by her side. In practice, he was said to have been constantly drunk and quite unsuited to be trusted in any such role. Believing that his wife was too close to her secretary David Riccio, Darnley, with co-conspirators murdered Riccio at Holyrood Castle. Darnley was later found murdered in the garden of a house in Edinburgh, in which he was lodging. The house was destroyed by an explosion. Mary Stuart continued to inflict damage on her own reputation when she married James Hepburn, Earl of Bothwell after he was accused and subsequently acquitted of murdering Darnley. The marriage was not looked upon with favour by members of the Scottish government and the Lords of Congregation (part of the Scottish system of government) imprisoned Mary in Leven Castle whilst her new husband fled the scene and the couple never reunited.

Had Mary Stuart remained in Scotland at this point then the outcome for her might have been entirely different but she escaped from Leven Castle in Scotland and her small army was defeated by the Protestants; she fled into exile in England where her presence became a thorn in the flesh for Elizabeth. It was much more difficult for the queen of England to ignore the needs and claims of Mary Stuart once she lived in the same realm. The presence of Mary Stuart in England was regarded, by Protestant members of the Privy Council in particular, as being a constant threat to the safety of Elizabeth and the stability of the realm. William Cecil, Lord Burghley, Elizabeth's chief minister and Francis Walsingham, Philip Sidney's father-in-law were responsible for repeatedly bringing the dangers posed by a possible rival to the attention of Elizabeth. The former queen of the Scots, she had abdicated in 1567 and was a member of the Guise family considered to be responsible for the massacre of Huguenots and the beginning of the French wars of religion. Mary Sidney would surely have taken an interest in the debates surrounding fears over the possible treachery of Mary Stuart. Elizabeth finally agreed to the execution of Mary Stuart after much persuasion and some would say plotting! The execution took place on 8 February 1587, within days of Philip Sidney's funeral. There has even been a suggestion that Philip Sidney's funeral had been deliberately delayed to coincide with the death of Mary Stuart in order to distract the attention of the population but also to provide a contrast: to illustrate how England buried their loyal and pious martyrs[1]. Queen Elizabeth was to some extent ambivalent about Mary Stuart's treatment but was said to be bitter and angry that her ministers had virtually tricked her into signing the death warrant of her cousin. During the final years of her reign Elizabeth was said to be haunted by the death and profoundly regretted the part which she had played in the killing.

Mary Sidney's mother had been one of Elizabeth's closest supporters and in her role as a lady-in-waiting she had taken care of her through illnesses such as smallpox. Could it be that Mary Sidney herself had seen and recognised

1 Woodward, J, 1997.

the pain felt by Elizabeth, not just physical pain, but the torment she must have experienced in connection with Mary Stuart's execution? Perhaps her choice of the Cleopatra story for translation was to do with offering comfort to her queen. As mentioned previously this play was translated, by Mary Sidney, from French into English. Although Sidney's first version was published in 1592 it is likely that she had been working on the translation for some months at least. Five years earlier the execution of Mary Stuart had taken place. Is it possible that Mary Sidney's choice of translation could be her way of offering solace to Elizabeth and supporting her for having the courage to carry out a task which went against nature? During the closing scenes of her translation of Cleopatra, Sidney shows the Egyptian women servants pleading with the queen of Egypt to give up the idea of taking her own life, for the sake of her children, for the wellbeing of her subjects and to secure succession. Cleopatra takes the asp and puts it to her breast thus putting feelings before duty and leaving Egypt open for Roman occupation. Is it possible that Elizabeth would see this as a message of support? That when she carried out the execution of the former queen of Scots she put country before feelings and thus helped to ward off the threat of a much dreaded civil war.

7
The Sidneys and Poems from Antiquity

The Sidney Psalms

Mary Sidney's translations of the psalms were perhaps her greatest achievement and the accomplishment for which she should have been most celebrated. The reasons why this did not happen are complex and can only be guessed at. Although the manuscript version of her psalms circulated during the 17th century a printed version did not appear until 1823, and by that time things had moved on and the Sidney name had diminished further into obscurity. With the greatly increased interest in feminism during the 20th century Mary Sidney continued to be unnoticed, almost certainly because her literary achievement was embedded in a deeply religious narrative which no longer held widespread appeal. It might be expected that the Anglican Church would foreground her translations given the paucity of women acknowledged in their history but sadly this has not happened, so far. Yet the history of literature is inextricably entwined with the history of religion. The Bible itself is literature: a collection of stories following the lived history of a particular group of people. The drama that we enjoy so much today, on our screens or in the flesh, has its roots in medieval mystery plays which presented the stories from the Bible in an accessible and visible form and were often performed in the grounds of churches and cathedrals. With Philip's belief, extolled in *The Defence* that the psalms were the highest form of poetry, and with Mary's poetic versification of the psalms, the two Sidneys joined forces and helped to weave a new chapter in the history of poetry. Mary did what great writers and artists have a reputation for doing: she took a traditional text and transformed the structure and content with a new translation to make something new and fresh and appropriate for her own time. The impact it had on the metaphysical poetry of the next era was profound. It is, therefore, worthwhile having some understanding of the history and nature of the psalms in order to recognise this development in English poetry.

Why were the Sidneys so engaged with the translation and encouragement of psalm reading and what has this to do with the world of literature? From our 21st century perspective it is hard to recreate or imagine the interest and religious fervour surrounding the construction, the messages and translation of these ancient poems in the Elizabethan world. In Mary Sidney's day the psalms functioned in many ways: they were popular songs sung by people of all ages and from all walks of life; their repetition provided a sense of attachment to a community and an identity. The Reformation had dispensed with the idea that it was necessary for an ordinary individual to approach communicating God through some kind of intermediary. Previously, prayers had to be addressed through certain channels, for example by asking a priest or churchman to intercede or by pleading with a saint to interact with God on behalf of the believer. The Reformation swept away those ideas and some Christians believed it was possible to approach the creator without asking a priest, bishop or even the pope to intercede on their behalf. As a consequence the psalms increased in significance even more. They were written using the first person and provided a direct narrative between the 'I' of the poems and God. Psalms could be seen to refer directly to the lived experience of the speaker and their sense of the awareness of the presence, or otherwise, of God: 'Why standeth so far off, O Lord, and hidest thy face in the needful time of trouble?' (Psalm 10, Coverdale) Furthermore, psalms were very often given a political interpretation and could be used to express protest, as when they were used by political prisoners or, what we might refer to today as, prisoners of conscience. Kathleen Swain has shown how psalms 'functioned as political vehicles, as media of education and popular culture, and as literary texts…' It is quite easy to detect the political nature of some psalms: 'Deliver me from my enemies, O god; defend me from them that rise up against me. O deliver me from the wicked doers, and save me from the bloodthirsty men' (Psalm 59, Coverdale).

During the Reformation interest in the psalms crossed class boundaries and they could be recited by individuals from all sections of society. As they were full of word pictures people of all ages could tap into and explore them as reflections of their own feelings and states of mind. They had an intimacy and immediacy which seemed to address the hopes and fears of people across all walks of life, ranging from expressions of fear to thankfulness and joy: 'The snares of death compassed me round about, and the pains of hell got hold upon me' (Psalm 116. Coverdale), 'For strangers are risen up against me; and tyrants…' (Psalm 54, Coverdale), 'O God, my heart is ready, my heart is ready; I will sing, and give praise…' (Psalm 108, Coverdale). They reflect a spiritual yearning felt by individuals 'Like as the hart desireth the water-brooks, so longeth my soul after thee, O God'(Psalm 42, Coverdale).

In his *Defence* Philip Sidney described the desired approach to enable a full appreciation of these poems: that the merry should rejoice by singing the psalms and those who are sad should turn to them for consolation. During the 16th century the psalms were turned into a focus for meditation. In the circles in which the Sidneys and their like moved there were high levels of literacy, and texts were becoming more readily available because of the increased use of printing. But it was not the same for a large section of the population who did not have the opportunity to learn to read and write and were still without easy access to the printed word. For them the destruction of pictures, statues and other forms of religious visual culture, by Henry VIII and his men, had the effect of denying a focus for their meditation. Pictures, statues, rood screens and all the paraphernalia associated with their local churches were lost to congregations, despite the fact that much of it had been gathered through their community effort and, in a sense, belonged to the public. The wide range of artefacts and images in churches had been an important part of communicating the content of biblical text. It says so much about King Henry VIII that he should believe that everything was his to destroy. Perhaps there was a hope amongst at least some of the translators that their poems or psalms could be remembered and recited as word pictures for illiterate sections of the population.

The psalms have elements of poetry, song and prayer absorbed into each one. They originated in the oral traditions of the Hebrew people living in the area we now call Israel; at other times in the past it has been known as Palestine. Part of their use had always been for communal singing. Although many of these poems had been passed on, possibly for centuries, by word of mouth, it is known that a proportion were written down in the 5th century BCE during the time of the Hebrew King David. Whilst the authorship of many of the psalms is anonymous as many as eighty three are attributed to this king. Once written in the Hebrew language the psalms were included in the Hebrew Bible or Tanakh, still used by followers of the Jewish faith today. This Hebrew Bible was adopted by Christians and transformed into the Old Testament part of the Christian Bible. Within the Old Testament the psalms remained in a discrete chapter but during the Reformation the development of printing allowed for the proliferations of psalm books: just pamphlet size copies of the Book of Psalms, called *The Psalter*.

When Elizabethans, including the Sidneys, translated the psalms they were using a literary form that had also emerged from Middle Eastern cultures surrounding Israel. The same type of poetry has been found among the archaeological sites of ancient Babylon (present day Iraq). Some of the psalms written in Hebrew are thought to date back to a period as early as 900 – 500 BCE but these poems continued to emerge over the centuries, up to and including the period covered by the New Testament, that is, during the 1st century CE. The Biblical *Book of Psalms* was first translated into Greek in the 3rd century BCE during the ascendancy of the Greek empire. This version of The Bible is referred to as The Septuagint. Five centuries later demand grew for a Latin translation of The Bible to cater for the needs of the citizens of the Roman Empire, as Greek became displaced. This eventually led to the production, in the 4th Century AD, of St Jerome's full Latin translation referred to as The Vulgate. It was authenticated by the pope and became the authorized biblical text until the Reformation.

Control over biblical translation ended during the Reformation and multiple editions appeared in vernacular languages. So *The Psalter* began to appear in languages other than Latin too, containing all one hundred and fifty psalms. The first complete bible to be translated into English was accomplished by Miles Coverdale in 1535. He had taken over the task which was begun by William Tyndale and the availability of printing allowed for multiple versions to be published. This was the English translation used by Philip and Mary Sidney for their version of the psalms. Mary also deliberately used the Geneva Bible for her translation. Written during the Reformation in Geneva it provided the version most closely associated with the followers of Calvin. Calvinists identified the poems as containing the theological and doctrinal knowledge necessary to understand their faith. They were the battle cry of the Huguenots in France and the Sidneys identified with their cause and sought to offer solace to beleaguered European Protestants.

Context: Psalms in the Elizabethan Court

In courtly circles, during the reign of Elizabeth translating psalms from the Latin had become a regular pastime. There were literally hundreds of different translations. As this activity was intimately associated with the sacred it was regarded as being open to females as well as males. There was a built in sense of godliness in the process so the virtue of a woman was not challenged by her participation. There is some evidence to suggest that Mary Sidney understood Hebrew and could therefore translate from the original although the suggestion is far from conclusive. Hebrew poetry was distinguished by the use of parallelism: that is one line of poetry corresponding with another line, so a thought presented on one line is repeated in different words on the next line. The second line of a verse repeats the thought in the first line. For example: "I said, I will take heed to my ways, that I offend not in my tongue. I will keep my mouth as it were with a bridle, while the ungodly is in my sight" (Psalm 39, Coverdale). Rhyme was not a feature of Hebrew poetry but it was a notable aspect of the Sidney translation and they came to be regarded as being particularly special, a view which was acknowledged in the time in which they were written. Before his death Philip completed psalms 1-43, Mary went on to translate 44-150. The highly regarded poet John Donne recognised the exquisite nature of the Sidney psalms and wrote a poem in praise of the work: *Upon the Translation of the Psalmes by Sir Philip and the Countess of Pembroke his sister*:

> This Moses and this Miriam…
> Two by their bloods, and by Thy Spirit one;
> A brother and a sister, made by Thee
> The organ, where Thou art the harmony.
> Two that make one John Baptist's holy voice,
> And who that Psalm, 'Now let the Isles rejoice;
> Have both translated, and applied it too,
> Both told us what, and taught us how to do…

What set out as a joint venture between brother and sister was curtailed by the death of Philip. However, Mary took up the project and ran with it until the final version of the Sidney psalms was presented to the queen.

A gift for the queen

There was also a family precedent for using psalms as a public form of protest. John Dudley and Robert Dudley had both translated psalms expressing vengeance whilst they were imprisoned in the Tower of London; as Protestants they readily associated with the cries for deliverance and punishment of enemies in these poems. During the early Tudor period in the

Psalm 40

mid-16th century, the psalms of David were seen to represent the problems of an individual facing threat from various quarters, including treacherous courtly intrigue. There were fears of enemies within and without the country. There was a sense in which the succession and line of David had been challenged in the Israelite monarchy in the same way as there had been attempts to undermine Elizabeth's succession. The association of King David, with these devotional poems, was especially important for the subjects of Queen Elizabeth. Strong parallels between the two monarchs had therefore been drawn, though David was king in around 500 BCE. The dual role of David as poet and king was emphasized in the Elizabethan era. The theological notions of 'election' and a people chosen by God for a purpose permeate Old Testament thinking about David and his psalms. There is also a sense in which Elizabethan Calvinists inherited the ideas and applied them to their own situation. They seemed not to have any difficulty regarding themselves as elected by God to represent the truth of their outlook and Mary's task was to ensure the queen remembered her responsibilities, as had the Hebrew King David.

In a way Mary's version of the psalms reinforces the purpose of the Protestant warrior but in some translations there seemed to be a blurring of what makes a psalm intensely religious or what gives it a more secular flavour. Some writers stress that it is not easy to picture some of the Sidney psalms in a ritual setting as they are not appropriate for congregational reciting. But the experimentation with lyric in translations of the psalms had a major impact as poetry developed in the vernacular with the proliferation of the writing of sonnets and other secular poetry. In this way the psalms permeated English literary traditions. Did the Sidney psalms provide a bridge between religious and secular lyrics? Their work has been referred to as paraphrasing the original pieces, or providing poetic meditation on the psalms rather than translation. It is undeniable that in her rendering of the Hebrew poems Mary Sidney has created poetry of great beauty in her effort to capture the message of the pieces:

> Our potter he
> Knows how his vessels we
> In earthy matter lodged this fickle form:
> Fickle as glass,
> As flow'rs that fading pass,
> And vanish so,
> No not their place we know,
> Blasted to death with breath of blust'ring storm.

Sidney signed the volume containing her poems and psalms 'By the sister of the Incomparable Sidney'. This was by way of a self-authorization. By claiming the close link with the renowned figure of her brother she could promote her own versions of the psalms. In summoning his name and referring to the 'pure spirit' she could evoke her brother's causes. If one aim still remained at the forefront of the 'things to do' list of Mary Sidney, it had to be keeping alive the aim of supporting European Protestants and, in so doing, keeping a weather eye on Spain. By the late 1590s Elizabeth was taking some steps to withdraw from the Dutch war. In 1601 Henry Herbert, Mary's husband, died. This was to mark another major milestone in her life as her extant, printed works date before that time, so, as far as is known, the collection prepared for the queen was Sidney's last direct written effort to influence the direction of travel in foreign policy. By 1603 there was a new monarch as the queen died in that year, two years after Herbert. As a widow the countess's position in society shifted, as her son William took centre stage.

To The Angel Spirit

One particular section of Mary Sidney's *Antonie* script has caused some scholars to interpret the verse as Mary expressing sexual desire for her brother. It occurs in the final stages of the play when Cleopatra longs for physical union with Antony, her lover. Those who read sexual innuendoes between brother and sister into the *Antonie* text may also turn to the poem *To the Angel Spirit* by Mary Sidney for supporting evidence. While the play was a single authorship venture there is some discussion over the extent of Mary and Philip's collaboration over the translation of the psalms. Philip was responsible for translating some of them before he left for the Low Country. Mary Sidney translated the remaining psalms and completed the presentation manuscript with two poems: *To the Angel Spirit* and *Even Now That Care*. *To the Angel Spirit* was dedicated to her brother and acted as a sort of Preface to the translation. There are two versions of the script of the poem in existence today: one attached to the manuscript appeared with the 1599 collection of psalms and the other emerged as a print version in 1623 amongst the papers of Samuel Daniel. The two versions differ and while they both point towards close collaboration in the matter of the written work, some readers regard the manuscript version, in particular, as being an erotic evocation of love and union between the mourner and object of the mourning with the following line in the first stanza: 'My muse with thine, itself dared to combine'. The 17th century commentator, John Aubrey, writing a century after Philip's death, quoted gossip that a child had been the result of a physical union between the brother and sister. It appears that there is a complete lack of evidence in support of this claim. However, rumours surrounding a close physical relationship circled around the pair. Whilst some 20th century scholars speak of the dangers of projecting psychoanalytic theories back to 16th century verse others believe that some of the language is heavily explicit. Some language may operate at an unconscious level but the question must be asked, what are the chances of Mary Sidney deliberately writing about sexual love between herself and her brother in a text to be delivered to the queen alongside the translation of Biblical text? Any such association remains in the realm of conjecture.

What is of importance is the incredible beauty of this poem and Mary's very real effort to show that she had inherited the right to edit Philip's work and that in matters of faith and adherence to religion and the spirit they acted as one. The translation is a 'joint work', 'inspired by thee'. It is a combination of 'My muse with thine', and it is also one with the 'divine'. The poem clearly expresses a sense of the profound love between the brother and sister but care has to be taken to make sure that this focus does not distract from a wider appreciation of the eleven stanzas of the piece. Sidney has evoked King David in her poem for several reasons. Most obviously because there was a belief that the psalms were inspired by God and written by King David, during what was believed to be the golden age of the Hebrew period of kingship.

So here then, Sidney was drawing a parallel between King David and her queen. Elizabeth had presided over forty years of relative stability in England as Sidney prepared her psalms for the monarch. 'Age after age' has admired the sacred tones of David's poems and the implication is that in England other voices aim to 'excel in holy rites performed'. Philip Sidney had expressed the view that the psalms were the highest form of poetry and therefore art. In this preface to the joint translation Sidney is presenting her brother as most worthy to complete this high and divine art for the queen and herself as the person most able to complete the process. It is apparent that this task was Sidney's final attempt to memorialise her brother in such a grand literary task, even though his greatness was such that more could be achieved had he lived:

> Immortal monuments of thy fair fame,
>   Though not complete...

Did Mary Sidney sense that the end of an era was approaching? Four years after her intention to present her psalms to Elizabeth, the queen's reign ended in 1603 when she died in old age, after which time it was Mary's son who became close to the new king. As mentioned previously Mary's husband had been dead for two years and there was a new Earl of Pembroke, William her son. He was setting his own agenda with the new monarch: times had moved onwards. In an amazingly personal final stanza Mary Sidney took her step back from public life. Her life's work done:

> Receive these hymns, these obsequies receive ;
>   If any mark of thy sweet sprite[1] appear,
>   Well are they borne, no title else shall bear.
> I can no more: Dear Soul, I take my leave;
>   Sorrow still strives, would mount the highest sphere
>   Presuming so just cause might meet thee there:
> Oh happy change, could I so take my leave!

> By the sister of that
> incomparable Sidney

Mary Sidney had fulfilled her ambition to complete the Sidney translation of these most precious poems. One more of Mary Sidney's translations appeared in 1600, after the psalms: her version of Petrarch's *Triumph of Death,* which she transformed from the Italian. This project though, was without the emotional intensity that the translated psalms captured.

Bearing in mind the quality and rarity (composed by a woman) of Mary Sidney's translations, it is a travesty and injustice that they have not received greater acclaim. Unfortunately the combined effort of monarch (Henry VIII) and church in Salisbury, and the surrounding area, had suppressed female education so the corollary of this would seem to have had an impact on the reception of women's writing. One hundred years after Sidney died officials

---

1 spirit.

within the cathedral revealed their stance on the ability of women and girls to benefit from education. When a charity was established to provide a school for orphan girls from church of England families the dean and chapter refused to act as trustees. The Godolphin School for girls was founded in Salisbury in 1726 by Charles and Elizabeth Godolphin. The girls were to be taught to read, write, dance and keep accounts. William Godolphin, a nephew of the founders, was chosen to administer the school after the refusal of the dean of the cathedral to be involved. There is a strong tradition which claims that the decision not to participate was made on the grounds that the idea of educating women was 'mere foolery and dreaming.' [1]

In an exploration of the idea of 'sacred parody' Beth Wynne Fisken[2] has given extraordinary insight into Mary Sidney's translation. Fisken has pointed towards the very different writing style between Mary and Philip. She argues that this is based, in part, on the way that Mary used secular poetry, particularly the sonnet sequence, rather than psalms for her model. In so doing Sidney conveys a sense of intensely personal love of the divine, which is usually confined to the realms of human feeling. The idea of sacred parody then was to encourage the individual to worship God with the passion of romantic love. The result of this led to a parallel between the psalms and sonnet sequences: in the former the lover entreats the beloved and in the latter the worshipper pleads with God. In her poem *To the Angel Spirit* and in her psalms Mary Sidney puts great emphasis on the communication of mystical love, that is a sense of awe and mystery surrounding individual and divine love. Fisken quotes the analysis of C.S. Lewis as claiming that the sonnet sequences were to do with prolonged lyrical meditation, rather than with telling a story, hence reinforcing the notion that Sidney was using the psalms as a model for meditation on the soul. A close reading of the psalms reveals the special skills which the Sidney siblings brought to their translations of these ancient poems.

The Sidney Psalter

The Greek verb psallein referred to the playing of a stringed instrument, and the noun psalmos extended this sense to refer to a song sung to music: a devotional song and the best kind of poetry, as Sidney says in *The Defence of Poesy*. The poet John Donne was full of praise for the Psalter too, as shown in his dedicatory poem quoted earlier in this chapter. He believed that psalms conveyed 'the highest matter in the noblest form'. Praise indeed from a revered poet and orator.

Eighteen manuscripts of the Sidney psalms survive today, but no contemporary printed version. It seems incredible to us that such a work of translation never achieved the apparent permanence of a neat printed version. However, the Psalter was widely circulated in manuscript form.

Today, we tend to value novelty and originality in writing and sometimes overlook the skill needed to translate works and the impact a new translation can have. Mary and Philip's versions are novel and ground-breaking with

---

1   The Dictionary of National Biography.
2   Fisken, B, 1989.

use of varied rhythms (metre) and rhyming schemes, line lengths and stanza arrangements. Only a few psalms follow the exact same format. Mary Sidney revised Philip's compositions after he died (Psalms 1 – 43) and the remainder are entirely her own work. They are so different from the King James Bible versions or the Book of Common Prayer (based on the earlier Coverdale bible).

Looking at a selection of Sidney psalms and comparing them with versions we are probably more familiar with is interesting. It reveals many differences in approach, many merits and also highlights occasional rhymes and phrases which might grate on the modern ear. Nevertheless, they are well worth reading for their poetic merit: their originality and their ability to reach out to the reader.

Two of Philip Sidney's psalms, edited by Mary Sidney Herbert

Psalm 13

This is one of many examples of Sidney's experimentation with line length, metre and rhyme to create an accessible, memorable psalm. The speaker is distressed and feels that God has neglected him in his pain and anguish. But it ends with an affirmation of trust:

> How long (O Lord) shall I forgotten be?
> What? Ever?
> How long wilt thou thy hidden face from me
> Dissever?
> How long shall I consult with careful sprite[1]
> In anguish?
> How long shall I with foes' triumphant might
> Thus languish?
> Behold me, Lord, let to thy hearing creep
> My crying.
> Nay, give me eyes, and light, lest that I sleep
> In dying.
> Lest my foe brag, that in my ruin he
> Prevail`ed
> And at my fall they joy that, troublous, me
> Assail`ed.
> No, no, I trust on thee, and joy in thy
> Great pity:
> Still therefore of thy graces shall be my
> Song's ditty.

The final rhyme of 'ditty' is unfortunate to a modern ear as we think of a ditty as a kind of nursery rhyme or maybe something a little frivolous. But, ignoring that, the psalm is interesting in the way it moves from question to declaration,

---

1   spirit

to pleas and finally to acceptance of God's love and concern. And it does this in a fresh way through rhyming couplets and starkly different line lengths. The one word lines stand out from the text and we read them with emphasis. The longer lines use the traditional iambic pentameter with a very regular five beats to the line.[1]

Compare the tone and form with the Coverdale version (also still used today in the Book of Common Prayer):

> How long wilt thou forget me, O lord, forever: how long wilt thou hide thy face from me?
> How long shall I seek counsel in my soul, and be so vexed in my heart: how long shall mine enemies triumph over me?
> Consider, and hear me, O Lord my God: lighten mine eyes, that I sleep not in death.
> Lest mine enemy say, I have prevailed against him: for if I be cast down, they that trouble me will rejoice at it.
> But my trust is in thy mercy: and my heart is joyful in thy salvation.
> I will sing of the Lord, because he has dealt so lovingly with me; Yea I will praise the name of the Lord most Highest.

The tone is sombre. The pleas and questions, like Sidney's version, reveal the anguish. His psalm, however, with its regular rhyme and insistent rhythm is easier to remember and the unusual layout adds to the impact. If read aloud the rhythm and fluidity are central in creating the feeling of a song.

Psalm 30

This psalm praises God for saving David, the speaker, from his enemies and for always being there for him: listening and responding.

The wording of the psalms in the King James Bible (first printed in 1611, much later than Coverdale and the Sidneys' translations) has been praised for its language and its striking cadences – its musicality. This psalm begins clearly:

> I will extol thee, O Lord; for thou hast lifted me up, and hast not made
>   my foes to rejoice over me.

'hast not made my foes' is awkward to say, but the sense is clear.

Compare this with Sidney's first verse:

> O Lord, thou hast exalted me
>   And saved me from foes' laughing scorn:
>   I owe thee praise, I will praise thee.

---

[1] See the Appendix for more information on metre.

He uses a regular iambic tetrameter rhythm, and the first and third line rhyme – yet there is a sense of a natural speaking voice. The third line helps to create this with the balanced phrasing: 'I owe' quickly followed by the affirmation – yes 'I will'.

There are some evocative lines in both versions. Verse 5 of the King James Bible version says 'weeping may endure for a night, but joy cometh in the morning.' Sidney's translation is lengthier and takes up a whole stanza, but it is similarly moving and creates a clear picture:

> Well may the evening clothe the eyes
>   In clouds of tears, but soon as sun
>   Doth rise again, new joys shall rise.

The diction and phrasing, such as the use of 'Well may' sounds down to earth and gives credibility to a speaking voice: we are compelled to listen. The phrase 'clouds of tears' is beautifully simple too and conjures up an exact picture. The verse is full of gentle soft 's' sounds (sibilants) which create a quiet, reverent feeling. Sidney changes the tone and mood towards the end of the psalm which rises to a climax in the final verse:

> Therefore my tongue shall never lack
>   Thy endless praise: O God, my king,
>   I will thee thanks for ever sing.

He changes the rhyme scheme in this verse, ending with a rhyming couplet. The final line is a little contorted – we would normally say 'I will sing thee thanks forever' but changing the word order keeps the steady rhythm going and makes the rhyme work. The important link between 'king' and 'sing' is emphasised: he promises to always sing the praises of God.

A selection of Mary Sidney Herbert's psalms

Mary is as inventive and original as her brother, and comparing her translations with other versions highlights her strengths and underlines her novel approach.

Psalm 57
Miserere Mei, Deus – an example of her unusual, experimental form

This psalm asks God for solace and refuge in difficult times and like many of the psalms ends   by praising God and affirming his power and mercifulness. The first verse showcases Mary's skill in creating an unusual verse form and a simple speaking voice:

> Thy mercy Lord, Lord, now thy mercy show:
>   On thee I lie;
>   To thee I fly.
> Hide me, hive me, as thine own,

Till these blasts be overblown,
Which now do fiercely blow. [1]

Compare this with the King James version:

Be merciful unto me, O God, be merciful unto me; for my soul trusteth
in thee; yea in the shadow of thy wings will I make my refuge until these
calamities be overpast.

The Coverdale version opens similarly, then in the second half ends
with: 'and under the shadow of thy wings shall be my refuge, until this
tyranny be over-past.' The overall sense of all three is the same but the layout
of Mary's psalm is very effective in clearly conveying the sense and enabling
her, for example in the shorter lines 2 and 3, to emphasise her point simply.
The rhyme of 'lie' and 'fly' cement this point: the psalmist relies on God and
will always seek his comfort. The simple vocabulary makes for a more intimate
feel, although the speaker does vary the tone: for example, the end of this verse
is more declamatory with the drama of 'blasts' which 'fiercely blow'. Overall
the psalm with its nine verses is easy on the ear with its musical beats, and
easy to remember because of her skilful use of rhyme and rhythm.

Psalm 84 – Mary's musicality: creating a rhythmic, expressive psalm.

This is a joyful psalm of praise and comparing versions shows Mary's skill in
creating such a different style of translation. Here are the three openings:

Coverdale:

O how amiable are thy dwellings: thou Lord of hosts!
My soul hath a desire and longing to enter into the courts of the Lord: my
heart and my flesh rejoice in the living God.

King James:

How amiable are thy tabernacles, O Lord of hosts!
My soul longeth, yea , even fainteth for the courts of the LORD; my heart
and my flesh crieth out for the living God.

Poem of Mary Sidney- first verse:

How lovely is thy dwelling,
Great god, to whom all greatness is belonging!
   To view thy courts, far, far from any telling
My soul doth long, and pine with longing
      Unto the God that liveth,
      The God that all life giveth,

---

1   She begins with a ten syllable line, then two shorter lines of four syllables, two lines
of seven syllables and a final line of six syllables, with a steady beat throughout and a
rhyming scheme which she sustains throughout the poem.

My heart and body doth aspire,
Above delight, beyond desire.

The Coverdale psalm has a simplicity and directness; the King James version is more melodramatic (crieth, fainteth) and elaborate (tabernacles). Mary's version is longer but her use of repetition is so clever and effective, like musical notes or tunes which a composer repeats but varies slightly: 'Great god' echoed in 'all greatness'; 'long' echoed in 'longing'; 'life' echoed in 'liveth' and the more obvious and insistent repetition of 'far, far'. Mary Sidney creates patterns and parallels - the effects of which are less easy to explain, like trying to pin down the impact of a piece of music. But, we hear a speaking voice and enjoy its sound while being unaware of the intricacy of her poetic methods.

Towards the end of the psalm the Coverdale version simply states: ' I had rather be a doorkeeper in the house of my God : than to dwell in the tents of ungodliness'; the bible version uses the more dramatic 'tents of wickedness' whereas Mary's second last verse ends with:

I count it clearer pleasure
    To spend my age's treasure
Waiting a porter at thy gates
Than dwell a lord with wicked mates.

Occasionally, some of Mary Sidney's lines may sound a little forced, the sense twisted to extort a rhyme that fits, a little like a musician striking the wrong note The use of 'mates' , for example, is surprising to us and seems to undercut the strength of the assertion with a colloquialism which we recognise. Perhaps it would have had more strength and impact in the 17th century. Our reaction to the language is bound to be different today. But the sense is clear and the originality and accessibility of her translation deserves praise.

Psalm 88 – a memorably simple and song-like psalm

This is a personal plea to God asking him to listen and to help. The King James version is sonorous, economical and has dramatic impact:

O Lord God of my salvation, I have cried day *and* night before thee;
Let my prayer come before thee: incline thine ear unto my cry;
For my soul is full of troubles; and my life draweth nigh unto the grave.

Mary's approach is very different; she has a more elaborate opening, with an extended description of how night descends and the 'golden wealth' of the sun' is then locked up – such a vivid description:

My God, my Lord, my help, my health,
    To thee my cry
    Doth restless fly,
        Both when of sun the day
        The treasures doth display,

And night locks up his golden wealth.

Mary carries on in a second verse which corresponds to lines two and three of the King James version.

> Admit to presence what I crave:
>> Oh, bow thine ear
>> My cry to hear,
>>> Whose soul with ills and woes
>>> So flows, so overflows,
> That now my life draws nigh the grave.

The repetition of 'so flows, so overflows' is very effective: the sounds created are fluid and so aptly convey the outpouring of anxiety, the flooding out of emotion. The rhyme and insistent rhythm in the poem works well too, to conjure up a voice propelled towards darkness. There are thirteen verses in all in Mary's translation and we are moved by the revealing of personal woes.

The Coverdale version is less memorable than Mary Sidney's and the King James psalm. It lacks the sense of an anguished voice and it lacks the interesting phrases of Sidney's. It is direct and simple, qualities which are admirable and which the Sidney psalms often exhibit to great effect, but we are not drawn into the psalm in the same way as with Mary's. Here it is:

> O Lord God of my salvation, I have cried day and night before thee: O
> let my prayer enter into thy presence, incline thine ear unto my calling.
> For my soul is full of trouble; and my life draweth nigh unto hell.

Psalm 117 – Laudate Dominum – an acrostic psalm (a word puzzle)

Mary experiments with form and just a cursory glance at any of her psalms reveals how each arrangement is so different. This psalm is visually striking; there are some forced rhymes and inverted phrases made to fit her tight pattern but the impact is dramatic.

> **P** raise him that aye
> **R** emains the same
> **A** ll tongues display
> **I** ehovah's fame.
> **S** ing all that share
> **T** his earthly ball:
> **H** is mercies are
> **E** xposed to all,
> **L** ike as the word
> **O** nce he doth give,
> **R** olled in record,
> **D** oth time outlive.

Making use of the initial letters to spell out the Latin translation of Laudate Dominum together with the regular line length and rhythm make the sentiments easy to remember. She is not out to impress with any grandiose language; many poets would strain after a grander word than 'ball' (globe?) but the alliterative 'rolled in record ' expands the image and connects us with the idea of the earth as a ball rolling and the sense of time passing: days rolling around as the earth moves. She is celebrating the fact that the word of God has been recorded and recognised and will last for ever.

In the King James version the use of 'endureth' conveys the everlasting nature of God's word:

> O Praise the Lord, all ye nations: praise him, all ye people.
> For his merciful kindness is great towards us; and the truth of the Lord
> *endureth* for ever. Praise ye the Lord.

This is powerful and direct, but Sidney's version has merit and novelty in its slogan like approach.

Psalm 130 – Mary's version of a well-known psalm

This psalm was a popular one for writers to translate – it is one of the 'penitential psalms' asking God for forgiveness and redemption.

Here are the first few lines of the Coverdale version:

> Out of the deep have I called unto thee, O Lord: Lord hear my voice
> O let thine ears consider well: the voice of my complaint.
> If thou, Lord, wilt be extreme to mark what is done amiss; O Lord, who
> may abide it?

Here is Mary's version (the first two verses of a six verse psalm):

> From depth of grief
>   Where drowned I lie,
> Lord, for relief
>   To thee I cry:
> My earnest, vehement, crying, praying,
> Grant quick, attentive hearing, weighing.
>
>
> O Lord, if thou
>   Offences mark,
> Who shall not bow
>   To bear the cark?[1]
> But with thy justice mercy dwelleth,
> And makes thy worship more excelleth,

---

[1] burden

The final two lines of the first verse are powerful: the bold beat of the lines emphasising how heartfelt a cry this is, followed by an emphatic declaration that God is listening. We have to read these lines speedily, but with an insistent rhythm that presses home the sense. She questions God simply: who would not be bowed down if God always marked every offence? The verse ends with the assertion that God is both just and merciful.

Mary's version is simple but she elaborates to emphasise the depth of anguish. Her use of rhyme is not awkward, but perfectly fits the sense. It is a quietly dramatic opening to the psalm, full of memorable play on sound in a convincing, sincere prayer.

Psalm 136 A hymn like psalm using her range of poetic techniques

This is a psalm of praise, asking everyone to praise God for the wonders of his creation and his saving of Israel. Mary's use of repetition in this psalm echoes the King James version which repeats 'for his mercy endureth for ever' at the end of each verse; Mary's refrain is 'For his bounty endeth never'. The rhythm in her version dominates – a simple heartbeat rhythm in lines 1 and 3 of each stanza: Lub-dub, Lub-dub, Lub-dub, Lub-dub. She then cleverly alters the metre in lines 2 and 4 which draws our attention to the refrain.[1] The King James version begins with :

> O give thanks unto the Lord; for he is good: for his mercy endureth for
>   ever.
> O give thanks unto the God of gods: for his mercy endureth for ever.
> O give thanks to the Lord of lords: for his mercy endureth for ever.
> To him who alone doeth great wonders: for his mercy endureth for ever.
> To him that by wisdom made the heavens: for his mercy endureth for
>   ever.
> To him that stretched out the earth above the waters; for his mercy
>   endureth ever.

Mary's first three verses are:

> Oh, praise the Lord where goodness dwells,
>   For his kindness lasteth ever:
> Oh, praise the God all God excels,
>   For his bounty endeth never.
>
> Praise him that is of lords the Lord,
>   For his kindness lasteth ever:
> Who only wonders doth afford,
>   For his bounty endeth never;
>
> Whose skilful art did vault the skies,
>   For his kindness lasteth ever:

1 Mary uses iambic tetrameter in lines 1 and 3, then trochaic tetrameter in lines 2 and 4.

> Made earth above the waters rise,
>   For his bounty endeth never;

Mary's psalm contains some evocative lines such as 'Whose skilful art did vault the skies'. This is more elaborate than 'made the heavens' and a range of images are captured in the 'vault of skies': the medieval notion of the heavens being vault shaped, semicircular and not infinite. The verb vault also proclaims God's power: his ability to reach and shape the heavens in one giant leap or vault.

The psalms are very different in their impact. Mary is skilfully using a range of poetic techniques: the play on sound and repetition; the use of regular rhythm and rhyme to hammer home a message. The bible version is memorable too: declamatory and sombre with wonderful images, such as 'him that stretched out the earth above the waters'; but Mary's ability to use poetic techniques and often to simplify wording whilst retaining a richness of sense makes her psalm both fascinating and accessible.

A Renaissance aristocratic woman:
Mary's language and imagery

Mary would have been skilled in embroidery and needlework: skills which she would have had time to practise. Michele Osheraw[1] argues that her knowledge of embroidery stitches influenced the varied, imaginative layout of her poems as well as her diction. Mary herself said in one of her dedicatory poems at the beginning of the Psalter, referring to her brother: ' But he did warp, I weaved this web to end;' as well as ' And I the cloth in both our names present'. She uses the language of stitching and clothing here, but it is interesting to speculate on the influence of needlecraft on the shape of many psalms, far-fetched though this may initially seem. For example, Osheraw argues that Psalm 134 is one of many influenced by embroidery stitches and it does seem plausible. In this psalm the shape is similar to some styles of clustered openwork, as Osheraw says, where ' pairs of linen strands [are] grouped into clusters and gathered at their centre; this cinching is made by a working thread wrapped twice (generally) around the cluster strands.'[2]
The longer lines descend to this cinched middle and then the shape allows us to ascend back to the final longer (octameter) line – a mirror of the opening. Here is the whole poem:

Psalm 134
Ecce nunc

> You that Jehovah's servants are,
> Whose careful watch, whose watchful care,
>   Within his house are spent;
>   Say thus with one assent:

1 Osheraw, M, 2015.
2 Ibid.

' Jehovah's name be praised.'
Then let your hands be raised
  To holiest place,
    Where holiest grace
      Doth aye
        Remain:
      And say
        Again,
    'Jehovah's name be praised.'
Say last unto the company,
          Who tarrying make
          Their leave to take,
    'All blessings you accompany,
From him in plenty shower`ed
Whom Zion holds embowere`d
  Who heav'n and earth of nought hath raised.

We have looked at a small selection of Sidney psalms which demonstrate her virtuosity and her creative approach to translation which is shown throughout the whole Psalter. Throughout the collection she boldly experiments with line lengths and arrangement, with rhythms and rhymes, with use of sound for impact and use of everyday language. Occasionally phrases jar, as if she is forcing the experimentation and sometimes perhaps trying too hard to be a little different but the Psalms are a wonderful testament to her skill and sensitivity and her ability to put an individual stamp on the translations.

The King James versions and the Coverdale versions have dominated for centuries, together with some occasionally banal modern translations where the commendable rationale was to make the sense clear to the audience. However, the loss of the 'music 'of the psalms in some of these more recent translations is sad. Sense and sound are linked and turning to Mary Sidney's strikingly different translations brings this home to us and we enjoy the music of her verse as well as grasping the meaning. Read the psalms aloud and we appreciate even more the lilting musical qualities which are so integral to the Sidney psalms.

Why has Mary Sidney Herbert never been accorded more recognition or praise? Her brother's reputation and works are published, recognised and studied. Is it simply because as a woman she was not expected to succeed in the public realm? Or is it partly because her translations were unusual, innovative and ahead of their time? Or was she diffident and over modest and did not want, or feel it appropriate, to overshadow her brother?

However, Mary has undoubtedly left an unsung legacy. George Herbert's experiments with form, not just line lengths and rhythms, but creating differently shaped poems with visual impact – an impact which influences how we read a poem – were perhaps inspired by reading the Psalter. In his final creative years Herbert lived near Wilton House and was known to visit; it is highly likely that he gained access to a Psalter manuscript. His poems, of course, are not translations, their content is original but there is such an uncanny likeness in experimentation that it is not far-fetched to assume she had a strong influence on the style of his verse.

8
George Herbert

When thou dost purpose ought (within thy power)
Be sure to do it, though it be but small
Extract from Herbert's poem *The Church Porch*

Herbert certainly followed his own advice and in his relatively short life of thirty nine years wrote memorable, often experimental and strikingly fresh poems which still give pleasure, and consolation today – anything but a small achievement.

He is a distant relative of Philip Sidney and Mary Sidney Herbert: a great nephew of Mary through her marriage to Henry Herbert the 2nd Earl of Pembroke. George Herbert's grandfather Edward Herbert, later Lord of Cherbury, was Henry Herbert's brother. George Herbert's father Richard Herbert was an MP and a sheriff and deputy lieutenant of the Welsh county of Montgomery. It may have been a very privileged background, like the Sidneys, but as with many families at the time, the loss of family members often hit hard. Herbert's grandfather died when he was only a few weeks old and his father died when he was three, leaving his mother Magdalene Herbert pregnant with her tenth child.

Mrs Herbert moved from Wales first to Shropshire and then Oxford, finally setting up house in Charing Cross in 1601. The moves must have been unsettling for George and the family but Magdalen ensured that they were well cared for. The fascinating *Kitchin Booke,* which records household details such as expenditure, visitors, meals and such like covers the first few months of the family settling in to London life. It gives us a picture of a well- to- do family who were possibly living beyond their means, according to a later comment from one of the sons, Edward.[1] There were twenty six members of the household including the family and staff and the book written by the steward, John Gorse, and signed off on many pages by Mrs Herbert, records meals served and items bought. For example on 2 July 1601 'one crabbe and one lobster' were purchased for 2s 6d, amongst thirteen other items such as 'half a Greene fishe' (7d), 'one Pyke' (12d) and a 'bunch of Passneps' – total expenditure was ten shillings and nine pence.[2] Visitors names are recorded, such as the composers William Byrd and John Bull, and there is evidence that Herbert was tutored at home in the Classics, as would have been normal for someone of his background. That summer George was provided with a

1   From https://oxforddnb.com
2   Charles, A, 1974.

George Herbert

grammar book; he was also to study a work by a Roman statesman: 'Cato Senior'. Classical education began at a young age and the study of Latin and Greek dominated. As well as being able to read the extracts pupils had to compose pieces themselves and speak in the languages - quite a skill, and testing intellectually. Pupils were trained in use of rhetoric and oratory and the spoken word was important.

By all accounts Herbert was a hard-working and able student who became a scholar at Westminster school at the age of twelve and later went to Trinity College Cambridge, graduating in 1613 in second top place out of 193 graduates. What was then to become of him? He became a Lecturer in Rhetoric and then in 1620 he secured the post he coveted: University Orator. This involved making speeches to visiting dignitaries including James I. He must have had excellent public speaking skills: an awareness of audience and the politics involved, together with the ability to make an impact with apt and creative use of language. These qualities are displayed in many of his poems: the reader or listener really connects with the dramatic speaking voice.

During his spell as Orator he spent six months as the elected MP for Monmouthshire, a short-lived interlude which was then followed by a typically privileged career move into the church: becoming an ordained deacon (probably in 1624) and later a canon at Lincoln Cathedral (1626). In this diocese he carried out some public duties such as the delivery of an annual sermon in the cathedral. He was able to draw an income from the Lincolnshire parish of Leighton where he was appointed prebendary (a prebend was a stipend or salary, a word originally from the Latin praebenda) and he helped to raise funds to rebuild the disused church. [1] Another source of income at the time, and one which he retained all his life was a 'preferment' or a share in a rectory in Montgomeryshire. His final position was in Salisbury as parish priest for the Bemerton and Fugglestone areas. So here was the distant relative of the Pembrokes finally living in the same Wiltshire area that had nourished Mary Sidney and Philip Sidney, and which became the environment where he gathered together much of his now well known religious verse and created a collection known as 'The Temple' (published after his death).

This quick sketch of his life shows the advantages that a near aristocratic background brought for him; the education he received and the circles he moved in were obviously formative. In London, for example he must have met John Donne the poet and preacher who was well-known to his family; after Mrs Herbert died Donne gave an oration at the memorial service, as well as

---

[1]   For further information about his life see https;//www.oxforddnb, the Oxford Dictionary of National Biography online.

left: The statue of George Herbert on the exterior of Salisbury Cathedral.
right: A window depicting George Herbert at Salisbury Cathedral.

dedicating one of his poems to her. These family connections would have played a part in shaping his thinking and his expectations about his career. But all the connections in the world cannot make a great poet. However, the legacy of the Herbert – Sidney family is striking and George is not the only family member to have excelled in the arts. His eldest brother Edward was a poet and philosopher. On the Sidney side both Robert and William (brothers of Philip) were poets, and further down the line another Mary Sidney, niece to Mary Sidney Herbert who through marriage became Lady Mary Wroth, wrote a prose romance and was the first woman to write a sonnet sequence. We talk of a 'Bloomsbury set' of artists in the early 20th century and here we have a 'Wilton set'.

There is no doubt that this extended Herbert - Sidney family nurtured many talented writers. George Herbert is one of the best known and well loved, and extensively studied. What is it about Herbert which attracts readers several hundred years after his death? We need to look closely at some of his poetry for the answers.

Early Latin verse

Herbert was schooled in Latin and Greek from an early age. There would be nothing unusual amongst the educated in being able to translate classical texts and to speak the language. However, to produce poems of quality in another language is a rarer skill. Herbert, we believe, wrote some of the early poems whilst at Westminster. The collection of forty epigrams was written in response to Melville's long poem. Melville's work supported Puritan views that the church was becoming too Roman Catholic in its practices such as its use of song, its reverence of the cross and other icons. The frontispiece of the work, published after Herbert's death, has the title 'The Muses' Reply' and contains three dedications: to King James, Charles, Prince of Wales and the Bishop of Winchester, followed by the epigrams.

The collection is called: *Epigrams in Defence of the Discipline of Our Church* and the first poem is politely addressed to the king (Herbert is ever the politician) and humbly explains why he is writing lots of short poems:

> Since a thousand matters, it is agreed, beat upon your mind
> And the world hangs upon its work;
> And because I am afraid to wear you out with long
> and laboured verses,
> Instead of one large and complete song, CAESAR,
> I shall give you bits and pieces.
> While you are beating down the *Cathars*,[1] with
> your bearing and your books,
> I am glad of the crumbs from your table.

The original Latin verse is beautifully concise:

> Cum millena tuam pulsare negotia mentem
> Constet, & ex illa pendeat orbis ope;
> Ne te productis videar lassare Camoenis,
> Pro solido, CAESAR, carmine frusta dabo.
> Cu`m tu contundis *Catharos*, vultu'que librisque,
> Grata mihi mensae sunt analecta tuae.

Throughout the collection a clear speaking voice emerges, sometimes gently goading and sometimes directly critical. Herbert deals with all aspects of Melville's views and counters them with arguments. For example in Epigram 23 he defends sacred music: 'O Music, filled with a hundred Graces,

---

[1] The Cathars refers to a Christian sect which were persecuted by the Catholic church in the 12th – 14th century but in the time of James 1 it was a term used to denigrate the Puritans.

The food of more glorious spirits,' and he talks specifically about the beauty of the psalms and how nature marvels at the sound:

> The nearby sea marvels at the sound,
> And Jordan itself halts its waters in amazement;

After drawing us in with lyrical descriptions he ends on a more barbed note, complaining about the Puritan emphasis on the spoken word and a neglect of music:

> Do you block your crude ears, new flock,
> And fail to hear? Clamouring against the songs
>   To make more space
>   For wearing out your pulpits?
>
> But who can find it surprising
> That minds which are drums disturbing the public peace,
>   Filled with resounding discord,
>   Should tolerate no harmony?

This is a resounding critique. For Herbert, music was very important, as was respect for Anglican ritual. His pithy epigram 24 is strongly worded – directed at Melville:

> So, blasphemous man, you call sacred songs
>   lowing, do you?
> I would rather low than bray.

Epigram 36 is addressed 'To the Innocent Who Have been Led Astray' and ends with a brilliant, simple, but pointed criticism of the leaders of this movement:

> Innocent minds, whose pure life is led
>   Among the waters of the world with a clear shining faith,
> Far be it that my words should wound your natural chastity;
>   These songs censure your leaders alone.
> My only plea is this: would that you had
>   Their eyes, and they your hearts.

The more mature Herbert would probably have edited this collection of poems and made them pithier, but they exude a daring, youthful confidence and they contain strong lines such as these from Epigram 37:

> For if I wished to cut you with my verse,
> And to vomit forcefully all the anger
> That has been stored up in me by the disdain your friends
> Showed for the Church, and by their abuse of Athens
> (And who would not be roused by this quarrel?)

I would by now have thoroughly destroyed you:
With fiery Latin Muses, or the crackling Greek one;
Every single line, refusing ink,
Would have been drawn in seething lead,
Branding with a hundred scars
Your ungodly groans and your fine grimaces:

However in epigram 39 – *To his Most Serene Majesty* – we see the politically astute poet at work. Herbert praises the King and encourages him to defeat 'the furious foe' and to overturn 'whatever projects heresy is fostering'.

The final poem is dedicated to God. Here is the last line which expresses a sentiment which recurs in much of his verse.

What I write, and the pleasure I give, if I do so, is all yours.

The Latin version of this, with its sonorous tones, is worth quoting:

Quod scribe, & placeo, si placeo, tuum est.

The Sacred Grove is another collection of Latin verse which contains advice on how to live our lives; some poems faintly reminiscent of the self help guides published today. Poem 21 'On the Glutton' sums up starkly in its final line:

Anyone who longs to die before his time – he'll[1] seek you out.

There are several poems about human nature such as the dangers of pride, about hollow eloquence ('silk in your words') and reflections on many aspects of religion, plus criticisms of the papacy.

Memoriae Matris Sacrum
(A Sacred Gift in memory of My Mother)

This is a moving collection of Latin poems which was probably composed in the months following his mother's death in June 1627 and then published later that year together with John Donne's 'Sermon of Commemoration for the Lady Danvers' (Magdalen had remarried in 1609 to Sir John Danvers).[2] The first poem in the sequence shows the depth of his grief:

Ah mother, from what spring might I weep for you?
    What drops could count out my griefs?
Next to my tears, the neighbouring Thames seems dry
    And I dryer than your chorus of virtues.
If I were poured, still burning, into a river black with grief
    I could not make ink enough for your praises.

---

1   The 'he' is Gluttony personified.
2   Drury, J, and Moul, V, 2014.

> For this alone I write in thanks: that you are for me not only
> Mother: now Sorrow delivers these Metres.

There are nineteen poems in all including six in Greek, and Herbert uses a range of verse styles and rhythms. It is worth reading the whole sequence which reveals his love and admiration for his mother. In the second poem he is down-to-earth, lavishing praise on her domestic skills, her ability to run the home efficiently; also, he praises her writing and speaking skills '..a wonderful harmony of sense and expression', and her compassion – ' A general balm for the anxious heart'.

In Poem 11 he sustains an image of himself as 'a felled tree'. With his mother alongside him he was strong :

> But now I lie open to my fate, exposed without my mother
>   to the blasts of the wind,
>   Unsteady, my motion surpassing even the salt sea.

They are moving personal poems and very accessible in translation. Obviously they lose something of the rhythm and shape of the original Latin verse but they show strong, raw feelings about loss.

Poem 10 makes clever use of simple imagery to stress this momentous loss, building the poem round the image of a weary, wet traveller (everyman) in gloomy weather who after her death rejects the minor irritations of the British climate and turns to overwhelming tears at the loss of his 'Great Mother' (so much neater and more impressive a phrase in Latin: Magna Mater). Here is the full text of the poem:

> Surely up to now the gloomy south winds
> And the Sky sad and heavy with rain
> And British earth reduced to mud
> -All these the traveller has stressed unfairly.
> But now at your death, Great Mother,
> He quite rightly rejects the damp air he breathes in
> Resentfully, and blows out the offending mouthful.
> For now Country, City and Court weep for you:
> For you now, England, and the two Gaelic lands,
> Yes, even ancient Wales weeps,
> All three drawing down the tears of an earlier age
> For fear they should come too late for your virtues.
> There is no clear corner anywhere,
> The sea no longer girts us round, but floods us all.

The final two lines are so vivid: a sea of tears drowning everyone. The traveller's complaints about the damp British weather are totally submerged in the floods of tears. The collection is a heartfelt memorial to a much loved mother.

The Temple

This is Herbert's better known collection which he assembled in the last few years of his life (1630 – 1633) when he served as rector in charge of 'Fugglestone with Bemerton.' Fugglestone church can be seen on the side of the main A36 road near Wilton House and the church at Bemerton, now a suburb of Salisbury, still exists together with the imposing rectory opposite and its long garden leading down to the banks of the Nadder. Salisbury has a thriving George Herbert Society[1] which uses the Bemerton church for readings and meetings.

St Andrew's Church, Bemerton

Herbert's links with the Herbert family in Wilton House had solved his agonising dilemma about what he should do for employment. He veered towards a religious calling but was also torn by the pull of the court and the university, though when Philip Herbert offered him this parish as a country parson he settled in the area. He had married Jane Danvers in 1629 and they were joined in Bemerton rectory by his three orphaned nieces. Despite illnesses this was a productive three years for Herbert, not only writing and editing his poems but producing a guide to being a country parson, which is still in print today: *A Priest to the Temple* or *A Country Parson*. This is very revealing about his cares and concerns but the poems also reveal his dilemmas – and much more – in a striking, innovative way.

Herbert entrusted his English poems to Nicholas Ferrar, a close friend, and modestly said to him that he could publish them 'if he think it may turn to

1 www.georgeherbert.org.uk

the advantage of any dejected poor soul'[1]. The first edition of *The Temple* was published in the year he died, 1633, and ran to six editions in eight years - a success then, and still read today in our generally more secular society. So, what is the lasting appeal of Herbert's poetry? Let us look at a selection.

The poem *Jordan (1)* focuses on poetic language: how should a poet express himself? He opens with arresting questions about how we should write; he debates this and then celebrates plainness in the final lines.

> Who says that fictions only and false hair
> Become a verse? Is there in truth no beauty?
> Is all good structure in a winding stair?
> May no lines pass, except they do their duty
>   Not to a true, but painted chair?
>
> Is it no verse, except enchanted groves
> And sudden arbours shadow coarse-spun lines?
> Must purling streams refresh a lover's loves?
> Must all be veil'd, while he that reads, divines,
>   Catching the sense at two removes?
>
> Shepherds are honest people; let them sing:
> Riddle who list, for me, and pull for Prime:[2]
> I envy no man's nightingale or spring;
> Nor let them punish me with loss of rhyme,
>   Who plainly say, *My God, My King.*

Herbert hammers home the point that fancy language (the 'purling streams') does not make a poet. He often chooses simple diction and homely images ('painted chair') and avoids the embellished style – 'enchanted groves' and 'sudden arbours'. His question 'Is all good structure in a winding stair?' says it all so neatly. The finale, as often with Herbert, sums up with a religious reference and here there is a positive endorsement of plain speaking: who needs more than the simple declaration of '*My God, My King*'?

Jordan (2) is another brilliant poem on the same theme. He reflects that initially he sought out 'quaint words, and trim invention' and his writing was 'Curling with metaphors'. What an apt phrase which conjures up diverse images of fancy, tangled curls, or the ornate decorative curls on manuscripts, and also an image of toe-curling embarrassment – cringing at purple passages in poetry! Herbert later reflects that 'Nothing could seem too rich to clothe the sun,'; but in the last verse he concludes with:

---

1   Drury, J. and Moul, V, 2015.

2   Shepherds were often associated with the singing of pastoral poetry. Here Herbert says they can sing his thoughts which are: Sing in a riddling way as you wish, or try to gain the winning card (Primero was a card game), and become top dog, but he does not envy those poets who have to be inspired by the usual prompts – romantic nightingale images or features of spring.

But while I bustled, I might hear a friend
Whisper, *How wide is all this long pretence!*
There is in love a sweetness ready penned:
Copy out only that, and save expense.

Several of Herbert's poems have become celebrated hymns: they are accessible, simple and show how good he was at creating verse that is memorable and rhythmical and impressive when set to music. *Antiphon (1)* has the chorus of 'Let all the world in ev'ry corner sing' and the whole song is based on Psalm 95 (O come, let us sing unto the Lord). Herbert's verses are short and clear with no wordy elaboration. The point is made. Here is verse 1:

The heav'ns are not too high,
His praise may thither fly:
The earth is not too low,
His praises there may grow.

Herbert also wrote his version of Psalm 23: 'The God of love my shepherd is'. Together with the poem 'The Elixir: 'Teach me my God and King', and the hymn from *Praise (2)* they remain favourite church hymns today. Here is the opening to *Praise (2):*

King of Glory, King of Peace,
        I will love thee;
Ant that love may never cease,
        I will move thee.

The rhythm is regular: seven syllables in the longer lines with four beats or stresses to the line; and the shorter line with four syllables and two main stresses. However, when we read the shorter lines we tend to emphasise each word and slow down to take in the sense. The overall structure is clever but simple. Here are the second and third verses:

Thou hast granted my request,
        Thou hast heard me:
Thou didst note my working breast,
        Thou hast spar'd me.

Wherefore with my utmost art
        I will sing thee
And the cream of all my heart
        I will bring thee

The verses alternate between what I (Herbert)says, and Thou's response (God). Six verses move between I and Thou and the last verse changes:

Small it is, in this poor sort
          To enrol thee:
Ev'n eternity is too short
          To extol thee.

A quiet and positive ending, extolling God. What a wonderfully structured and deceptively simple form.

Speaking of form (the arrangement of words and lines and stanzas) Herbert is well known for shaping some of his poems so that visually the form echoes the sense of the verse. In the 1960s there emerged a form of verse called concrete poetry, which does just this. At the time it was celebrated as innovative: write a poem about a skyscraper block and shape the lines and length to create a picture of the skyscraper, or it could be a river or a waterfall. However the Greeks got there first and even Herbert, experimental though he was, was not the first to play with the impact of how a poem looks. Nevertheless several of his poems are skilfully formed to capitalise on this shaping. For example, the well known *Easter-wings* takes the shape of birds in flight:

Lord, who createdst man in wealth and store,
          Though foolishly he lost the same,
                    Decaying more and more,
                              Till he became
                                        Most poor:
                              With thee
                    O let me rise
          As larks, harmoniously,
And sing this day thy victories:
Then shall the fall further the flight in me.

My tender age in sorrow did begin:
          And still with sicknesses and shame
                    Thou didst so punish sin,
                              That I became
                                        Most thin.
                              With thee
                    Let me combine,
          And feel this day thy victory:
For if I imp my wing on thine,
Affliction shall advance the flight in me.

The birds are in flight horizontally, as in Herbert's original manuscript, which was a double spread with each poem on a separate page facing the other. Apparently a printer in 1633 turned the shape into two equilateral triangles, a kind of hourglass shape, but whichever version you read the wonderful marriage of sense and shape is shown: we descend in tone and volume to the centre of each verse and then rise joyfully at the end. The centre of the first verse is the short line stating that man has become 'most poor' having squandered 'wealth and store'. But we rise joyously at the end, like larks, singing about the victory of the resurrection. The second verse begins with Herbert's despair at his own sin and sickness; we descend to the midpoint where he has become 'most thin' (physically and mentally fragile) and then we rise again when he asks to join in the victories and imp (implant) his own wing on God's so that his upward, joyous flight can be advanced. By becoming closer he will soar again and the 'affliction' he has felt will be the catalyst enabling him to get closer to God. Read the poem aloud and you will sense the rhythm and feel the decline and joyous rise in each verse.

Commenting on poetry and 'translating' it like this can make it seem banal. The poet says it all so much better in such a concise, fascinating form. Also, there is often ambiguity in poetry and the sense is open to multiple interpretations which enriches the poem and allows us to celebrate our differing responses. Herbert can be deliberately teasing and ambivalent. For example, what is meant by 'the fall further the flight in me'? Literally, the lark descends and then takes off again, energised by singing. The fall also reminds us of the 'fall' of man and the sins which Christ atoned for. There are many different ways in which we can respond to a poem like this and interpreting a narrative can be challenging, but we certainly feel the rhythms here, hear the sounds and sense the mood changes.

There are several other poems where shape is cleverly linked with sense, such as *The Altar* which is shaped like a solid altar: a table with strong supports. Herbert also uses the ancient tradition of Echo poems as a neat way of dramatising a dialogue: in the poem *Heaven* the Echo responds to each question with a one word answer. Here is the opening:

> O who will show me those delights on high?
>   *Echo.*   I.

The poem carries on with five more questions before:

> Then tell me what is that supreme delight?
>   *Echo.*   Light.
> Light to the mind: what shall the will enjoy?
>   *Echo.*   Joy.
> But are there cares and business with the pleasure?
>   *Echo.*   Leisure.
> Light, joy, and leisure; but shall they persever?
>   *Echo.*   Ever.

This is a positive poem where the final answer crystallises the pleasures of heaven and promises everlasting light and hope, and it is so neatly structured. The Echo replies using the last syllable of the preceding line, a genuine, meaningful echo. We also admire Herbert's skills in poems such as *Iesu* (the original spelling of Jesus), a riddling poem which describes how Jesus is in his heart and his whole person. Let the poem speak for itself:

Iesu

IESU is in my heart, his sacred name
Is deeply carv'ed there: but th'other week
A great affliction broke the little frame,
Ev'n all to pieces: which I went to seek:
And first I found the corner, where was *I,*
After, where *ES,* and next where *U* was graved.
When I had got these parcels, instantly
I sat me down to spell them, and perceiv'ed
That to my broken heart he was *I ease you,*
           And to my whole is *IESU.*

Herbert sustains the unusual image of a picture frame (the heart) breaking into pieces and then ends with relief – his heart is mended.

Many of Herbert's poems dwell on religious dilemmas and particularly his own torments and doubts. We do not need to identify with his Anglican beliefs to appreciate and sympathise with his need for comfort, certainty and reassurance. He often takes us on a harrowing journey but a poem's ending usually offers some resolution and peace. There are many great poems, but we will focus on a few rather than try to glance at them all.

In *Affliction*(1) Herbert begins joyfully, celebrating his faith and his anticipation of joys to come:

When first thou didst entice to thee my heart,
           I thought the service brave:
So many joys I writ down for my part,

In the fourth verse he speaks of being given 'milk and sweetnesses' and how his days were 'straw'd with flowers and happiness'. But then he catalogues the problems: 'consuming agues', loss of friends and family and feeling stressed and rudderless which he expresses with such vividness:

Thus thin and lean without a fence or friend,
I was blown through with ev'ry storm and wind.

He was tempted by 'The way that takes the town' but accepted the calling. But he is not sure how to cope with the responsibility of priesthood:

Now I am here, what thou wilt do with me
           None of my books will show:

Herbert does not reach out for the grand image to convey his feelings but the next lines spell out the problems in a down to earth way:

I read, and sigh, and wish I were a tree;
           For sure then I should grow

> To fruit or shade: at least some bird would trust
> Her household to me, and I should be just.[1]

And the final verse contains a disturbing resolution which leaves us with doubts:

> Yet, though thou troublest me, I must be meek;
>> In weakness must be stout.
> Well, I will change the service , and go seek
>> Some other master out.
> Ah my dear God! though I am clean forgot,
> Let me not love thee, if I love thee not.

There is tension in this final verse and a quiet colloquial 'Well' introduces the dramatic notion that he will seek another master. Then we hear his voice and the gentle address to a God he feels has forgotten him. The final line with its clear balance of two opposing halves expressed in simple monosyllabic diction, provides a kind of resolution, but not quite. Which route will he take? We are, however, impressed by his sincerity: he will not commit if he cannot wholly give of himself, a quality of honesty and humility which endears him to us and ironically shows how worthy he is of his role.

Many of Herbert's poems focus on his doubts about his own worthiness, his uncertainties about his role and his relationship with God. We hear the anguish in his voice; in *Denial*, for example, he is praying to God, asking him to listen and to give him direction. The opening lines plainly show his state of mind:

>> When my devotions could not pierce
>>> Thy silent ears;
> Then was my heart broken, as was my verse:

He uses a musical image to convey how lost he is; his soul is 'Untuned, unstrung'. His 'feeble spirit' is:

>> Like a nipt blossom, hung
>>> Discontented.

The way Herbert arranges his lines- their length and position on the page and the resultant visual impact - is important. We read and understand the poem differently because of the arrangement. Sometimes his poems are tidied up by printers and each line starts neatly from the left margin. But look at the first three lines of the poem here. We linger a little on 'pierce' because it is at the end of the line, then the shorter central line with its emphasis on silence is quietly dramatic. Moving the third line towards the left so that it is separate, emphasises the narrative change marked by 'Then'; and the understated 'heart broken' stands out from the poem. Herbert's placing of phrases is never accidental: it impacts on our reactions to his poems.

---

[1]   i.e. justified in my choices.

He ends the poem with musical references again, and asks God to help him sort out his thinking (what he referred to in the second verse as his 'bent thoughts, like a brittle bow')

> O cheer and tune my heartless breast,
> Defer no time;
> That so thy favours granting my request,
> They and my mind may chime,
> And mend my rhyme.

In *The Collar* his anguish is expressed with more sound and fury. He is railing against the restrictions of his role, the priest's collar which defines him. There is much 'choler', or anger in the poem too. He batters his listener with a startling opening:

> I struck the board, and cri'd, No more.
> I will abroad.
> What? shall I ever sigh and pine?
> My lines and life are free; free as the road,
> Loose as the wind, as large as store.
> Shall I be still in suit?

Question after question tumbles out as he loudly bewails what he sees as his failure to achieve anything worthwhile. He chafes at the restrictions of his role, and shows the turmoil of his thoughts about freedom and his doubts about the debate he is having. This is all beautifully resolved at the end with the calm final lines:

> But as I raved and grew more fierce and wild
> At every word,
> Me thoughts I heard one calling, *Child*
> And I repli'd , *My Lord.*

The poem is shaped as one continuous verse and the use of questions draws the listener in. The poet is troubled and his thoughts fly in all directions, so there are no neat verse forms here. It's not the easiest of poems to unpick and each line throws out so many images and ideas, but hear it spoken and its impact is strong.

There are many poems about sin and love, redemption, mortality and the transience of life. These are not stuffy poems which preach at the reader or dusty, dry descriptions of his beliefs or excessively descriptive passages about church ritual. They speak in a direct way to the reader, or preferably the listener. They need to be heard. To appreciate *The Agony* there is no need to look up the passage in the bible describing Christ's agony on the Mount of Olives. Here Christ is 'A man so wrung with pains' carrying the sins of the world and then dying on the cross, his side pierced with a pike, spilling blood. The last two lines speak of the Love that God has and how :

Love is that liquor sweet and most divine,
Which my God feels as blood; but I, as wine.

The reference is to the communion – the drinking of wine to remind us of
Christ's blood and suffering.

Redemption is a skilful poem which tells the story of Christ's descent
to earth and how he was crucified to redeem everyone's sins. To state just
that is to miss the richness of an allegory – the telling of a simple story in
an unusual way, a story that has underlying meanings and which makes us
reflect on wealth and earthly ambitions and what we really value. The imagery
sustained throughout the sonnet is of worldly things: buying and selling and
taking possession. The speaker is looking for his landlord, in heaven and then
in wealthy places but finally finds him dying amongst thieves and murderers.
Here is the whole poem:

Having been tenant long to a rich Lord,
    Not thriving, I resolved to be bold,
    And make a suit unto him, to afford
A new small-rented lease, and cancel th'old.
In heaven at his manor I him sought:
    They told me there, that he was lately gone
    About some land which he had dearly bought
Long since on earth to take possession.
I straight return'd, and knowing his great birth,
    Sought him accordingly in great resorts;
    In cities, theatres, gardens, parks, and courts:
At length I heard a raggèd noise and mirth
    Of thieves and murderers: there I him espied,
    Who straight, *Your suit is granted,* said, and died.

There are many uplifting and positive poems, full of praise and joy, and
many that offer us a mixture of pain and pleasure. For example *Virtue* begins
with:

Sweet day, so cool, so calm, so bright,
The bridal of the earth and sky:
The dew shall weep thy fall tonight;
                For thou must die.

The next two verses speak of roses which bloom but whose 'root is ever in its
grave', and spring which fades and music which has its 'closes'. But the final
verse offers hope to the virtuous:

Only a sweet and virtuous soul,
Like season'd timber never gives;
But though the whole world turn to coal,
                Then chiefly lives.

The virtuous soul survives the fires of judgement day. It is a smoothly lyrical poem with liquid 'l' sounds and soft 's' sounds; only the harsh sound of 'coal' grates deliberately. The final line of each verse is altered slightly and we move from 'For thou must die' to the emphatic 'And thou must die' to 'And all must die', and then the quietly matter of fact 'chiefly lives'.

Herbert writes about the transience of life in several poems, but they are not morbid or self pitying. In *Life* he builds the poem around the image of a small bunch of flowers which, beautiful though it is, withers in his hand. The last verse ends with:

> Farewell dear flowers, sweetly your time ye spent
> Fit, while ye lived, for smell or ornament,
>   And after death for cures.
> I follow straight without complaints or grief,
> Since if my scent be good, I care not , if
>   It be as short as yours.

What a wonderfully simple and memorable line: 'if my scent be good'. A short life well lived is celebrated here.

Herbert often uses simple, natural imagery: fruits, trees, flowers - but he is not tempted to over elaborate. There are no wordy details or lavish expressions. In *The Flower*, for example, he speaks of his 'shrivel'd heart' which has 'recovered greenness'. Later in the poem he celebrates the return of his inspiration and his appreciation of nature:

> And now in age I bud again,
> After so many deaths I live and write;
>   I once more smell the dew and rain,
> And relish versing.............................

The order of poems in *The Temple* was arranged by Herbert himself before he died and tellingly the final poem celebrates love. Unlike Sidney's very different love sonnets this is about sacred love. Here Herbert is reconciled with God and is given love and reassurance.

Love (3)

> Love bade me welcome: yet my soul drew back,
>   Guilty of dust and sin.
> But quick-ey'd Love, observing me grow slack
>   From my first entrance in,
> Drew nearer to me, sweetly questioning,
>   If I lack'd anything.
>
> A guest, I answer'd, worthy to be here:
>   Love said, You shall be he.
> I the unkind, ungrateful? Ah my dear,
>   I cannot look on thee.

Love took my hand, and smiling did reply,
   Who made the eyes but I?

Truth Lord, but I have marr'd them: let my shame
   Go where it doth deserve.
And know you not, says Love, who bore the blame?
   My dear, then I will serve.
You must sit down, says Love, and taste my meat:
   So I did sit and eat.

Herbert is remembered in Salisbury Cathedral in a beautiful window behind the high altar. There is also a stone carving of him in one of the niches above the West door. It shows a lean ascetic looking character looking down on the Cathedral Close. In the distance are the water meadows, still grazed today in the traditional manner, introduced not long after Herbert's death. They are 'drowned' or flooded twice a year to encourage the early grass growth which the sheep still crop today. Apparently, he walked over these water meadows to evensong at the cathedral two or three times a week and the paths he walked are still there.

The Rectory, Bemerton

The rectory in Bemerton was bought in the 1980s by another writer Vikram Seth who renovated the house. He has written several award winning novels and much poetry, some of which cleverly echoes Herbert's verse forms. The poem *Host* describes how having bought 'the old house' he worries that

Herbert's ghost-like presence might influence his style. In the second verse his concern is shown in a dialogue between the rain and the speaker – a to-ing and fro-ing reminiscent of Herbert's dramatic voices. The end of this verse concludes simply and effectively: Seth accepts that Herbert might influence his writing style but he wryly and quietly acknowledges that he could do worse than accept such influence.

In the final verse Seth sums up the problems experienced in this house: the pleasures and the losses and the physical events such as floods and an invasion of moles. He has shared not only the place with Herbert but also some of the pain. The final two lines draw a moving and apt conclusion, painting a picture of Herbert - the 'host' - standing in the shadows, keeping watch while Seth writes.[1]

Herbert's poems can be lyrical and emotional, but controlled and organised as well as being intriguing and often argumentative. His influence on poets today is still strong: such accessible, colloquial and dramatic verse provides a model of what poets might aspire to, as Seth shows in his poem 'The Host'.

Poets tend to become pigeon holed: Beat poets of the 20th century, Romantic poets of the late 18th and early 19th century or Modernists of the 20th century and so on. Herbert is often given the label 'metaphysical' and sorted with other 17th century poets such as John Donne, Henry Vaughan and Andrew Marvell. The label was coined by Samuel Johnson and is shorthand for poets who used unusual 'conceits' (figurative language) often taken from science or the everyday, rather than the more traditional images. Think of Herbert's use of 'coal' in the poem *Virtue* quoted earlier – he is not a poet who dwells on babbling brooks or elaborate romantic images. It also embraces the idea of a poet who argues but who often exposes contradictions and uncertainties. A label can help us to look at poems and be aware of particular facets. However, labels can become constricting and we may spend time looking for features which fit the label. Just reading Herbert's verse, aloud if possible, helps us to appreciate the ideas and debates, the sounds and rhythms and images, and above all, to enjoy the thought-provoking and often moving poems.

It is not far-fetched to celebrate Herbert's verse and to link this with a legacy from Mary Sidney Herbert. They were both connected by places in common: Salisbury and Wilton House, but of more importance, there is a clear family connection and Mary Sidney's experiments with verse form are echoed and developed by Herbert. There are of course dramatic differences: Mary Sidney had Calvinist leanings whereas Herbert took on the 'collar' of an Anglican priest and his poetry is full of self-examination. But he deserves his place alongside the other Sidney Herberts : innovators all.

---

[1] See rsliterature.org/library-article/love-bade-me-welcome for a complete version of the poem .

9
Mary Sidney's Legacy

Pembroke's Men

In the world of politics which Henry Herbert inhabited both in Wales and as part of his management of his estates in the South-West of England he had the reputation for being brusque, tactless and belligerent. He is said to have alienated everyone with whom he came into contact: beginning with foes and ultimately working his way through his friends. Within the county of Wiltshire he was isolated, having antagonised the gentry in the surrounding area. What is interesting is the contrast between this hostile environment and the one created by his wife in her domain of the house at Wilton. The evidence of Henry's *modus operandi* in his dealings with his landowning and council responsibilities does not point towards a person who might initiate the patronage of the arts. Yet the supportive networks that emanated from the inspiration of the countess evidently had an impact on the earl. Perhaps he enjoyed the additional status afforded to the household because of the connections with the world of art. Under Sidney's influence Henry Herbert became patron of one of the travelling troupes of actors who became known as the Earl of Pembroke's Men.

In 1923 Sir Edmund Chambers wrote in his history *The Elizabethan Stage* that Shakespeare worked as one of Pembroke's Men and that it was after the collapse of Pembroke's Men that he joined the more famous company of Chamberlain's Men. This idea has been repeated by other scholars but it is a matter of dispute that has not been resolved. Biographical information about Shakespeare is far from complete and researchers have yet to find hard evidence about what he was doing between 1585 and 1594; so discussion of his whereabouts during this period is reliant on speculation. Shakespeare disappears from view after 1585 until there are records of his activity again in 1594, at which time he is noted as being a performer in plays produced by Chamberlain's Men. A lot of the discussion is centred on the uncertainty concerning exactly when companies associated with Shakespeare were formed and which companies might have actually worked in tandem. Further evidence about Pembroke's Men emerged in a will, which came to light in the mid-twentieth century. The will was completed on 23 August 1592 and concerned the estate of Simon Jewell, a man who lived in Shoreditch, London where two public playhouses 'The Theatre' and 'The Curtain' had been built in the 1570s. Jewell was one of Pembroke's Men; his will names five other possible members of the group but Shakespeare is not one of them.[1]

1 George, D. (1981)

MARY SIDNEY

Countess of Pembroke

from the extremely rare Print
engraved by Simon Pass

Mary Sidney Herbert

Further details in Jewell's will supports the narrative that Pembroke's Men was formed as a specific response to the outbreak of the plague in 1592 which closed London Theatres. It was therefore begun as a travelling company. The ban on performances in London lasted for two years. Indeed the performance record of Pembroke's Men, now housed in the British Library, shows that they left London for a tour of the provinces visiting Leicester in the autumn. Early in 1593 they were in Bewdley, then Ludlow and Shrewsbury, all places associated with the Pembroke dynasty. In June and July they were in York and Rye in Sussex. By the first half of 1594 they were back in London and bankrupt. Before their tour in 1592 they had spent £80 on a range of necessary items, including costumes. The money also covered horses and wagons purchased to transport the company; everything had to be pawned or sold. The costs of the tour had proved too much for Pembroke's Men and there is direct evidence that they also had to sell shorter versions of longer texts which they had used for performance. There is a possibility that the company recovered as there is a reference dating back to 1597 referring to Pembroke's Men making an agreement to play at The Swan, in London, for a year. A patron was a necessity as an official seal of approval for a drama company but beyond that the part played by the patron of the company is unclear, and whether or not there was financial support involved in this case is unknown but thought to be unlikely other than for payments made by audiences at a production. The discussions over Simon Jewell's will are of great interest partly because they illustrate that, even so many years after the era, new evidence does emerge from time to time and new ways of looking at old evidence. There are questions which remain unanswered about Pembroke's Men, including why did the earl set up the company in his name so late in life? The answer almost certainly lies with the expanding influence of the countess, in the literary world.

William, third Earl of Pembroke

Whilst Henry allowed a drama company to be associated with his name all the evidence points towards the Sidney clan as having the literary ability in the Wilton branch of the Herbert family. Mary's influence can be perceived particularly in the association of her eldest son and heir to the Wilton empire, William. His story has been touched on before in relation to a disastrous affair with one of Elizabeth's young women at court. But William lived well into middle age and throughout his adult life he was acknowledged as being the most important patron of the arts of the era. When his father died in 1601, William was twenty one and already very popular and well known at court. When he was christened at St. Mary's Church, Wilton, twenty days after his birth at Wilton House, his status was assured with the choice of godparents for the new baby. They were Elizabeth the queen, Robert Dudley Earl of Leicester and Ambrose Dudley Earl of Warwick. In the presence of the queen, William had his first introduction to Oxford University when he was twelve years old which started an association which lasted through his life. On January 29th 1617 he was made Chancellor of the university: a college was renamed in his honour, Pembroke College.

William's affair with Mary Fitton had unforeseen consequences. For Mary, no doubt they were permanent and life changing. She gave birth to a son who only lived for a very short time. In her circle she was known as the woman made pregnant by and rejected by the Earl of Pembroke. Not even the threat of complete exile from court could change his mind about the refusal to marry her: William's career, during Elizabeth's lifetime was finished. He was sent to the Fleet prison where he was held for a month, between 25 March and 25 April, and then sent back to his country seat in Wilton. Anyone who knows the scenic beauty of Wilton and the surrounding countryside may not see that as much of a punishment but his mother was furious with him. She had taken great care over his upbringing with his education being attended to by renowned figures such as her fellow playwright Samuel Daniel. He had been prepared to inherit the vast Herbert fortune and he had adopted the literary refinements of the Sidney branch of the family. William wrote a collection of his own verse. He had military training and could excel at the tilt, as his uncle Philip had before him. He had imbibed the culture of the young Protestant elite but his downfall must have appeared to be quite complete at this stage. Unlike Mary Fitton though, William was to be offered a second chance which he seized.

When James I of England acceded to the throne on the death of Elizabeth in 1603 William and his younger brother Philip made the journey to Scotland in order to accompany the new king to his seat of power at Westminster. Thus began a new and close relationship. After two visits made by James to Wilton House, during the first year of his reign, William was once more welcomed to court and soon became a gentleman of the Privy Chamber: one of the men with closest access to the king. In such an influential position, with the family name of Sidney in the background, and the knowledge that here was a man with an appetite for the arts, the number of books dedicated to him were numerous. He became a patron to famous figures such as Ben Jonson, Richard Burbage and Edward Allyn. After his relative George Herbert repeatedly failed to find a career William sponsored him for the post of rector at Bemerton near Salisbury, and enabled his seat in the House of Commons. Thus providing the most auspicious conditions for George to continue with his writing and it was during the latter phase of his life that George became most prolific and successful with his poetry. Perhaps the most celebrated link that William and his brother have with the literature of the age is the fact that Shakespeare's first folio published in 1624 is dedicated to the two brothers, William and Philip. Mary need not have worried about the career of her eldest son as his success at court continued well into the reign of Charles I. William died suddenly in 1630 and his brother Philip then became heir to the Pembroke estate.

Robert and Barbara Sidney (née Gamage)

Another interesting family avenue to explore in relation to the Sidney literary legacy is the life and work of Robert Sidney, uncle to William and the younger brother of Mary and Philip. Like Philip he had been heavily involved in the military support of Protestants in Europe and had been appointed commander of the English garrison at Flushing. He had married

Barbara Gamage and the couple had eleven children. On 15 October 1587 a daughter born to Robert and Barbara, was named Mary, after her artistic aunt. The family lived in the Sidney home on the banks of the River Thames, Baynard's Castle. The house no longer exists, unlike some of the other Sidney dwellings which still stand today. Robert had very little influence at court during Elizabeth's reign and looked to his sister Mary to put forward his case when needed. However, as with his nephew William, his fortunes improved greatly on the accession of James I, when he became Baron Sidney of Penshurst. His advancement during James's reign continued with Robert gaining the titles Earl of Leicester and Viscount Lisle of Penshurst. He was known to be particularly close to his sister and despite his military activity and busy family life, Robert expanded on the family tradition of writing poetry.

Baynard's Castle

In the later part of the 20th century a fascinating discovery was made. A note book containing poetry which originated in the Elizabethan era had been found in Warwick Castle. By 1973 it was discovered that the book had formerly been part of a collection in the library at Penshurst and the author was none other than Robert Sidney. It is speculated that the document might have found its way to Warwick as it was the seat of an earlier Earl of Leicester, or it might have been transported there because of the connections Fulke Greville had with Warwick Castle[1]. In 1975 Robert Sidney's poems appeared for sale at a London auction and eventually found their way to the British Library collection, where they are now housed. Robert's note book was, of course, hand written and contains a number of revisions and crossings out; added to which a sentence which states 'For the countess of Pembroke' has led scholars

---

1   Kelliher, W, and Duncan-Jones, K, 1975.

to voice the opinion that when Robert wrote his collection of poems it was his intention to pass them to his sister Mary for her opinion, before they were written in a final form. Gary Waller has made a study of the poems and songs contained in the text and he points towards the influence of both Philip and Mary in their construction. In particular he notes the mutual interest in 'formal experimentation' reflected in Robert's songs and Mary Sidney's psalms[1]. The collection of Robert Sidney's poems is of great significance as it is the largest body of original work to have survived in the handwriting of the author, more than any other English poets of the Elizabethan era.

Robert's close association with King James meant that he had constant access to the court and was frequently required to be there when not at his post in Flushing, where he was the governor. Once she was old enough, Mary, his daughter, joined the court circle and participated in masques which were part of the entertainment scene. William Herbert acted alongside her and other prominent courtiers; a close relationship developed between the two cousins. William and Mary were not strangers to each other when their relationship developed in young adulthood as Mary Wroth (as she became on her marriage day) had spent time with her aunt's family at Wilton during her childhood. Mary Wroth must have regarded her aunt Mary as being a second mother to her during those long periods when she supported Barbara, her mother, throughout Robert Sidney's long absences from home. In the year 1604 the two cousins both had marriages arranged for them by their parents. Their respective partners were regarded as being sufficiently well placed in society with the correct level of status and breeding. Mary was married to Robert Wroth of Loughton Hall in Essex. The alliance was not necessarily looked upon as a success. Mary and her new husband seemed to be ill-matched from the start. He is said to have been devoid of interest in literature and the arts with the focus of his attention being on hunting.

It seems odd that the Sidney family should have settled for such an alliance bearing in mind the reputation that they had built. Perhaps the decision was based, in some degree, on the major advantage that Robert Wroth had in the eyes of the Sidney clan, which was that he was a Protestant with leanings towards Puritanism. But rumours about his lifestyle and drunken behaviour somewhat challenge the image. The playwright Ben Jonson, an admirer of Lady Mary Wroth, lamented that 'my Lady Wroth is unworthily married on a jealous husband'.[2] He was ten years her senior and said to be a wealthy landowner but when he died in 1614, ten years after the wedding, he left her with twenty three thousand pounds of debt. The consequences of being made a widow without an adequate income is illustrated by what happened to Mary Wroth. For the rest of her life she was to battle to try to overcome the debts left by her husband. Property ownership rights had such a deleterious impact on women of the day as her only child, a baby son, died when he was two years old, shortly after her husband Robert. Without a male child as a possible heir on the horizon, the Wroth estates passed to other members of the family leaving Mary without the wherewithal to pay the debt. The liability

1   For a further discussion see Waller, G. 1976.
2   Oxford Dictionary of National Biography.

remained with her for the rest of her life. Thus the death of her husband had placed her in the iniquitous position of inheriting his debts but not his assets. Her financial position was in complete contrast to that of her cousin William as he was one of the richest men in England, as his father had been before him.

Mary Wroth

Robert Wroth had not been shy about pronouncing on the discontent which he felt as the husband of Mary Wroth and he had communicated that message to her father shortly after the marriage. William had married his wife Mary Talbot in 1604, the same year as his cousin Mary had wed Robert Wroth. Whether it was unhappy marriages or a mutual love of the arts which brought them together is not certain but it is known that after her husband's death William and Mary had two children together named William and Catherine. It is possible that their affair began before the death of Robert Wroth. William the great literary patron, son of Mary Sidney, formed an alliance with his first cousin who became the most prolific female writer of the seventeenth century. Mary Wroth's *Urania* was the first known full length work of fiction written by an Englishwoman. She named her longest piece of writing after her great friend and relation, Susan de Vere, Countess of Montgomery: *The Countess of Montgomery's Urania.* Susan de Vere was the wife of Mary Sidney's youngest son, Philip.

Urania had a mixed reception from the audiences at the time. It was written in prose interspersed with songs and poems. The main plot was based around the personalities of Pamphilia and Amphilanthus. There are sub plots and diversions from the story line. Characters with fictional names were recognisably modelled upon individuals from the society in which Mary Wroth moved. With the principal relationship being between two first cousins it is widely thought that there is a clear autobiographical element in the narrative. As this element of the story was reminiscent of her liaison with her cousin William, it is unlikely that this aspect of the piece caused annoyance among readers. However, where the story line was interpreted as repeating other notorious scandals of the day, those implicated took exception. One John Chamberlain described Wroth as taking 'great libertie or rather licence to traduce whom she pleased'. There is written evidence to show that Wroth attempted to withdraw her books from the public because of her belief that the content was being misrepresented and her intentions misconstrued. After the 17th century print run another version did not appear until late in the 20th century. Today the text of *Urania* is studied in literature departments in universities across Britain and America. The text is vast and rambling but there is great interest in reflecting on this major work of romance written by a Jacobean woman, a stepping stone along the way to the modern novel. In addition to *Urania,* Mary Wroth was the first woman to write a sonnet sequence, *Pamphilia and Amphilanthus.* Consisting of over a hundred sonnets the sequence was first published alongside *Urania,* in the 1621 printed edition of the book. It was later treated as a separate work. Mary Wroth was also known for her play *Love's Victory* and for her patronage of a number of writers. Ben Jonson dedicated his play *The Alchemist* to her.

In her writing Wroth has perhaps stimulated more interest in the modern era as she moved away from the mainly religious concerns of her aunt. But Mary Wroth was a further step away from the generation for whom it was not unheard of to die for upholding a particular faith. Had Mary Sidney Herbert's ventures into the literary world enabled her niece to take women's writing to another phase of authorship where both men and women operate on more equal terms? The answer must surely be in the affirmative. Mary Wroth's work is considered to be exceptional in many ways. The *Urania* and the sonnet sequence are secular pieces in the main. That is not to say that they are not influenced, to the same extent, by the Protestantism and religiosity of the Sidney outlook. The dominating theme of the poems is an exploration of love. In the example which follows though there are noteworthy echoes of the subjects dear to the heart of Wroth's aunt Mary:[1]

> You blessed Starres, which doe Heauen's glory show,
> And at your brightnesse make our eyes admire:
> Yet enuy not, though I on earth below,
> Inioy a sight which moues in me more fire.
> I doe confesse such beauty breeds desire
> You shine, and clearest light on vs bestow:
> Yet doth a sight on Earth more warmth inspire
> Into my louing soule, his grace to know.
> Cleare, bright, and shining, as you are, is this
> Light of my ioy: fix't stedfast, nor will moue
> His light from me, nor I chang from his loue;
> But still increase as [th'eith] of all my blisse.
> His sight giues life vnto my loue-rould [eyes],
> My loue content, because in his loue lies.[2]

In Elizabethan poetry 'starrs' were often synonymous with eyes, so both the human face and the heavens are called to mind. The line 'I doe confesse such beauty breeds desire' is sometimes quoted as illustrating one of the ground breaking aspects of Wroth's work as she was able to express notions of female desire, a concept which was supressed both before and after her writing. Yet there is something about this sonnet which reminds the reader of examples from Mary Sidney's metrical psalms. The boundary between human and divine love is obscure and there is a longing for both. The language reflects Wroth's Calvinist heritage: 'soul' and 'grace'. There is no doubt about Wroth's pride in her origins and her intention to be associated with her aunt and uncle. The frontispiece for *Urania* is headed *The Countesse of Mountgomeries Urania. Written by the right honourable the Lady Mary Wroath, Daughter to the right noble Robert Earl of Leicester, And neece to the ever famous, and renowned Sr Philips Sidney knight. And to ye most exell[n]t Lady Mary Countesse of Pembroke late deceased.*

---

1 Quotations from Mary Wroth's work used in this chapter are taken mostly from early documents which use a different script to that of today.
2   Wroth, M, 1621

Much of Mary Worth's work is dominated by more secular tones and in this writing the progress that the niece made in moving forward in her exploration of fiction can be seen most readily. Wroth was able to take her writing into another sphere, writing original pieces with a forthright analysis of sensation and feelings. She broke away from the constant need to keep her work grounded in classical works, religion and philosophy. In his book about Wroth, Gary Waller claims that her early widowhood enabled her to live with a degree of autonomy which she would not have had if her husband had survived[1]. It is very likely that this had an impact on the freedom of expression within her work. Despite *Urania*'s length and complexity a few short extracts should help to convey something about the character of her writing. The following sonnet articulates the passion present in her writing:

How like a fire doth love increase in me?

How like a fire doth love increase in me?
   The longer that it lasts the stronger still,
   The greater, purer, brighter; and doth fill
   No eye with wonder more than hopes still bee.

Bred in my breast, when fires of Love are free
   To use that part to their best pleasing will,
   And now impossible it is to kill
   The heate so great where Love his strength doth see.

Mine eyes can scarce sustaine the flames, my heart
   Doth trust in them my passions to impart,
   And languishingly strive to shew my love.

My breath not able is to breath least part
   Of that increasing fuell of my smart;
   Yet love I will, till I but ashes prove.

The nature of the narrative of *Urania* is such that the sonnets and songs are very often sad and fairly mournful as they reflect on difficulties faced by the participating characters. There are exceptions and, particularly in the prose, wit and humour penetrate the script. This can be observed in a section when the shepherdess Celina and the Prince of Venice, Leurenus, fall in love with each other within moments of meeting; it is love at first sight. The prince attempts to woo Celina with a song but her response shows that she is unimpressed. The extract begins with the song of the prince:

Haue I lost my liberty,
And my selfe, and all, for thee
O Loue?
Yet wilt thou no fauour giue

1   Waller, G, 1976.

In my losse thy blame will liue;
Alas remoue.

Pitie claimes a iust reward,
But proud thoughts are thy best guard
Once smile:
Glory tis to saue a life
When deceiuers are in strife
Which to beguile.

Your gaine hath my paine begot,
But neglect doth proue my lot,
O turne,
Say it was some other harme,
And not your still sought for Charme
Did make me burne.
Thus may you all blame recall,
Sauing me from ruins thrall
Then loue
Pitie me, Ile no more say
You to cruelty did sway,
But loyall proue.

Else be sure your tricks Ile blaze,
And your triumph Castle raze
Take heed,
Conquerours cannot remaine
Longer then mens hearts they gaine,
Worse will you speed.

You a King set vp by loue,
Traytors soone may you remoue
From by,
Take this counsell serue loues will
And seeke not a heart to kill,
Least both doe cry.

She heard him, and liked neither, his tune nor words, her heart another
was flying, or staying but to flie further, as taking breath for a longer
iourney. He looked towards her, she from him, he went as to her, she
rose and walked towards the Groue; he followed and sigh'd, she went
on, and was deafe to his sorrow; he cried to her, she was silent, and
answered not, as not taking his words to her. He ouertooke her, and
with teares told her his paine; she was sorry for him, and could be so, her
owne being so great. Hee said her sight had killed him: she answered, he
liued yet (and she hoped should) to be cured of that wound.

He said, none but she could cure him. She replide, shee was an ill Chirurgion, else she would not be vncured. Alas, said he, pity me. O pitie, said she, haue compassion on me. It is you deere Shepheardesse (sigh he) can and must pitie me. Pitie, said she, hath so little acquaintance with mee, as I cannot inuite her to me, how then shall I spare so much to you? Your first sight (said he) murdred mee. Alas that first sight, said she, should hurt vs both; it is my case, and certainely this is but a charitable paines you take, to helpe me to discouer my paine, which is so intollerable, and past remedie, as both with our best (and I thinke addition of) wits cannot relate or discouer[1]

Mary Wroth has been the subject of intensive study in recent years. It is not surprising that there is a great deal of interest in her work. What is extraordinary is that it took until the late 20th, early 21st century for Wroth to enter the canon of literature and take her place alongside other writers of the era. George Herbert was contemporaneous with Wroth but he gained extensive acknowledgement for his abilities at a much earlier stage. Was this because George Herbert's poetry was rooted in religious belief? The church of England has certainly made every effort to enhance his status with memorials in his former church in Bemerton and at Salisbury cathedral. Perhaps perceptions about sexual morality played their part during times when female virtue was the primary consideration when judging women; so it may have appeared to be unthinkable to applaud Wroth's work. Yet scholars have begun to see signs, in George Herbert's poetry, that he was on occasion, heavily influenced by Wroth's writing in *Pamphilia to Amphilanthus*. Her volume was printed in 1621 whilst Herbert's collection appeared, after his death, in 1633. Comparing two of Wroth's sonnets that appear early in her sequence, with *The Flower* by Herbert, R. Pritchard concludes that the latter poet has used Wroth's sonnets comprehensively in forming his own poem. Pritchard argues that similarities in the use of language, imagery and ideas in the three poems mean that it is not feasible to call the parallels coincidence[2]. George Herbert and Mary Wroth were the generation that followed the Sidney siblings. They both built on the Sidney - Herbert legacy and there is a possibility that Herbert was influenced by Wroth.

Samuel Daniel: *Cleopatra.*

A certain amount of controversy surrounds the description of a 'Wilton circle' or 'Wilton set'. Some writers have taken the terms to mean that there was a defined group of people, centred around the countess, who deliberately sought to ensure that literature maintained classical Greek and Latin traditions rather than allowing the development of an English form as represented by Shakespeare and others. This idea has been debunked by other authors, seeing this as a myth attributing too much power to what was, in reality, a group of aspiring poets, and they regard the notion of a 'Wilton

1   Wroth, M. 1621.
2   Pritchard, 1996.

circle' to be a much looser description, simply referring to the fact that there seemed to be a network of individuals, associated with literature and writing of some kind, in varying forms of contact with Sidney. The contact ranged from writing a sentence or two of dedication in a work or, in the case of Daniel, writing a play about a topic of Mary Sidney's choice as a companion to her own creation. There is a sense in which she was his patron but the relationship was more than that as Daniel was a tutor for her children so his work was based primarily at Wilton House. He is possibly the writer, apart from Philip, with whom she worked most closely. In his dedication to *Cleopatra* Daniel wrote about Mary Sidney's influence on his work:

> Loe here the worke the which she did impose,
> Who onely doth predominate my Muse:
> The starre of wonder, which my labours chose
> To guide their way in all the course I use.
> Shee, whose cleere brightnes doth alone infuse
> Strength to my thoughts, and makes me what I am;
> Call'd up my spirits from out their low repose,
> To sing of state, and tragicke notes to frame. (Dedication: Daniel *Cleopatra*)

Contemporary writers Jane Stevenson and Peter Davison have invented the phrase 'female deviceship' to explain activities involving elite early modern women that are not covered by authorship or patronage; works that communicated a woman's intentions without necessarily being created by her own hand. Perhaps Daniel's *Cleopatra* falls into this category. Despite Daniel revising the play many times, Mary Sidney is said to have had a considerable influence on the end product. It is interesting as the play is referred to as a closet drama even though it was written by a man. It is in the same style as *Antonius*, which relies on the structure of traditional Greek theatre. Those who believe there was a tightly knit circle emanating from Wilton regard this play as being of the type encouraged by Philip Sidney in his *Defence of Poesy*, an imitation of the ancient European theatre rather than an innovation in the English literary tradition. However, drama groups at London University have recently taken part in modern productions of the play which have emphasised the political nature of the text, leading to the conclusion that the private spaces where closet drama flourished encouraged opportunities for intellectual independence rather than being caught up in an obsession with preserving the status quo. This thinking transforms the way of thinking about closet drama. It was not a feminine pursuit to while away time for those disengaged from society. Indeed a stronger statement is justified: in *Cleopatra* Daniel continued the political themes which Sidney had introduced into her play and in the final stages of Daniel's play the empire of the Ptolemies comes to an end with Daniel making a clear link between Cleopatra's mistakes and the downfall of the Ptolemies. Neither Sidney nor Daniel shied away from political messages and their dramas were almost certainly intended for a wider audience than a small côterie of intellectuals at Wilton House.

19 October 1593 is the date on which Daniel's play was entered into the Stationers' Register. It was printed alongside two of his earlier manuscripts

Delia and the *Complaint of Rosamund*. It is noticeable that women featured prominently in this work. Both *Delia* and the *Complaint of Rosamund* express similar themes to *Cleopatra* with monarchs retrospectively able to understand that their actions have wreaked destruction on their realms. Compared to Sidney's rendering of the Egyptian story there is a closer focus on Egypt rather than Rome in Daniel's version. For example, he does not include the chorus of Roman soldiers and Octavian is a distant figure unlike Sidney's depiction of him as a tyrant. The effect of this shift of emphasis makes the issue of succession the crux of the play. The ultimate message is from the chorus that the dangers of sensuality and luxury have brought about the devastation of the state with the question of who will succeed not being addressed until the eleventh hour. By which time it is too late to find a way out of the inevitable loss of a nation to an empire builder. It raises a parallel question that was exercising members of the Privy Council and their associates: who would take over the throne of England after Elizabeth I? Far from holding back a development in English literature Mary Sidney and Samuel Daniel were raising the stakes. As a writer with conviction, Sidney was using classical literature for the purposes of making a commentary on the politics of the day. She was not trying to limit the scope of the new English forms of drama and curtail the likes of a Shakespeare or a Marlowe. With Shakespeare's first plays being produced in the early 1590s Sidney and Daniel could not have known the eventual extent of his success and influence. Instead Sidney was part of the same movement in which Shakespeare and Marlowe took part. They were engaged in writing historical dramas, in part, to provide a critique of the rule of leaders and monarchs.

Shakespeare's *Antony and Cleopatra* was written towards the end of the first decade of the seventeenth century, approximately fifteen to twenty years after Sidney. Did Sidney influence Shakespeare's play? Following their detailed analysis of the plays in question Marie-Alice Belle and Line Cottegnies would say 'yes'. In their introduction to Sidney's translation they point out that it has been accepted for some time that Shakespeare used Sidney as a source for two Roman plays: *Julius Caesar* and *Antony and Cleopatra*. They agree that the latter play contains an assortment of similarities in the use of vocabulary which suggest that Sidney's writing was most definitely a source. Furthermore, there are multiple verbal echoes of Daniel's version in Shakespeare's treatment of the story. An interesting fate awaited yet another version of the play written by Philip Sidney's long standing admirer Fulke Greville. Several years after he wrote his *Antony and Cleopatra*, having been inspired by Sidney and Daniel, he destroyed the only copy of the piece by burning the entire manuscript. Naturally Fulke Greville did not give a clear reason for his motivation in this act but there is speculation that it had something to do with going too far in criticism of the state.

More Shakespeare connections....

The Shakespeare legend is so strong due to the quality and prolific nature of his works that it is inevitable that questions are asked as to how much contact other Elizabethan and Jacobean writers might have had with the great man. Of course extensive biographical information about his life simply does not exist. Although his plays may offer hints about the character of the man there are no claims that he wrote about his own experience except possibly in *The Tempest* where at the conclusion of the play Prospero gives up his art and leaves the stage. There have been claims that if any details about Shakespeare's life can be elicited from his writing then look in the direction of his sonnets. It has been widely accepted that Shakespeare dedicated his sonnets to the eldest son of Mary Sidney, William Herbert and that Herbert can be identified as the anonymous young man of the poems. Shakespeare dedicated his First Folio to the Herbert brothers: William and Philip. It is plausible and legitimate to claim that the sonnets are fictional and personalities other than Herbert have been suggested as being the young man of Shakespeare's sonnets. The First Folio refers to the playwright's first edition of the collection of his plays published in 1623.

In *Philip's Phoenix* Margaret Hannay discusses evidence that there were further connections between the Sidney Herberts and the bard. In the second half of the 19th century William Cory was employed as a Greek tutor at Wilton House for the young George, Earl of Pembroke. He was reportedly told by the then lady of the house, Lady Herbert, that a letter existed written by Mary Sidney to her son William, asking him to bring James I to Wilton House to see a production of *As You Like It.* Sidney planned, apparently, to use the event to petition the king on Raleigh's (also spelt Ralegh) behalf. The Sidney family regarded Raleigh as an ally and during the first year of the reign of James I Raleigh was incarcerated in prison awaiting trial under threat of execution; it is highly likely then that Mary Sidney would have attempted to facilitate his release. It is known also that during the same year the king spent a significant amount of time at Wilton House between August and October as he was advised to stay away from London due to another outbreak of the plague. Furthermore, records based at the British Library show that the King's Men (this had morphed from Lord Chamberlain's Men), Shakespeare's acting troupe, did indeed play before the king at Wilton House on 3 December 1603, for which they earned the fee of thirty pounds. Due to the status of the venue and as the performance was in front of the king there is a high probability that Shakespeare took part on that day. This certainly points towards Mary Sidney and her sons being active in encouraging the early performances of the plays of William Shakespeare.

Translating Petrarch: *The Triumph of Death*

There is still in existence today one more translation which Mary Sidney wrote after *Antonius,* although the precise date is uncertain. Some scholars choose 1595 as the date when her translation of Petrarch's *The Triumph of Death* was completed in manuscript form while the date 1600 has been settled on by other specialists in the field. The 1600 date is particularly interesting as that would place the final translation after the anticipated presentation of the Psalms to Elizabeth. Either way the choice of Petrarch, at this stage in her life, is thought provoking. It has already been mentioned that the psalms were part of the final effort to influence the queen over foreign policy. It is quite clear why Mary would have chosen Petrarch as a suitable option: it was consistent with her life's obsessions. Francesco Petrarch was the great Italian humanist and poet responsible for stimulating the European and specifically English interest in the sonnet form. Born in 1304 he lived in Florence, Tuscany and Avignon. His sonnets became the exemplar for the enthusiastic profusion of poetry written during the Renaissance. He had lived during the fourteenth century and there is a sense in which his life had been deeply affected by the plague or Black Death which swept across Europe during that era, in wave after wave.

As a young man Petrarch is said to have fallen in love with Laura when they were both present in the congregation at a service in the Church of Claire d'Avignon, during the spring of 1327. The love that he felt for Laura was unrequited and, like many of Petrarch's contemporaries, she became a victim of the plague and died. The image of Laura remained central to Petrarch's love poems which were admired across the continent. Laura was an idealized symbol for the object of the poet's love. She may or may not have been an actual person. It was to Laura that Petrarch addressed the *Triumph*. Petrarch's work was written in two chapters: with chapter one containing one hundred and seventy two lines and the second chapter one hundred and ninety. The last few lines reveal a trope or theme which will have struck a chord with Sidney:

> Ladie (quoth I) your words most sweetlie kinde
> Have easie made, what ever erst I bare,
> But what is left of you to live behind,
> Therefore to knowe this, my onlie care,
> If sloe or swift shall com our meeting-daye.
> She parting saide, As my conjectures are,
> Thou without me long time on earth shall staie. (Chapter 2, lines 185-190)[1].

The text of Sidney's translation is regarded as being close to the original in terms of structure and presentation of ideas but the evidence is overwhelming that, once again, it is not just for reasons of her sense of loss that the countess chose this particular text to write in English. The poem was one of a series by Petrarch all referred to as *Trionfi*. They covered the themes of Love, Chastity, Fame, Time and Eternity. There was already an established tradition to use the imagery of Petrarchan poems in visual and poetic representations of Queen Elizabeth. The idealized love Petrarch had for Laura provided a useful vehicle of expression for praise of the monarch. The poem of Sidney's choice is quite obviously concerning mortality as the queen approaches what was in Tudor times, a grand old age. Within the text the voices of the Poet, Death and Laura are not always easy to distinguish. Their descriptions cover ideas such as the nature of death being the conqueror of all things, how to prepare for the inevitable and specifically the demise of Laura, although she is referred to as 'Ladie' and not mentioned by name. One clear reading of the translation is to see this as an attempt on the part of the countess to enter the political arena; she is presenting a challenge to the idea that females should only be involved

---

1 Clarke, Danielle, Renaissance Women Poets.

in private and domestic spheres. It is not surprising then to come across lines
where the 'I' of the text observes:

> From India, Spaine, Gattay, Marocco, Coome,
> So manie Ages did together falle.
> That worlds were fill'd, and yett they wanted roome,
> There sawe I, whom their times did happie calle,
> Popes, Emperors, and kings, but stranglie growen,
> All naked now, all needie, beggars all.
> Where is that wealth? Where are those honors gonne?
> Scepters and crounes, and roabes, and purple dye
> And costlie myters, sett with pearle and stone?
> O wretch, who doest in mortall things affye:
> (yet who but doeth) and if in end they dye
> Them-selves beguil'ed, they find but right, saie I.

The Sidney and Dudley families' concerns for the duties of rulers are
reflected in these lines as is the overriding apprehension to do with succession.
How does a populace replace a tyrannical and inappropriate leader? Danielle
Clarke[1] has carried out an intricate study of this translation and points out
that, although Mary Sidney appears to have made what might be referred to
as an 'accurate' translation she has actually made numerous 'interventions'
in the text where she uses the vocabulary from Calvin's commentary on the
Psalms, from Philip Sidney's poetry and from the Geneva Bible. All of these
sources would be recognised by Elizabethan readers as being associated with
Protestant beliefs thus reinforcing the sense of the text in terms of presenting
a critique of misguided rulers. It is not suggested that Elizabeth's reign is
seen here in entirely negative terms but it is rather a cautionary tale about
possibilities. In this way Mary Sidney can be seen to be leading the way for
women writers to express their views through the subtle medium of literature.
She was not just providing a means by which her brother's views could be
conveyed. Mary Sidney had deeply held opinions and beliefs about the mix
of politics, monarchy and Protestantism which she expounded through her
creative writing using inventive and original means.

Puritans: a new heaven and a new earth

One of the episodes in Philip Sidney's biography which does much to
illustrate the adventurous aspect of his character is the desire that he
had to accompany Sir Francis Drake on his voyages of exploration to the West
Indies in 1585. Fulke Greville wanted to go as well but the queen had other
ideas about Sidney's usefulness to the crown and he and Greville were not
allowed to set sail. Perhaps Philip Sidney had caught some of the Huguenot
fervour with their desire to set up a refuge for themselves in Florida in the late
1560s. Part of the aim of Drake's trip was to attack Spanish towns on both sides
of the Atlantic. The voyage was linked to Sir Walter Raleigh's plans to travel

1   Clarke, D. 1997.

to Virginia, the previous year, but he did not reach his goal either. Escaping the political and religious environment through travel was exercising the minds of Elizabethans looking for new opportunities. Towards the end of the sixteenth and into the seventeenth century zealous Protestants who had come to be known as Puritans had started thinking in serious ways of the idea of a new heaven and a new earth; concepts mentioned in the New Testament Book of Revelation. Some Elizabethans regarded this as being a hope for a future afterlife, a world beyond death. For others it referred to an actual possibility, a new world in reality where there was an end to corrupt rulers and the beginning of leadership which suited their religious aspirations. There were hopes that New England would embody their desires.

Whilst Philip Sidney did not make the long and hazardous journey to the West Indies or New England, one Anne Bradstreet did and her experience provides a fascinating angle on the Sidney network and legacy. Anne Bradstreet was born in England in 1612, during the lifetime of Mary Sidney but well after Philip's death. She sailed to New England with her family, leaving Southampton for the three month journey on board one of the so-called 'pilgrim fathers' ships, the 'Arbella'. Before leaving Bradstreet would doubtlessly have heard a famous sermon preached by John Winthrop at the dockside about their destination being chosen by God to be their 'city on a hill'. The link with Sidney was not just through religion; the link becomes clearer when it is known that before her marriage Anne was named Anne Dudley. She was the eldest daughter of Thomas Dudley governor of the Massachusetts Bay Company. Her half-brother Joseph became governor of Massachusetts. There was a family tradition that they were descended from John Dudley, Duke of Northumberland, beheaded on 22 February for his attempt to make his daughter-in-law, Jane Grey, queen. The idea was that Anne Bradstreet shared the same grandfather as Philip and Mary. This seems to be highly plausible but what matters is that Bradstreet portrays Sidney as the person that she most admires because of the values he upheld, her perception of the family connection and his reputation as hero of the Elizabethan age.

Why should Bradstreet's opinion of Philip Sidney be of significance? Anne Bradstreet (née Dudley) is known as the first woman writer of a book written in America, the title being *The Tenth Muse Lately Sprung up in America*. Bradstreet then, plays a critical role in the history of American writers as she was America's first female published poet. Her ability was recognised in her day and she still has a reputation for having created scholarly and intellectual verse which very often addressed the European and American political landscape: for example, *Dialogue Between Old England and New* and following Sidney convention, *In Honor of that High and Mighty Princess Queen Elizabeth of Happy Memory*. A full version of each of these poems is included in an appendix at the end of the chapter. In the Dudley-Sidney tradition Bradstreet was highly educated with knowledge of Greek, Latin, French and Hebrew.

Bradstreet's admiration for Philip Sidney is expressed in two poems. In one poem he is named: *An Elegy upon Sir Philip Sidney*, but in the other poem: *The Four Ages of Man* he is identified by a description of the manner of his death. In the first version of the *Elegy* Bradstreet refers in a direct manner to the family relationship:

> Let, then, none disallow of these my straines
> Which have the self-same blood yet in my veines.

In the second edition of the piece this was changed to:

> Then let none disallow of these my straines
> Whilst English blood yet runs within my veins.[1]

This change has caused some commentators to doubt the link between the families but there might have been other reasons for the tweaking of the text here when so many factors point towards a bloodline connection, not least of which is sharing a name. There is though no doubt that Bradstreet was reinforcing the Sidney legend of the protestant hero in her new home in America:

> The more I say the more thy worth I stain,
> Thy fame and praise is far beyond my strain
> O Zutphen, Zutphen that most fatal City
> Made famous by thy death, much more the pity:
> Ah! In his blooming prime death pluckt this rose
> E're he was ripe, his thread cut Atropos.
> Thus man is born to dye, and dead is he,
> Brave Hector, by the walls of Troy we see.

There is some amusing and rather ambiguous discussion of Sidney's work *Arcadia* in Bradshaw's writing:

> Witness Arcadia penned in his youth,
> Are not his tragick Comedies so acted,
> As if your ninefold wit had been compacted.
> To shew the world, they never saw before,
> That this one Volume should exhaust your store;
> His wiser dayes condemned his witty works,
> Who knows the spels that in his Rhetorick lurks,
> But some infatuate fools soon caught therein,
> Fond Cupids Dame had never such a gin,
> Which makes severer eyes but slight that story,
> And men of morose minds envy his glory:
> But he's a Beetle-head that can't descry
> A world of wealth within that rubbish lye,
> And doth his name, his work, his honour wrong,
> The brave refiner of our British tongue,
> That sees not learning, valour and morality,
> Justice, friendship, and kind hospitality,
> Yea and Divinity within his book,

---

1   For poems by Anne Bradstreet see https://www.poetryfoundation.org/

Such were prejudicate, and did not look.

Bradstreet seems to have had mixed feelings about *Arcadia*! Her judgements may have been affected by speculation about the identity of the lovers in the story and how chaste (or not) Astrophel and Stella were in their forms as represented in Sidney's book. The final six lines of the poem under the heading *Epitaph* dispel any thoughts the reader might have that Bradstreet believed in anything other than the virtuous nature of the hero of Zutphen:

> Here lies in fame under this stone,
> Philip and Alexander both in one;
> Heir to the Muses, the Son of Mars in Truth,
> Learning, Valour, Wisdome, all in virtuous youth,
> His praise is much, this shall suffice my pen,
> That Sidney dy'd 'mong most renown'd of men.

For all sorts of reasons it would be of such benefit to know how familiar, if at all, Bradstreet was with the writing of Mary Sidney or even Mary Wroth. There can be little doubt though that Bradstreet had imbibed a message about Philip Sidney that his sister Mary would have heartily endorsed. Bradstreet's image of the courtier is reinforced again in *The Four Ages of Man*. Writing in 1642 she presents portraits of characters to illustrate youth at its best and at its most challenging. Youth in the most positive form is illustrated by the attributes of Philip:

> Mine education, and my learning's such,
> As might my self, and others, profit much:
> With nurture trained up in virtue's Schools;
> Of Science, Arts, and Tongues, I know the rules;
> The manners of the Court, I likewise know,
> Nor ignorant what they in Country do.
> The brave attempts of valiant Knights I prize
> That dare climb Battlements, rear'd to the skies.
> The snorting Horse, the Trumpet, Drum I like,
> The glist'ring Sword, and well advanced Pike.
> I cannot lie in trench before a Town,
> Nor wait til good advice our hopes do crown.
> I scorn the heavy Corslet, Musket-proof;
> I fly to catch the Bullet that's aloof.
> Though thus in field, at home, to all most kind,
> So affable that I do suit each mind,
> I can insinuate into the breast
> And by my mirth can raise the heart deprest.
> Sweet Music rapteth my harmonious Soul,
> And elevates my thoughts above the Pole.
> My wit, my bounty, and my courtesy
> Makes all to place their future hopes on me.

Like Mary Sidney Anne Bradstreet was a wife and mother. In *The Four Ages of Man* there is a sense in which she evokes part of Mary Sidney's translation of *The Discourse on Life and Death* which begins with a contemplation of the 'voyage' of life from the cradle to the grave. Mary Sidney writes about the passion of youth and the battle between a life of virtue or vice. Bradstreet gives a detailed description of the youth she chose to provide the exemplar of goodness, and that is Philip. Bradstreet portrays a vivid picture of an individual who has embarked upon the life of vice:

> This is my best, but youth (is known) alas,
> To be as wild as is the snuffing Ass,
> As vain as froth, as vanity can be,
> That who would see vain man may look on me:
> My gifts abus'd, my education lost,
> My woful Parents' longing hopes all crost;
> My wit evaporates in merriment;
> My valour in some beastly quarrel's spent;
> Martial deeds I love not, 'cause they're virtuous,
> But doing so, might seem magnanimous.
> My Lust doth hurry me to all that's ill,
> I know no Law, nor reason, but my will;
> Sometimes lay wait to take a wealthy purse
> Or stab the man in's own defence, that's worse.
> Sometimes I cheat (unkind) a female Heir
> Of all at once, who not so wise, as fair,
> Trusteth my loving looks and glozing tongue
> Until her friends, treasure, and honour's gone.
> Sometimes I sit carousing others' health
> Until mine own be gone, my wit, and wealth.
> From pipe to pot, from pot to words and blows,
> For he that loveth Wine wanteth no woes.
> Days, nights, with Ruffins, Roarers, Fiddlers spend,
> To all obscenity my ears I bend,
> All counsel hate which tends to make me wise,
> And dearest friends count for mine enemies.
> If any care I take, 'tis to be fine,
> For sure my suit more than my virtues shine.
> If any time from company I spare,
> 'Tis spent in curling, frisling up my hair,
> Some young *Adonais* I do strive to be.
> *Sardana Pallas* now survives in me.
> Cards, Dice, and Oaths, concomitant, I love;
> To Masques, to Plays, to Taverns still I move;
> And in a word, if what I am you'd hear,
> Seek out a British, bruitish Cavalier.
> Such wretch, such monster am I; but yet more
> I want a heart all this for to deplore.
> Thus, thus alas! I have mispent my time,

My youth, my best, my strength, my bud, and prime,
Remembring not the dreadful day of Doom,
Nor yet the heavy reckoning for to come,
Though dangers do attend me every hour
And ghastly death oft threats me with her power:
Sometimes by wounds in idle combats taken,
Sometimes by Agues all my body shaken;
Sometimes by Fevers, all my moisture drinking,
My heart lies frying, and my eyes are sinking.

Writing about the stage before 'Youth', in her section on 'Childhood, there is a certain earthiness and honesty about Bradstreet's writing that has an echo of the displeasure relating to parenting in the early years, that Sidney had expressed in her translation of 'The Discourse'. Here are Bradstreet's reflections:

Ah me! conceiv'd in sin, and born in sorrow,
A nothing, here to day, but gone to morrow,
Whose mean beginning, blushing can't reveal,
But night and darkness must with shame conceal.
My mother's breeding sickness, I will spare,
Her nine months' weary burden not declare.
To shew her bearing pangs, I should do wrong,
To tell that pain, which can't be told by tongue.
With tears into this world I did arrive;
My mother still did waste, as I did thrive,
Who yet with love and all alacrity,
Spending was willing to be spent for me.
With wayward cries, I did disturb her rest,
Who sought still to appease me with her breast;
With weary arms, she danc'd, and *By, By,* sung,
When wretched I (ungrate) had done the wrong.

The question remains as to how much Bradstreet knew about the women writers in her extended family and how she felt empowered by their efforts. Despite their lives overlapping for just a few years and the fact that they lived, during adult years, on separate continents, Mary Sidney and Anne Bradstreet had a certain amount of life experience in common. They both wrote whilst attending to family life and in their writing there is evidence of both classical learning and reference to the vagaries of human existence. Indeed the beginning of what would later be known as the study of child development and psychology can be discerned. Publishing also features in a narrative of both of their lives. As outlined in previous chapters Sidney published her work and that of her brother. Bradstreet's is an extraordinary tale as without her knowledge, her brother-in-law Reverend John Woodbridge travelled to England in 1649 with a copy of her writing in his luggage. It was Woodbridge who then, again without the permission of the author, arranged to have her poems published by a bookseller in London under the title *The Tenth Muse*

Lately Sprung up in America, or Several Poems, compiled with great variety of Wit and Learning, full of delight. The poems were a great success in Old England and New England. One vast difference though between Sidney and Bradstreet lies in their public expression of love. For Mary Sidney all of her efforts in that direction were reserved for the brother she loved and lost. For Anne Bradstreet, however, her poem about her affection for her husband is frequently quoted as the best example of her writing so it is fair to end the discussion of her here with the piece:

To My Dear and Loving Husband

If ever two were one, then surely we.
If ever man were loved by wife then thee.
If ever wife was happy in a man,
Compare with me, ye women, if you can.
I prize thy love more than whole mines of gold,
Of all the riches that the East doth hold.
My love is such that rivers cannot quench,
Not ought but love from thee give recompense.
Thy love is such I can no way repay;
The heavens reward thee manifold, I pray.
Then while we live, in love let's so persever,
That when we live no more, we may live ever.

It is extraordinary that this woman related to and admiring of Philip Sidney, began the process of establishing and initiating a literary tradition in the New World. The young courtier could not have imagined the extent of his literary influence through the promulgation of his work by his sister. Mary Sidney, however, had some idea of their success and she had lived to observe the family name gain a high reputation for learning and the love of literature. There were numerous books with dedications written to her, she was patron to successful poets of the day and she saw a number of her works in print form. Furthermore she saw the next generation, especially her son William and niece Mary, take up the cause of the defence of poetry and the arts.

Mary Sidney's post-Pembroke life

The age gap between Mary and her husband Henry was such that she was a widow for a considerable length of time. At the death of her husband there was another shift in how Mary Sidney spent her days. She had inherited a number of estates from her husband and, according to his will, they were hers as long as she did not marry again. The management of those estates became a focus for her, rather than her writing. She remained a wealthy woman and also spent time visiting Europe. She had a long term man friend, a doctor, Matthew Lister, by all accounts her equal in intelligence and knowledgeable within his field. She is said to have engaged in leisure activities such as dancing, shooting and card playing. It seems that she was able to enjoy life without the cares and responsibilities which haunted her younger days. In our present time when the ownership of property is out of the reach of so many, as indeed it was in Elizabethan England, it appears to be a mark of a sense of excessive entitlement and possibly greed, that inspired Mary Sidney to build a new hunting lodge, Houghton House, in Bedfordshire where King James stayed as her guest not long before her final illness. The world that she had entered when marrying a Herbert had done the trick of securing her fortune and Mary Sidney had played her cards with care.

Houghton House

Mary was amongst the last members of the 'old guard' of courtiers and gentlewomen pressing for the furthering of the Protestant cause. Perhaps it was a matter of relief to her that after the completion of her Psalms and the death of Elizabeth there was closure in relation to her brother Philip's untimely death and she could take a step back from the responsibilities associated with this aspect of her life. Although she had a profound sense of disappointment that her son William had disgraced himself at court with the Fitton affair, with the change of monarch her son had the chance to restore his reputation and she could look forward to the family status becoming more secure in the days ahead. It must have been gratifying for her to observe that William took an increasing interest in patronage of the arts and to see her niece, Mary Wroth, take up a writing project that was modelled on the writing of an uncle whom she did not personally know. Mary Sidney had passed on her love of the arts. The diplomatic nature of the way she had set about making her voice heard was laid bare when she was held up as a paragon in comparison with her niece by a certain Sir Edward Denny. Denny believed that Wroth had bruised

Salisbury Cathedral

his reputation by including scandalous material related to him in *Urania*. He was effusive in his praise of Mary Sidney's rendering of holy psalms but was able to fall back on arguments which dogged female writing until the last century in his condemnation of Wroth, particularly the questioning of her mental capacity. For Denny, Wroth should have followed her aunt and not entered the secular arena where women did not belong; her writing was proof that women had no place in literature other than that of a religious kind. The problem in sustaining appreciation of Mary Sidney's great work of art, the Psalms, has been that for many in churches and beyond, women had no right of involvement there either.

In relation to the most famous of all of the Elizabethan poets, William Shakespeare, it is not known what contact, if any, Sidney had with him before or after her patronages diminished. She did not live to read the dedication to both of her sons (William and Philip) written by William Shakespeare in the 1623 folio of his work. It has been said that she persuaded Shakespeare to write his sonnets. There is also speculation that William Herbert was actually so close to Shakespeare that he is the one referred to as 'WH' in a version of Shakespeare's sonnets published in 1609 and that Mary Fitton was the 'dark lady' of the sonnets, beloved by both Shakespeare and Herbert. Unless further evidence is found this remains guesswork.

The final chapter of this book has undertaken the task of evaluating Mary Sidney's legacy and as with all life writing, when delineating the achievements of a person at the centre of a narrative, as she is here, it is important to be clear about what is being claimed in terms of heritage. The arguments associated with her abilities are related specifically to a literary heritage and a belief that she was one of the very significant women who opened the way for female authorship. Other exceptional women had gone before her, such as the religious mystic, Julian of Norwich, 1343-1416, and very many women have followed in their footsteps. Collecting all of their stories contributes to a balanced view of their accomplishments alongside male writers.

After her death from smallpox at her London home in Aldersgate Street, Mary was buried under the choir steps at Salisbury Cathedral; her husband had been buried within the same building. There is something poignant about the setting of her interment. No doubt it would have been deemed fitting for her to have a place in the structure which held such status in a certain Christian world. It is likely that it would have appealed to the side of Mary that enjoyed pomp and status. There can be no doubt about her devotion to her faith. But evidence of her having a significant connection with the cathedral during her life time has yet to emerge. Indeed Salisbury cathedral was regarded as being at the conservative end of the spectrum in the adaptations made to accommodate the new church in England; the Sidneys held more radical views about church organisation and structure. A memorial for Mary should do justice to the inventive and creative streak that was part of the Sidney make-up. It was as if the Sidneys stood at the edge of a new world which their learning and position in society afforded them. Their writing explored new possibilities and in the material world they looked out beyond England to forge alliances.

There is a possibility that the spot where Mary lies was once marked by a very small monument but it seems to be especially sad that in the building in which she is buried there is nothing to mark her exceptional translations of biblical texts in the form of the psalms. What a missed opportunity! The magnificient cathedral could be seen from the high ground of her estate but most probably Mary did not look in that direction for religious solace during her lifetime. Her spiritual home was in Wilton a few miles from the cathedral city. Wilton was the place where she shared so much with her brother and her family: it was their Arcadia, their domain in the spectacularly beautiful Wiltshre countryside. A place where each sibling individually put their own stamp on their writing which takes its rightful place in the history of literature written in English.

Appendix

Ben Jonson: To Penshurst

Thou art not, Penshurst, built to envious show,
Of touch or marble; nor canst boast a row
Of polished pillars, or a roof of gold;
Thou hast no lantern, whereof tales are told,
Or stair, or courts; but stand'st an ancient pile,
And, these grudged at, art reverenced the while.
Thou joy'st in better marks, of soil, of air,
Of wood, of water; therein thou art fair.
Thou hast thy walks for health, as well as sport;
Thy mount, to which the dryads do resort,
Where Pan and Bacchus their high feasts have made,
Beneath the broad beech and the chestnut shade;
That taller tree, which of a nut was set
At his great birth where all the Muses met.
There in the writhèd bark are cut the names
Of many a sylvan, taken with his flames;
And thence the ruddy satyrs oft provoke
The lighter fauns to reach thy Lady's Oak.
Thy copse too, named of Gamage, thou hast there,
That never fails to serve thee seasoned deer
When thou wouldst feast or exercise thy friends.
The lower land, that to the river bends,
Thy sheep, thy bullocks, kine, and calves do feed;
The middle grounds thy mares and horses breed.
Each bank doth yield thee conies; and the tops,
Fertile of wood, Ashore and Sidney's copse,
To crown thy open table, doth provide
The purpled pheasant with the speckled side;
The painted partridge lies in every field,
And for thy mess is willing to be killed.
And if the high-swollen Medway fail thy dish,
Thou hast thy ponds, that pay thee tribute fish,
Fat aged carps that run into thy net,
And pikes, now weary their own kind to eat,
As loath the second draught or cast to stay,
Officiously at first themselves betray;
Bright eels that emulate them, and leap on land

Before the fisher, or into his hand.
Then hath thy orchard fruit, thy garden flowers,
Fresh as the air, and new as are the hours.
The early cherry, with the later plum,
Fig, grape, and quince, each in his time doth come;
The blushing apricot and woolly peach
Hang on thy walls, that every child may reach.
And though thy walls be of the country stone,
They're reared with no man's ruin, no man's groan;
There's none that dwell about them wish them down;
But all come in, the farmer and the clown,
And no one empty-handed, to salute
Thy lord and lady, though they have no suit.
Some bring a capon, some a rural cake,
Some nuts, some apples; some that think they make
The better cheeses bring them, or else send
By their ripe daughters, whom they would commend
This way to husbands, and whose baskets bear
An emblem of themselves in plum or pear.
But what can this (more than express their love)
Add to thy free provisions, far above
The need of such? whose liberal board doth flow
With all that hospitality doth know;
Where comes no guest but is allowed to eat,
Without his fear, and of thy lord's own meat;
Where the same beer and bread, and selfsame wine,
This is his lordship's shall be also mine,
And I not fain to sit (as some this day
At great men's tables), and yet dine away.
Here no man tells my cups; nor, standing by,
A waiter doth my gluttony envy,
But gives me what I call, and lets me eat;
He knows below he shall find plenty of meat.
The tables hoard not up for the next day;
Nor, when I take my lodging, need I pray
For fire, or lights, or livery; all is there,
As if thou then wert mine, or I reigned here:
There's nothing I can wish, for which I stay.
That found King James when, hunting late this way
With his brave son, the prince, they saw thy fires
Shine bright on every hearth, as the desires
Of thy Penates had been set on flame
To entertain them; or the country came
With all their zeal to warm their welcome here.
What (great I will not say, but) sudden cheer
Didst thou then make 'em! and what praise was heaped
On thy good lady then, who therein reaped
The just reward of her high housewifery;

To have her linen, plate, and all things nigh,
When she was far; and not a room but dressed
As if it had expected such a guest!
These, Penshurst, are thy praise, and yet not all.
Thy lady's noble, fruitful, chaste withal.
His children thy great lord may call his own,
A fortune in this age but rarely known.
They are, and have been, taught religion; thence
Their gentler spirits have sucked innocence.
Each morn and even they are taught to pray,
With the whole household, and may, every day,
Read in their virtuous parents' noble parts
The mysteries of manners, arms, and arts.
Now, Penshurst, they that will proportion thee
With other edifices, when they see
Those proud, ambitious heaps, and nothing else,
May say their lords have built, but thy lord dwells.

Mary Sidney Herbert: The Doleful Lay of Clorinda

Ay me, to whom shall I my case complain,
That may compassion my impatient grief?
Or where shall I unfold my inward pain,
That my enriven heart may find relief?
     Shall I unto the heavenly pow'rs it show,
     Or unto earthly men that dwell below?

To heavens? Ah, they, alas, the authors were,
And workers of my unremedied woe:
For they foresee what to us happens here,
And they foresaw, yet suffered this be so.
     From them comes good, from them comes also ill,
     That which they made, who can them warn to spill.

To men? Ah, they, alas, like wretched be,
And subject to the heavens' ordinance:
Bound to abide whatever they decree.
Their best redress is their best sufferance.
     How then can they, like wretched, comfort me,
     The which no less need comforted to be?

Then to myself will I my sorrow mourn,
Sith none alive like sorrowful remains:
And to myself my plaints shall back return,
To pay their usury with doubled pains.
     The woods, the hills, the rivers shall resound
     The mournful accent of my sorrow's ground.

Woods, hills, and rivers now are desolate,
Sith he is gone the which them all did grace:
And all the fields do wail their widow state,
Sith death their fairest flow'r did late deface.
      The fairest flow'r in field that ever grew,
      Was Astrophel; that was, we all may rue.

What cruel hand of cursed foe unknown,
Hath cropped the stalk which bore so fair a flow'r?
Untimely cropped, before it well were grown,
And clean defaced in untimely hour.
      Great loss to all that ever him did see,
      Great loss to all, but greatest loss to me.

Break now your garlands, O ye shepherds' lasses,
Sith the fair flow'r, which them adorned, is gone:
The flow'r, which them adorned, is gone to ashes,
Never again let lass put garland on.
      Instead of garland, wear sad cypress now,
      And bitter elder, broken from the bough.

Ne ever sing the love-lays which he made:
Who ever made such lays of love as he?
Ne ever read the riddles, which he said
Unto yourselves, to make you merry glee.
      Your merry glee is now laid all abed,
      Your merry maker now, alas, is dead.

Death, the devourer of all the world's delight,
Hath robbed you and reft from me my joy:
Both you and me and all the world he quite
Hath robbed of joyance, and left sad annoy.
      Joy of the world, and shepherds' pride was he,
      Shepherds' hope never like again to see.

O Death, that hast us of such riches reft,
Tell us at least, what hast thou with it done?
What is become of him whose flow'r here left
Is but the shadow of his likeness gone:
      Scarce like the shadow of that which he was,
      Naught like, but that he like a shade did pass.

But that immortal spirit, which was decked
With all the dowries of celestial grace:
By sovereign choice from th' heavenly choirs select,
And lineally derived from angels' race,
      Oh, what is now of it become, aread.
      Ay me, can so divine a thing be dead?

Ah no: it is not dead, ne can it die,
But lives for aye, in blissful Paradise:
Where like a new-born babe it soft doth lie,
In bed of lilies wrapped in tender wise,
     And compassed all about with roses sweet,
     And dainty violets from head to feet.

There thousand birds all of celestial brood,
To him do sweetly carol day and night:
And with strange notes, of him well understood,
Lull him asleep in angel-like delight;
     Whilst in sweet dream to him presented be
     Immortal beauties, which no eye may see.

But he them sees and takes exceeding pleasure
Of their divine aspects, appearing plain,
And kindling love in him above all measure,
Sweet love still joyous, never feeling pain.
     For what so goodly form he there doth see,
     He may enjoy from jealous rancor free.

There liveth he in everlasting bliss,
Sweet spirit never fearing more to die:
Ne dreading harm from any foes of his,
Ne fearing savage beasts' more cruelty.
     Whilst we here, wretches, wail his private lack,
     And with vain vows do often call him back.

But live thou there still happy, happy spirit,
And give us leave thee here thus to lament:
Not thee that dost thy heaven's joy inherit,
But our own selves that here in dole are drent.
     Thus do we weep and wail, and wear our eyes,
     Mourning in other's, our own miseries.

Philip Sidney: Sonnet 31 from the collection *Astrophel and Stella*

With how sad steps, O moon, thou climb'st the skies;
   How silently, and with how wan a face.
   What, may it be that even in heav'nly place
That busy archer his sharp arrows tries?
Sure, if that long-with-love-acquainted eyes
   Can judge of love, thou feel'st a lover's case;
   I read it in thy looks; thy languished grace
To me, that feel the like, thy state descries.
   Then even of fellowship, O moon, tell me,

Is constant love deemed there but want of wit?
Are beauties there as proud as here they be?
Do they above love to be loved, and yet
    Those lovers scorn whom that love doth possess?
    Do they call virtue there ungratefulness?

METRE

The metre of a poem refers to its rhythm and in traditional verse this often follows set patterns of stressed and unstressed syllables to create a 'beat'. Looking at the opening lines of Sidney's sonnet 32 he follows the convention of ten syllables to the line with five stressed syllables and five unstressed syllables. This is the well-used 'heartbeat' rhythm, formally called iambic pentameter. Looking closely at the lines and trying to unpick the rhythm we can use a **U** symbol for an unstressed syllable and / for a stressed:

U   / U /   U   / U / U /
Leave me, O love which reaches but to dust,
U   /   U   /   U / U / U /
And thou, my mind aspire to higher things;

This is the underlying pattern. The units of rhythm are called 'feet' and here there are five feet, each foot has one stressed and one unstressed syllable: a iambic pattern. As each line contains five feet the term pentameter is used. Obviously, we vary the way it is said otherwise it would sound very stilted; poets and readers play with the rhythmical framework to give variety to the sounds and the sense.

There are many other rhythmical patterns such as trochaic where the foot consists of /u and there are formal names for the line lengths too. A line of poetry with only three feet would be trimeter, four 'feet' tetrameter and so on.

Modern poetry often dispenses with these formal frameworks but poets still enjoy playing with and often subverting some of the traditional formats. The sonnet form, for example, with its iambic rhythm and concise structure is still popular with poets: a challenging format to copy and to adapt.

Anne Bradstreet: A Dialogue between Old England and New

New England.
Alas, dear Mother, fairest Queen and best,
With honour, wealth, and peace happy and blest,
What ails thee hang thy head, and cross thine arms,
And sit i' the dust to sigh these sad alarms?
What deluge of new woes thus over-whelm
The glories of thy ever famous Realm?

What means this wailing tone, this mournful guise?
Ah, tell thy Daughter; she may sympathize.

Old England.
Art ignorant indeed of these my woes,
Or must my forced tongue these griefs disclose,
And must my self dissect my tatter'd state,
Which Amazed Christendom stands wondering at?
And thou a child, a Limb, and dost not feel
My weak'ned fainting body now to reel?
This physic-purging-potion I have taken
Will bring Consumption or an Ague quaking,
Unless some Cordial thou fetch from high,
Which present help may ease my malady.
If I decease, dost think thou shalt survive?
Or by my wasting state dost think to thrive?
Then weigh our case, if 't be not justly sad.
Let me lament alone, while thou art glad.

New England.
And thus, alas, your state you much deplore
In general terms, but will not say wherefore.
What Medicine shall I seek to cure this woe,
If th' wound's so dangerous, I may not know?
But you, perhaps, would have me guess it out.
What, hath some Hengist like that Saxon stout
By fraud and force usurp'd thy flow'ring crown,
Or by tempestuous Wars thy fields trod down?
Or hath Canutus, that brave valiant Dane,
The regal peaceful Sceptre from thee ta'en?
Or is 't a Norman whose victorious hand
With English blood bedews thy conquered Land?
Or is 't intestine Wars that thus offend?
Do Maud and Stephen for the Crown contend?
Do Barons rise and side against their King,
And call in Foreign aid to help the thing?
Must Edward be depos'd? Or is 't the hour
That second Richard must be clapp'd i' th' Tower?
Or is it the fatal jar, again begun,
That from the red, white pricking Roses sprung?
Must Richmond's aid the Nobles now implore
To come and break the tushes of the Boar?
If none of these, dear Mother, what's your woe?
Pray, do not fear Spain's bragging Armado.
Doth your Ally, fair France, conspire your wrack,
Or doth the Scots play false behind your back?
Doth Holland quit you ill for all your love?
Whence is this storm, from Earth or Heaven above?

Is 't drought, is 't Famine, or is 't Pestilence?
Dost feel the smart, or fear the consequence?
Your humble Child entreats you shew your grief.
Though Arms nor Purse she hath for your relief—
Such is her poverty,—yet shall be found
A suppliant for your help, as she is bound.

Old England.
I must confess some of those Sores you name
My beauteous Body at this present maim,
But foreign Foe nor feigned friend I fear,
For they have work enough, thou knowest, elsewhere.
Nor is it Alcie's son and Henry's Daughter
Whose proud contention cause this slaughter;
Nor Nobles siding to make John no King,
French Louis unjustly to the Crown to bring;
No Edward, Richard, to lose rule and life,
Nor no Lancastrians to renew old strife;
No Crook-backt Tyrant now usurps the Seat,
Whose tearing tusks did wound, and kill, and threat.
No Duke of York nor Earl of March to soil
Their hands in Kindred's blood whom they did foil;
No need of Tudor Roses to unite:
None knows which is the Red or which the White.
Spain's braving Fleet a second time is sunk.
France knows how of my fury she hath drunk
By Edward third and Henry fifth of fame;
Her Lilies in my Arms avouch the same.
My Sister Scotland hurts me now no more,
Though she hath been injurious heretofore.
What Holland is, I am in some suspense,
But trust not much unto his Excellence.
For wants, sure some I feel, but more I fear;
And for the Pestilence, who knows how near?
Famine and Plague, two sisters of the Sword,
Destruction to a Land doth soon afford.
They're for my punishments ordain'd on high,
Unless thy tears prevent it speedily.
But yet I answer not what you demand
To shew the grievance of my troubled Land.
Before I tell the effect I'll shew the cause,
Which are my sins—the breach of sacred Laws:
Idolatry, supplanter of a Nation,
With foolish superstitious adoration,
Are lik'd and countenanc'd by men of might,
The Gospel is trod down and hath no right.
Church Offices are sold and bought for gain
That Pope had hope to find Rome here again.

For Oaths and Blasphemies did ever ear
From Beelzebub himself such language hear?
What scorning of the Saints of the most high!
What injuries did daily on them lie!
What false reports, what nick-names did they take,
Not for their own, but for their Master's sake!
And thou, poor soul, wast jeer'd among the rest;
Thy flying for the Truth I made a jest.
For Sabbath-breaking and for Drunkenness
Did ever Land profaneness more express?
From crying bloods yet cleansed am not I,
Martyrs and others dying causelessly.
How many Princely heads on blocks laid down
For nought but title to a fading Crown!
'Mongst all the cruelties which I have done,
Oh, Edward's Babes, and Clarence's hapless Son,
O Jane, why didst thou die in flow'ring prime? —
Because of Royal Stem, that was thy crime.
For Bribery, Adultery, for Thefts, and Lies
Where is the Nation I can't paralyze?
With Usury, Extortion, and Oppression,
These be the Hydras of my stout transgression;
These be the bitter fountains, heads, and roots
Whence flow'd the source, the sprigs, the boughs, and fruits.
Of more than thou canst hear or I relate,
That with high hand I still did perpetrate,
For these were threat'ned the woeful day
I mocked the Preachers, put it fair away.
The Sermons yet upon record do stand
That cried destruction to my wicked Land.
These Prophets' mouths (all the while) was stopt,
Unworthily, some backs whipt, and ears crept;
Their reverent cheeks bear the glorious marks
Of stinking, stigmatizing Romish Clerks;
Some lost their livings, some in prison pent,
Some grossly fined, from friends to exile went:
Their silent tongues to heaven did vengeance cry,
Who heard their cause, and wrongs judg'd righteously,
And will repay it sevenfold in my lap.
This is fore-runner of my after-clap.
Nor took I warning by my neighbors' falls.
I saw sad Germany's dismantled walls,
I saw her people famish'd, Nobles slain,
Her fruitful land a barren heath remain.
I saw (unmov'd) her Armies foil'd and fled,
Wives forc'd, babes toss'd, her houses calcined.
I saw strong Rochelle yield'd to her foe,
Thousands of starved Christians there also.

I saw poor Ireland bleeding out her last,
Such cruelty as all reports have past.
Mine heart obdurate stood not yet aghast.
Now sip I of that cup, and just may be
The bottom dregs reserved are for me.

New England.
To all you've said, sad mother, I assent.
Your fearful sins great cause there's to lament.
My guilty hands (in part) hold up with you,
A sharer in your punishment's my due.
But all you say amounts to this effect,
Not what you feel, but what you do expect.
Pray, in plain terms, what is your present grief?
Then let's join heads and hands for your relief.

Old England.
Well, to the matter, then. There's grown of late
'Twixt King and Peers a question of state:
Which is the chief, the law, or else the King?
One saith, it's he; the other, no such thing.
My better part in Court of Parliament
To ease my groaning land shew their intent
To crush the proud, and right to each man deal,
To help the Church, and stay the Common-Weal.
So many obstacles comes in their way
As puts me to a stand what I should say.
Old customs, new Prerogatives stood on.
Had they not held law fast, all had been gone,
Which by their prudence stood them in such stead
They took high Strafford lower by the head,
And to their Laud be 't spoke they held 'n th' Tower
All England's metropolitan that hour.
This done, an Act they would have passed fain
No prelate should his Bishopric retain.
Here tugg'd they hard indeed, for all men saw
This must be done by Gospel, not by law.
Next the Militia they urged sore.
This was denied, I need not say wherefore.
The King, displeased, at York himself absents.
They humbly beg return, shew their intents.
The writing, printing, posting to and fro,
Shews all was done; I'll therefore let it go.
But now I come to speak of my disaster.
Contention's grown 'twixt Subjects and their Master,
They worded it so long they fell to blows,
That thousands lay on heaps. Here bleeds my woes.
I that no wars so many years have known

Am now destroy'd and slaughter'd by mine own.
But could the field alone this strife decide,
One battle, two, or three I might abide,
But these may be beginnings of more woe—
Who knows, the worst, the best may overthrow!
Religion, Gospel, here lies at the stake,
Pray now, dear child, for sacred Zion's sake,
Oh, pity me in this sad perturbation,
My plundered Towns, my houses' devastation,
My ravisht virgins, and my young men slain,
My wealthy trading fallen, my dearth of grain.
The seedtime's come, but Ploughman hath no hope
Because he knows not who shall inn his crop.
The poor they want their pay, their children bread,
Their woful mothers' tears unpitied.
If any pity in thy heart remain,
Or any child-like love thou dost retain,
For my relief now use thy utmost skill,
And recompense me good for all my ill.

New England.
Dear mother, cease complaints, and wipe your eyes,
Shake off your dust, cheer up, and now arise.
You are my mother, nurse, I once your flesh,
Your sunken bowels gladly would refresh.
Your griefs I pity much but should do wrong,
To weep for that we both have pray'd for long,
To see these latter days of hop'd-for good,
That Right may have its right, though 't be with blood.
After dark Popery the day did clear;
But now the Sun in's brightness shall appear.
Blest be the Nobles of thy Noble Land
With (ventur'd lives) for truth's defence that stand.
Blest be thy Commons, who for Common good
And thy infringed Laws have boldly stood.
Blest be thy Counties, who do aid thee still
With hearts and states to testify their will.
Blest be thy Preachers, who do cheer thee on.
Oh, cry: the sword of God and Gideon!
And shall I not on them wish Mero's curse
That help thee not with prayers, arms, and purse?
And for my self, let miseries abound
If mindless of thy state I e'er be found.
These are the days the Church's foes to crush,
To root out Prelates, head, tail, branch, and rush.
Let's bring Baal's vestments out, to make a fire,
Their Mitres, Surplices, and all their tire,
Copes, Rochets, Croziers, and such trash,

And let their names consume, but let the flash
Light Christendom, and all the world to see
We hate Rome's Whore, with all her trumpery.
Go on, brave Essex, shew whose son thou art,
Not false to King, nor Country in thy heart,
But those that hurt his people and his Crown,
By force expel, destroy, and tread them down.
Let Gaols be fill'd with th' remnant of that pack,
And sturdy Tyburn loaded till it crack.
And ye brave Nobles, chase away all fear,
And to this blessed Cause closely adhere.
O mother, can you weep and have such Peers?
When they are gone, then drown your self in tears,
If now you weep so much, that then no more
The briny Ocean will o'erflow your shore.
These, these are they (I trust) with Charles our king,
Out of all mists such glorious days will bring
That dazzled eyes, beholding, much shall wonder
At that thy settled Peace, thy wealth, and splendour,
Thy Church and Weal establish'd in such manner
That all shall joy that thou display'dst thy banner,
And discipline erected so, I trust,
That nursing Kings shall come and lick thy dust.
Then Justice shall in all thy Courts take place
Without respect of persons or of case.
Then bribes shall cease, and suits shall not stick long,
Patience and purse of Clients for to wrong.
Then High Commissions shall fall to decay,
And Pursuivants and Catchpoles want their pay.
So shall thy happy Nation ever flourish,
When truth and righteousness they thus shall nourish.
When thus in Peace, thine Armies brave send out
To sack proud Rome, and all her vassals rout.
There let thy name, thy fame, and valour shine,
As did thine Ancestors' in Palestine,
And let her spoils full pay with int'rest be
Of what unjustly once she poll'd from thee.
Of all the woes thou canst let her be sped,
Execute to th' full the vengeance threatened.
Bring forth the beast that rul'd the world with's beck,
And tear his flesh, and set your feet on's neck,
And make his filthy den so desolate
To th' 'stonishment of all that knew his state.
This done, with brandish'd swords to Turkey go, —
(For then what is it but English blades dare do?)
And lay her waste, for so's the sacred doom,
And do to Gog as thou hast done to Rome.
Oh Abraham's seed, lift up your heads on high,

For sure the day of your redemption's nigh.
The scales shall fall from your long blinded eyes,
And him you shall adore who now despise.
Then fullness of the Nations in shall flow,
And Jew and Gentile to one worship go.
Then follows days of happiness and rest.
Whose lot doth fall to live therein is blest.
No Canaanite shall then be found 'n th' land,
And holiness on horses' bells shall stand.
If this make way thereto, then sigh no more,
But if at all thou didst not see 't before.
Farewell, dear mother; Parliament, prevail,
And in a while you'll tell another tale.

Anne Bradstreet: In Honour of that High and Mighty Princess, Queen Elizabeth

Although great Queen, thou now in silence lie,
Yet thy loud Herald Fame, doth to the sky
Thy wondrous worth proclaim, in every clime,
And so has vow'd, whilst there is world or time.
So great's thy glory, and thine excellence,
The sound thereof raps every human sense
That men account it no impiety
To say thou wert a fleshly Deity.
Thousands bring off'rings (though out of date)
Thy world of honours to accumulate.
'Mongst hundred Hecatombs of roaring Verse,
'Mine bleating stands before thy royal Hearse.
Thou never didst, nor canst thou now disdain,
T' accept the tribute of a loyal Brain.
Thy clemency did yerst esteem as much
The acclamations of the poor, as rich,
Which makes me deem, my rudeness is no wrong,
Though I resound thy greatness 'mongst the throng.

No *Phoenix* Pen, nor *Spenser's* Poetry,
No *Speed's*, nor *Camden's* learned History;
Eliza's works, wars, praise, can e're compact,
The World's the Theater where she did act.
No memories, nor volumes can contain,
The nine *Olymp'ades* of her happy reign,
Who was so good, so just, so learn'd, so wise,
From all the Kings on earth she won the prize.
Nor say I more than truly is her due.
Millions will testify that this is true.
She hath wip'd off th' aspersion of her Sex,

That women wisdom lack to play the Rex.
Spain's Monarch sa's not so, not yet his Host:
She taught them better manners to their cost.
The *Salic* Law had not in force now been,
If *France* had ever hop'd for such a Queen.
But can you Doctors now this point dispute,
She's argument enough to make you mute,
Since first the Sun did run, his ne'er runn'd race,
And earth had twice a year, a new old face;
Since time was time, and man unmanly man,
Come shew me such a Phoenix if you can.
Was ever people better rul'd than hers?
Was ever Land more happy, freed from stirs?
Did ever wealth in *England* so abound?
Her Victories in foreign Coasts resound?
Ships more invincible than *Spain's*, her foe
She rack't, she sack'd, she sunk his Armadoe.
Her stately Troops advanc'd to *Lisbon's* wall,
Don Anthony in's right for to install.
She frankly help'd *Franks'* (brave) distressed King,
The States united now her fame do sing.
She their Protectrix was, they well do know,
Unto our dread Virago, what they owe.
Her Nobles sacrific'd their noble blood,
Nor men, nor coin she shap'd, to do them good.
The rude untamed *Irish* she did quell,
And *Tiron* bound, before her picture fell.
Had ever Prince such Counsellors as she?
Her self *Minerva* caus'd them so to be.
Such Soldiers, and such Captains never seen,
As were the subjects of our *(Pallas)* Queen:
Her Sea-men through all straits the world did round,
Terra incognitæ might know her sound.
Her *Drake* came laded home with *Spanish* gold,
Her *Essex* took *Cadiz*, their *Herculean* hold.
But time would fail me, so my wit would too,
To tell of half she did, or she could do.
Semiramis to her is but obscure;
More infamy than fame she did procure.
She plac'd her glory but on *Babel's* walls,
World's wonder for a time, but yet it falls.
Fierce *Tomris* (*Cirus'* Heads-man, *Sythians'* Queen)
Had put her Harness off, had she but seen
Our *Amazon* i' th' Camp at *Tilbury*,
(Judging all valour, and all Majesty)
Within that Princess to have residence,
And prostrate yielded to her Excellence.
Dido first Foundress of proud *Carthage* walls

(Who living consummates her Funerals),
A great *Eliza*, but compar'd with ours,
How vanisheth her glory, wealth, and powers.
Proud profuse *Cleopatra*, whose wrong name,
Instead of glory, prov'd her Country's shame:
Of her what worth in Story's to be seen,
But that she was a rich *Ægyptian* Queen.
Zenobia, potent Empress of the East,
And of all these without compare the best
(Whom none but great *Aurelius* could quell)
Yet for our Queen is no fit parallel:
She was a Phoenix Queen, so shall she be,
Her ashes not reviv'd more Phoenix she.
Her personal perfections, who would tell,
Must dip his Pen i' th' Heliconian Well,
Which I may not, my pride doth but aspire
To read what others write and then admire.
Now say, have women worth, or have they none?
Or had they some, but with our Queen is't gone?
Nay Masculines, you have thus tax'd us long,
But she, though dead, will vindicate our wrong.
Let such as say our sex is void of reason
Know 'tis a slander now, but once was treason.
But happy *England*, which had such a Queen,
O happy, happy, had those days still been,
But happiness lies in a higher sphere.
Then wonder not, *Eliza* moves not here.
Full fraught with honour, riches, and with days,
She set, she set, like *Titan* in his rays.
No more shall rise or set such glorious Sun,
Until the heaven's great revolution:
If then new things, their old form must retain,
Eliza shall rule *Albian* once again.

Her Epitaph.
Here sleeps the Queen, this is the royal bed
O' th' Damask Rose, sprung from the white and red,
Whose sweet perfume fills the all-filling air,
This Rose is withered, once so lovely fair:
On neither tree did grow such Rose before,
The greater was our gain, our loss the more.

Bibliography

Alexander, G. (2001). Sidney's Interruptions. *Studies in Philology*, 98(2), 184-204. http://www.jstor.org/stable/4174696

Andrews, M.C. (1972). Sidney's Arcadia and The Winter's Tale. *Shakespeare Quarterly*, 23(2), 200-202. https://www.jstor.org/stable/2868578

Aristotle, (2013*)*. Poetics, a new translation by Anthony Kenny. Oxford: Oxford University Press.

Aubrey, J. (2014) in Clark, A. (ed). Brief Lives. Project Gutenberg ebookhttps://www.gutenberg.org/files/47787/47787-h/47787-h.htm

Barker, F. (1986). So Rare a Gentleman: Sir Philip Sidney and the Forgotten War of 1586. *History Today*, 36(11), 40-46.

Bell, M. and Cottegnies, L. (eds.) (2017). Robert Garnier in Elizabethan England, Mary Sidney Herbert's 'Antonius' and Thomas Kyd's 'Cornelia'. Cambridge: MHRA Association.

Berry, E. (1989). Sidney's May Game for the Queen, *Modern Philology*, 86(3), 252-264. http;//www.jstor.org/stable/438028

Bi-Qi, B. L. (2001). Relational Antifeminism in Sidney's 'Arcadia', *Studies in English Literature 1500-1900*, 47(1), 25-48. https://www.jstor.com/stable/1556227

Bradstreet, A. (2000). To my Husband and Other Poems. New York: Dover Publications.

Blythe, R. (ed.) (2003). A Priest to the Temple or A Country Parson with Selected Poems, George Herbert. Norwich: Canterbury Press.

Blythe, R. (2005). George Herbert in Bemerton, from Divine Landscapes. Salisbury: Hobnob Press.

Brennan, M. (1982). The Date of the Countess of Pembroke's Translation of the Psalms. *The Review of English Studies*, 33(132), 434-436. http://www.jstor.org/stable/515841

Buxton, J. (1987). *Sir Philip Sidney and the English Renaissance*. London: Macmillan Press.

Campbell, G. (2010). Bible, The Story of the King James Version, 1611-2011. Oxford: Oxford University Press.

Charles, A.M. (1974). 'Mrs Herbert's Kitchin Booke', *English Literary Renaissance*, 4(1), 164-173. https://www.jstor.org/stable/43446793

Clarke, D. (1997). "Lover's Songs Shall Turne to Holy Psalmes": Mary Sidney and the Transformation of Petrarch. *The Modern Language Review,* 92(2), 282-294. https://doi. org/10.2307/3734802

Clarke, D. (1997). The Politics of Translation and Gender in the Countess of Pembroke's 'Antonie'. *Translation and Literature,* 6(2), 149-166. http://www.jstor.org/stable/40316853

Clarke, D. (ed.) (2000). Renaissance Women Poets. London: Penguin.

Coren, P. (2002). Edmund Spenser, Mary Sidney, and the "Doleful Lay." *Studies in English Literature, 1500-1900,* 42(1), 25-41. http://www.jstor.org/stable/1556139

Davis, J. (2004). Multiple 'Arcadias' and the Literary Quarrel between Fulke Greville and the Countess of Pembroke. *Studies in Philology,* 101(4), 401-430. http://www.jstor. org/stable/4174801

Daybell, J. (2005). Recent studies in sixteenth-century letters. *English Literary Renaissance,* 35(2), 331–362. http://www.jstor.org/stable/24463684

Dean, D. (1998). Review of: The Sound of Virtue: Philip Sidney's 'Arcadia' and Elizabethan Politics by Blair Worden, *History,* 83(272), 719-720. https://www.jstor. org/stable/24424722

Duffy, E. (2005). The Stripping of the Altars. New Haven and London: Yale University Press.

Duncan-Jones, K. and Kelliher, H. (1975). A manuscript of Poems by Robert Sidney: Some Early Impressions. *The British Library Journal,* 1(2), 107-144. https://www.jstor. org/stable/42553982

Duncan-Jones, K. (ed.) (2002). Sir Philip Sidney, The Major Works. Oxford: Oxford University   Press.

Dutton, R. (2002). The Revels Office and the Boy Companies, 1600-1613: New Perspectives. *English Literary Renaissance,* 32(2), 324-351. http://www.jstor.org/ stable/43447637

Drury, J. and Moul, V. (eds.) (2015). George Herbert, The Complete Poetry. UK: Penguin.

Drury, J. (2014). Music at Midnight, The Life and Poetry of George Herbert. London: Penguin.

Farrell, K. Hageman, E. and Kinney, A. (eds) (1988). Women in the Renaissance, Amhurst: The University of Massachusetts Press.

Fisken, B. W. (1989). The Art of Sacred Parody in Mary Sidney's Psalmes. *Tulsa Studies in Women's Literature,* 8(2), 223-239. https://doi.org/10.2307/463736

Freer, C. (1971). The Countess of Pembroke in a world of words. *Style,* 5(1), 37-56. http:// www.jstor.org/stable/42945082

Greenblatt, S.J. (1973). Sidney's 'Arcadia' and the Mixed Mode, *Studies in Philology*, 70(3), 269-278. http://www.jstor.com/stable/4173809

Goodrich, J. (2014). Royal Propaganda: Mary Tudor, Elizabeth Tudor, and the Edwardian Reformation. Faithful Translators: Authorship, Gender, and Religion in Early Modern England. 67-106. Northwestern University Press. https://doi.org/10.2307/j.ctv3znxvx.7

Grierson, H.J.C. and Bullough, G (eds.) (1966). The Oxford Book of Seventeenth Century Verse. Oxford: The Clarendon Press.

Hannay, M. P. (1990). Philip's Phoenix. Oxford: Oxford University Press.

Hannay, M. P. (1989). "Princes you as men must dy": Genevan Advice to Monarchs in the Psalmes of Mary Sidney. *English Literary Renaissance*, 19(1), 22-41. http://www.jstor.org/stable/43447265

Hannay, M. P. (1994). ⊚House-confinéd maids⊚: The Presentation of Woman⊚s Role in the ⊚Psalmes⊚ of the Countess of Pembroke. *English Literary Renaissance*, 24(1), 44-71. http://www.jstor.org/stable/43447745

Harrison, T. P. Jr. (1926). A source of Sidney's 'Arcadia', *Studies in English*, 6, 53-71. http://www.jstor.com/stable/20779369

Heaney, S. (1980). Selected Poems 1965-1975. London: Faber and Faber.

Hecht, P. J. (2013). Distortion, Aggression, and Sex in Mary Wroth's Sonnets, *Studies in English Literature, 1500-1900*, 53(1), 91-115. https//www.jstor.org/stable/41818885

Houlbrooke, R. (1998). Review of: The Theatre of Death. The Ritual Management of Royal Funerals in Renaissance England 1570-1625, by J. Woodward. *Renaissance Studies*, 12(4), 605-608. http://www.jstor.org/stable/24412589

Keenan, S. (2008). Poetry (chapter), Renaissance Literature, Edinburgh: Edinburgh University Press.

Kelliher, H. and Duncan-Jones K. (1975). A manuscript of poems by Robert Sidney: some early impressions. *The British Library Journal*, 1(2), 107-144. http://www.jstor.org/stable/42553982

Kewes, P. (2012). "A fit memorial for the times to come...": Admonition and topical application in Mary Sidney's 'Antonius' and Samuel Daniels' 'Cleopatra'. *The Review of English Studies*, 63(259), 243-264. http://www.jstor.org/stable/23263644

Knowles, M. D. (2012). "Now English denizend, though Hebrue borne": Did Mary Sidney Herbert, Countess of Pembroke, Read Hebrew? *Studies in Philology*, 109(3), 279-289. http://www.jstor.org/stable/41511149

Lamb, M. E. (1982). The Countess of Pembroke's Patronage. *English Literary Renaissance*, 12(2), 162–179. http://www.jstor.org/stable/43447074

Lamb, M. E. (1984). Three Unpublished Holograph Poems in the Bright Manuscript: A New Poet in the Sidney Circle? *The Review of English Studies*, 35(139), 301-315. http://www.jstor.org/stable/515763

Lamb, M. E. (2006). Recent Studies in the English Renaissance. *Studies in English Literature, 1500-1900*, 46(1), 195-244. http://www.jstor.org/stable/3844569

May, S. W. (2011). Marlowe, Spenser, Sidney and – Abraham Fraunce? *The Review of English Studies*, 62(253), 30-63. http://www.jstor.org/stable/23016333

Marroti, A. F. and May, S. W. (2011). Two Lost Ballads of the Armada Thanksgiving Celebration [with texts and illustration]. *English Literary Renaissance*, 41(1), 31-63. http://www.jstor.org/stable/43447703

Mattiessen, F. O. (2013). Translation: An Elizabethan Art. Boston. Reprint Services Corporation.

Mears, N. (2003). Courts, Courtiers, and Culture in Tudor England. The Historical Journal, 46(3), 703–722. http://www.jstor.org/stable/3133568

Mentz, S. (2000). Selling Sidney: William Ponsonby, Thomas Nashe, and the Boundaries of Elizabethan Print and Manuscript Cultures. *Text*, 13, 151-174. http://www.jstor.org/stable/30227764

Miller, P. (ed.) (1956) The American Puritans, Their Prose and Poetry, New York: Anchor Books.

Moore, R. E. (2010). Sir Philip Sidney's Defence of Prophesying. *Studies in English Literature 1500-1900*, 50(1), 35-62. http://www.jstor.org/stable/40658419

Nicolson, A. (2009). Arcadia, The Dream of Perfection in Renaissance England, London: Harper Perennial.

Nelson, A. H. (2009). Emulating royalty: Cambridge, Oxford, and the Inns of Court, *Shakespeare Studies*, 37, pp. 67-89.

Osherow, M. (2015). Mary Sidney's embroidered psalms, *Renaissance Studies*, 29(4), 650-670. https://www.jstor.org/stable/10.2307/26618819

Pender, P. (2011). The Ghost and the Machine in the Sidney Family Corpus. *Studies in English Literature 1500-1900*, 51(1), 65-85. http://www.jstor.org/stable/23028093

Poirier, M. (1947). Sidney's influence upon A Midsummer's Night's Dream, *Studies in Philology*, 44(3), 483-489. https://www.jstor.org/stable/4172809

Prichard, R. E. (ed.) (1992). The Sidney Psalms, Manchester, Carcanet Press Limited.

Pritchard, R. E. (1996). George Herbert and Lady Mary Wroth: A Root for 'The Flower'? *The Review of English Studies*, 47(187), 386-389. http://www.jstor.org/stable/518286

Prescott, A. L. (2008). Mary Sidney's "Antonius" and the Ambiguities of French History.

The Yearbook of English Studies, 38(1/2), 216-233. http://www.jstor.org/stable/20479331

Rhodes, N. (2013). Marlowe and the Greeks. Renaissance Studies, 27(2), 199-218. http://www.jstor.org/stable/24420152

Ricks, C. (ed.) (1993). The Penguin History of Literature, English Poetry and Prose 1540-1674. London: Penguin.

Roberts, J. A. (1984). Part II: Mary Sidney, Countess of Pembroke. *English Literary Renaissance*, 14(3), 426-439. http://www.jstor.org/stable/43447316

Salzman, P. (ed.) (2000). Early Modern Women's Writing, An Anthology 1560-1700. Oxford: Oxford University Press.

Schafer, E. (2015). Introduction: Attending to Early Modern Women as Theatre Makers. *Early Theatre*, 18(2), 125-132. http://www.jstor.org/stable/44122667

Seth, V. (2011). The Rivered Earth. London: Orion.

Shakespeare, W. (1971). Antony and Cleopatra, New Swan Shakespeare, Advanced Series, Harlow: Longman Group.

Shakespeare, W. (2008). Anthony and Cleopatra, Oxford: Oxford University Press.

Sidney, Sir P. (2013). An Apology for Poetry and Astrophel and Stella (ed. J.M. Beach), Austin: West by Southwest Press.

Sidney, Sir P. (1994). The Countess of Pembroke's Arcadia (The Old Arcadia) (ed. K. Duncan-Jones), Oxford: Oxford University Press.

Sidney, Sir P. & Sidney, M. (2009). The Sidney Psalter, The Psalms of Sir Philip and Mary Sidney, (eds. H. Hamlin, M. Brennan, M. Hannay and N. Kinnamon), Oxford: Oxford University Press.

Steinberg, T. L. (1995). The Sidneys and the Psalms. *Studies in Philology*, 92(1), 1-17. http://www.jstor.org/stable/4174504

Stillman, R. E. (1984). Justice and the 'Good Word' in Sidney's The Lady of May', *Studies in English Literature 1500-1900*, 24(1), 23-38. https://www.jstor.org/stable/450347

Streitberger, W. R. (2008). Chambers on the Revels Office and Elizabethan Theatre History. *Shakespeare Quarterly*, 59(2), 185-209. http://www.jstor.org/stable/40210263

Strickland, R. (1990). Pageantry and Poetry as Discourse: The Production of Subjectivity in Sir Philip Sidney's Funeral. *ELH*, 57(1), 19-36. https://doi.org/10.2307/2873244

Strong, R. C. (1958). The Popular Celebration of the Accession Day of Queen Elizabeth I. *Journal of the Warburg and Courtauld Institutes*, 21(1/2), 86-103. https://doi.org/10.2307/750488

Strycharski, A. (2001). Some Verses of Henry and Mary Dudley Sidney and Prince Edward's "Little Schol". *A Quarterly Journal of Short Articles*, 24(4), 249-254.

Swaim, K. M. (1999). Contextualizing Mary Sidney's Psalms. *Christianity and Literature,* 48(3), 253-273. https://www.jstor.org/stable/44312691

The Book of Common Prayer (1549), 1662 revision. Oxford: Oxford University Press.

Waller, G. (1976). The "Sad Pilgrim", The Poetry of Sir Robert Sidney". Dalhousie Review, 55, 689-705

Weiss, H. B. (1927). Thomas Moffett, Elizabethan Physician and Entomologist. *The Scientific Monthly*, 24(6), 559–566. http://www.jstor.org/stable/7786

West, D.(ed) (1997) *Horace, The Complete Odes and Epodes,* Oxford: Oxford University Press.

Wilcox, H. (2004). Herbert, George (1593-1633). *Oxford Dictionary of National Biography,* Oxford: Oxford University Press. https://doi.org/10.1093/ref:odnb/13025

Wroth, M. (1621) The Countess of Montgmery's Urania. London: British Library, Early English Books.

Younger N. (2008). If the Armada Had Landed: A Reappraisal of England's Defences in 1588. *History*, 93(311), 328-354. http://www.jstor.org/stable/24428393

Index